Mel Bay Presents

GUITAR INTERVIEWS

Compiled & Edited by Colin Cooper

The Best from

CLASSICAL
GUITAR
Magazine
Vol. One

Sergio & Odair Assad
Manuel Barrueco
Julian Bream
Leo Brouwer
Roland Dyens
Evangelos & Liza
Eliot Fisk
Oscar Ghiglia
Sharon Isbin
Nikita Koshkin
Los Angeles Guitar Quartet
Vladimir Mikulka
Christopher Parkening
Joaquin Rodrigo
Angel Romero
Pepe Romero
David Russell
Andrés Segovia
David Starobin
David Tanenbaum
Benjamin Verdery
John Williams
Zagreb Guitar Trio

Visit us on the Web at www.melbay.com
E-mail us at email@melbay.com

CONTENTS

Sérgio and Odair Assad 4

Manuel Barrueco 9

Julian Bream 13

Leo Brouwer 20

Roland Dyens 25

Evangelos and Liza 29

Eliot Fisk 32

Oscar Ghiglia 39

Sharon Isbin 44

Nikita Koshkin 50

Los Angeles Guitar Quartet 54

Vladimir Mikulka 58

Christopher Parkening 63

Joaquín Rodrigo 67

Angel Romero 71

Pepe Romero 74

David Russell 77

Andrés Segovia 83

David Starobin 88

David Tanenbaum 93

Benjamin Verdery 99

John Williams 104

Zagreb Guitar Trio 111

About the Editor 116

AUTHORS

CC Colin Cooper
JD John Duarte
CK Chris Kilvington
HH Horst Hentschel
BO Bauke Oosterhout

ACKNOWLEDGMENTS

These profiles first appeared in Classical Guitar Magazine. Writers in that publication customarily retain their copyright, but I am particularly indebted to Maurice Summerfield for the use of photographs from the archives of Classical Guitar Magazine at Ashley Mark Publishing Company. My grateful thanks also to Simon Turnbull for his invaluable help in preparing them for publication.

FOREWORD

The human voice is generally considered to be the most expressive of all instruments. The violin runs it close, but neither of them is much good when it comes to harmony – the solo voice not at all. The guitar can do this while remaining a superbly expressive instrument in its own right. Only a lack of volume and sustaining power holds it back.

Both the voice and the violin – and, of course the piano – have magnificent repertoires. The guitar cannot aspire to that level, and possibly never will. On the one hand, that is a disadvantage; on the other, the very nature of the instrument leaves the guitarist with unparalleled opportunities for individual expression. For the past 200 years or so guitarists and guitar makers alike have been exploring that unique facility, perhaps never more so than in our present age. It follows that the individual thoughts of prominent guitarists are likely to consist of somewhat more than a series of reactions to an existing repertoire, and it is on the basis of that belief that this book has come into being. There is more than one way of becoming a great guitarist, as I hope these pages will show.

The articles and interviews in this book have all appeared at one time or another in Classical Guitar magazine. They have not been revised in the light of further developments in an artist's career, and are therefore not to be considered as up-to-date biography; rather, they should be read as one looks at a photograph, in the spirit of 'this is how they were then'.

We have witnessed an explosion of guitar talent in the past two decades or so, and the number of good and even great guitarists now practicing their art would fill a second volume without difficulty. To those whose names do not appear on this all-too-short preliminary list, I can only offer my sincere regrets together with the promise that they will be included in a subsequent volume. When you consider that Classical Guitar magazine has been published monthly for nearly nineteen years, and that nineteen multiplied by twelve comes to two hundred and twenty-eight, the size of the problem will be apparent.

Before a second volume of classical guitar interviews can be considered, however, there will be a volume devoted to guitarists from South America, a special genre that includes Roberto Aussel, Carlos Barbosa-Lima, Paulo Bellinati, Jorge Cardoso, Abel Carlevaro, Alirio Díaz, Eduardo Falú, Egberto Gismonti, Jorge Morel, Ricardo Iznaola. It may be argued that some of these have their origins in Europe, and in any case are as much classical as South American. But total consistency in such an area as music is impossible; lines of demarcation are difficult to determine, and in any case are probably neither relevant nor desirable.

An old saying sometimes used by guitarists to defend themselves against critics is 'The dogs bark but the caravan moves on'. There are no barking dogs in these pages, only the considered thoughts of valued artists presented in the hope that they will nourish and encourage the efforts of all those aspiring guitarists who are trying to come to terms with an instrument whose almost infinite powers of expression compete with an equally infinite complexity.

Colin Cooper

SÉRGIO AND ODAIR ASSAD

I had arranged to interview Sérgio and Odair Assad in the café of the Hotel Cracovia in Kraków. Barely had we taken a preparatory sip of coffee when a representative of the Kraków Philharmonic Orchestra arrived to say that the time of the afternoon rehearsal had been brought forward and a car was waiting.

And that was it. No further opportunity presented itself. The concert took place, the Assad brothers played two concertos brilliantly, and afterwards there was a party. Sérgio and Odair left early the following morning, and my last chance had gone. There were to be other meetings, of course, but we were committed to an article about the brothers: I would have to write it on the basis of what I already knew about them.

Well, it was written and it was published; but since one of the perceived virtues of the face-to-face interview is that it allows artists to give their own opinions in their own words, I prefer to offer an earlier interview. It was conducted by Bauke Oosterhout, an engaging Dutchman who not only played the guitar himself but also acted as agent for other guitarists, among them the great David Russell. Bauke's early death was a tragic loss to the guitar community. CC

Odair Assad: I started playing the guitar when I was eight years old. Sérgio started at twelve. We played together from the beginning and, as you can see, we're still at it!

We didn't actually choose to learn the guitar, but my father needed a couple of guitarists. We didn't have lessons. In Brazil you don't usually study an instrument. By that I mean that when you buy, for example, a guitar, you go along to a teacher and have your first lesson with him, but in Brazil we do it more the natural way and fiddle around with it, picking up things here and there. You hear music around you all day. It's the custom to play choros in a small ensemble consisting of different instruments like the mandolin and the cavaquinho (a small 4-string guitar). Two guitars play the accompaniment, using chords and playing the bass lines in thirds with the thumb.

My father plays the mandolin. He became tired of looking for guitarists to accompany him and, as he is very fanatical about music, he bought us guitars and taught us a bit about harmony so that we could play together.

After a while my father was very surprised that we had progressed so rapidly, and didn't know what to teach us any more. He went in search of a teacher but couldn't find anybody. We lived in a small village near São Paulo. Reading music we learned ourselves.

By coincidence, a reporter heard us play and seemed very impressed by it. He was acquainted with the Abreu brothers and knew their teacher in Rio. He introduced us to Monina Távora, a former student of Andrés Segovia. She never taught us technique; only the music was important to her. She is a great lady and very special to me.

Monina Távora helped you to get your concert career going?

Courtesy GHS Records

Yes, she did. We played all over Brazil. After that competition in Bratislava, we were getting more concerts in Europe. The well-known Brazilian composer Marlos Nobre took us to Europe. He worked for Unesco in those days.

Did he write for you?
Not exactly. He transcribed one of his own piano pieces for us.

You both have a very relaxed way of playing and not

being bothered by technical problems at all.
Maybe that's because of our musical upbringing. We have our roots in Brazilian folk music. When we were young we didn't hear anything else and played only choros, sambas, etcetera. Most of it was just improvising, which is a very good basis for a musician.

You are really fast players.
Paco de Lucia plays a lot faster. It's never our intention to play fast on purpose, because we just play what we feel at that particular moment, but to other people it can seem very fast. We do get criticized a lot for it. Maybe when we were kids we made a joke of it because everybody was saying 'Look how fast those boys can play!' I don't feel I'm playing very fast, but experience it as quite natural and normal.

What we look for in music is a lot of expression and the sheer pleasure of playing. We enjoy playing very much. We take all the risks, because we never plan how we are going to play the music in concert. That way every concert is new for us, and maybe that gives it that spontaneous feeling. Sometimes we change things right in the middle of it. A few notes extra, or improvisation. It's ridiculous to plan, for example, your dynamics beforehand because they'll never go the way you wanted them. All these things are evident in the music itself, and this way it's a lot more alive and sparkling.

Also the influence of the audience can change your way of playing. That bit of magic that can exist between public and artist is very important. It's different in every country. There is quite a difference between an English and a Chinese audience. When we played in Hong Kong and Taiwan we were in doubt all the time. You stand up after having played a piece; looking at the people, we couldn't figure out whether they were smiling or sleeping. That does affect your playing. Only after the concert we knew if they liked it or not.

You never play solo?
No, not really. From the start we have always played together. Mind you, we don't practice together but only play together. We study our parts separately. When we do, we usually play different pieces at the same time!

Have you made any records in Brazil?
We did two. On the first, we play on one side with an orchestra. The other side, just the two of us. It was recorded many years ago. I don't recommend it to you. For the recording with the orchestra we had to go to a town in the north of Brazil. The orchestral players were quarrelling continuously, and we spent a long

time just recording one side. The other side we had to record with them the next day. That same night in the hotel I opened a beer can and nearly cut my thumb in half. Sérgio was jumping up and down in complete panic. It seemed to hurt him more than me. I was holding my thumb together with my other hand, afraid that a large chunk might fall off. A doctor stitched it together. Very badly, I might say. Months later we recorded the other side in Rio, but without the orchestra.

We did another album for — don't laugh — Coca-Cola. Actually it's a double album and they used it as a Christmas present for their business associates in Brazil. We recorded all the Villa-Lobos pieces written for guitar. I play one part solo, Sérgio the other part. Actually, Coca-Cola sponsored our first tour through the US.

Our third record was made in Belgium. This year (1986) we recorded an album in the US for Nonesuch Records, which contains South-American music including Piazzolla's *Tango Suite*. Next year we are going to do a record of only Brazilian music, also for Nonesuch.

Astor Piazzolla wrote Tango Suite for you. Did you commission it?
Sérgio Assad: No, we did not. Through our good friend Roberto Aussel, we were invited to the home of a mutual friend in Paris. Astor Piazzolla was there also, after a concert he had given that same night. We played a few arrangements of his music for him. He loved it and said he would compose a piece for two guitars, dedicating it to us. All this happened in the autumn of 1933. I had forgotten all about it, but to my surprise I received it through the mail in February 1984. It's a great piece of music and very suited to us. We have been playing it in our program ever since.

There is a bit of percussion on the guitar in the beginning which is written down only in a few markings, not indicating how to do it. It took days to figure it out.

Gnattali wrote a lot for you too.
Ah yes, a good friend and a very productive composer. At home he had stacks of music he wrote for guitar. Also chamber music, orchestral works etcetera. He is the type of guy who dislikes intensely going into battles with publishers about contracts and percentages. The result is that he never anything gets published, and it doesn't interest him a bit. We were actually the first ones who played his music outside Brazil, where he isn't well known either.

The new generation of composers, like Almeido

Prado, Marlos Nobre and Edino Krieger, are strongly influenced by European avant-garde music. Until a few years ago it was like a fever running through the Brazilian music world. Composers like Francisco Mignone have written music in every style. Camargo Guarniere is more in the style of Villa-Lobos, only more avant-garde. Another one is Lourenzo Fernandez, a more academic composer. There are only a few composers who didn't depart from traditional Brazilian music and have produced a unique repertoire. Gnattali always wrote Brazilian music, although the influences of North-American jazz are evident.

I do have the feeling these composers think they have to write contemporary music like everybody else in order to get recognized as serious composers, this being the reason for departing from the more popular Brazilian idiom. I think they are mistaken, because they are more at home in writing Brazilian music. But things are changing. Ten years ago everybody played avant-garde music. Nowadays it seems to be going out of fashion, and there is a comeback of more traditional music. Look at Leo Brouwer, for instance. I believe South Americans should write their own music and use the immense richness of our folk music based on European harmonies and African rhythms. This is very important to me, and that's why we play so much of it in our programs.

Once I spoke to a young composer and asked him whether he would compromise in order to be successful, and he replied he couldn't because he believed in the teachings of Alban Berg and that would be the future of music! This is the mentality of most of them. That's why I admire Gnattali so much. His music is pure Brazilian. He couldn't care less what people might think of him, and goes his own way. As I said before, things are changing. There are many more young composers than the ones I've mentioned and I'm astounded by the talent we have in our country, but it's very hard to make a living out of it. The only government-controlled TV channel is showing mostly cultural programs, and it is surprising to see so many people doing very good work. It's a pity most people watch the usual crap on the other channels. Well, it's more or less the same problem all over the world.

In Europe there seems to be a revival of interest in South American music. I only have to mention Astor Piazzolla. Piazzolla is very well known in Europe now. His group is playing in nearly every country, and very successfully. Meanwhile he has been playing and living in France for decades. It's only in the last few years that his group has become popular internationally.

What about Villa-Lobos?
Of course, we guitarists are very pleased with his compositions. What we tend to forget is that his other works are in fact a lot better. They are never played. A sad thing, because their quality is of a high standard.

You are also a composer. Your Three Brazilian Dances are in the Duo's program.
I usually do all the arrangements also. The Three Dances were an attempt to solve the shortage of instrumental music. Instrumental music is not so well accepted in Brazil. This is changing, due to groups playing a distinct type of music called 'jazz brasileiro', which is the most important music played in Brazil nowadays. It's difficult to define, but it's a mixture of classical, jazz and Brazilian music. Nearly a complete different thing altogether. I think this music is going to be a great success.

Egberto Gismonti and Hermeto Pascual are famous in this genre, and both play with their ensemble in Europe, especially in France. Gismonti wrote several things for guitar, published by Max Eschig in Paris, but these pieces are more in the style of the post-Webern period. He doesn't play this music himself, nor does anybody else for that matter. They are great musicians and we include their other music in our programs. Hermeto Pascual is writing a suite for us at this moment.

The Brazilian music goes down very well with the audiences in your concerts. Shall we get a lot more of it in the future?
If we can get the music, yes. In guitar concerts, only Villa-Lobos is played. Maybe too much of it. As I told you, Brazilian composers like Nobre, Prado and Guarniere write European music. Guarniere could write very well for guitar but has only written a study for the instrument. Getting a program together of exclusively Brazilian music is a near impossibility, and you can imagine how the situation is for a duo.

What we do is to press composers like Pascual, Gismonti and Gnattali to write for us or make arrangements of their music. Typical Brazilian music took form at the beginning of this century. Ernesto Nazareth and Chinquinha Gonzaga were the most important exponents. They wrote in a style with a syncopated rhythm, which later became the basic rhythm of the samba and choros. At this time the word choro didn't yet exist. Nazareth called it, for instance, 'tango brasileiro'. Others called it 'corta jaca'. In the thirties, ensembles were playing in the streets of Rio to the beautiful girls on the balconies. Mostly sad and sentimental music like waltzes and polkas. The more cheerful pieces were the ones with that particular syncopated rhythm. People called these players 'chorões' because people were crying when they listened to them. Choro comes from the Portuguese word 'choro', which means crying.

Turibio Santos has recorded a lot of Brazilian music. Music by Nazareth, João Pernambuco, Dilermando Reis, Nobre and Prado. People now are expecting a large part of Brazilian music in our programs. We enjoy playing it, so the solution is easy. The only trouble is getting the music now! Getting composers to write for us is our small contribution to enlarging the guitar repertoire.

You never play Bach. Why not?
I just don't like it for guitar. A lot of guitarists will disagree with me, but the phrasing you can do on keyboard is next to impossible to do on guitar. It doesn't do justice to his music. However, we do like playing French Baroque because it's more elegant and I know we can make a good job of it, despite what the musicologists might say of it. I can't say the same thing about Bach, so we never play it. On the subject of authenticity, I can only say that it is lost already by using a present-day guitar.

What do you think about the critics?
A very tender subject. In general they have been very favorable to us, although sometimes they see behind our music more than we know ourselves. Like somebody who is explaining the deeper meaning in a painting while it is all new to the painter himself.

I try to avoid reading reviews as much as possible. I don't see the use of them. People should make up their own minds whether they like a concert or not. The most important thing for me in a concert, whether I'm playing or listening, is the communication between artist and audience. Sometimes it's there, sometimes not. You never know when it is going to happen because it's spontaneous. If the critic doesn't feel it at that moment, he couldn't care less whether the rest of the audience likes it or not. You can find bad things in the best performance, and he can say that a particular note is not played rightly or the phrasing is not executed well or it doesn't fit the style of the period. So, reviews — what for? Many times I've been to a concert about which I've had my own opinion. Later I read the review, and I start wondering whether I have attended the same concert as the reviewer. I might have enjoyed it immensely, but this person did not. The critic gives a one-man opinion, but there are a lot more people in the audience. Why is his opinion the most important?

Where do you see yourself in ten years' time?
Growing potatoes somewhere in the jungle of Brazil! Sometimes the hassle of travelling around the world is annoying me. I long for the quietness of the countryside.

7

Photo by Beatriz Schiller

But you keep on playing as a duo.
Oh yes, of course, as long as nothing bad happens to one of us. When our agent in the US contracted us he asked us whether we weren't afraid we would end up like the Presti-Lagoya Duo and the Abreu Brothers. He used to be their agent also. How on earth can I know what is going to happen tomorrow, let alone in ten years' time? I don't want to look into the future.

Ambitious?
Not at all. We've rolled from one thing into another without going after things. I enjoy what I'm doing with my brother. We depend a lot on each other and have a certain responsibility. We get along very well together although we are completely different persons. Suppressing our individuality a little is a small price to pay for being together all the time.

Each going your own way — would that be possible?
It would be very difficult for me to play solo. We've been playing together professionally for the last ten years and you get used to each other so much. The few times I've played solo didn't satisfy me at all.

Incredible things can happen when you've been together and been playing together for such a long time. I remember the days when things didn't work out so well, but now it doesn't matter what Odair is doing with his phrasing, ritardandos or dynamics because I feel it at the same time and in the same form. He never gets me into problems.

Who follows whom?
Nobody. We don't divide our parts in a way that one plays the melody and the other one does the accompaniment. We take turns, and the one who has the most important part leads.

People always think you are twins because you look so much alike.
That question is asked over and over again. Odair has a nice answer to it, and will say 'Yes, we are twins but I was born four years later'.

Several times I've been with you just before you give your concert. Worries or nervousness I haven't noticed at all. Even a photo session ten minutes before going up doesn't affect you both. What's the secret?
We enjoy playing guitar, so what's the worry? I must admit that before our Wigmore Hall debut we felt a bit uneasy. All those great musicians that have played there!

Your careers are going very well.

Especially in the last few years. We are getting more offers than we can handle. In 1986 we have tours in the US, England, Scandinavia, Australia, the Far East, back to the US, and again Europe. In between we still play in Brazil. Somewhere in 1986 we have to make a new record in the US, with Brazilian works only. Our lives are in complete chaos!

BO

MANUEL BARRUECO

Manuel Barrueco's surname means 'Baroque', and certainly he plays the music of Bach and other composers of the Baroque very well indeed. To me, however, he is the supreme classicist in his approach to the instrument. The very way he strikes the string is delightful. His posture on the platform is one of total balance between the tension that every artist feels — a necessary tension if you are going to play the guitar at all — and a state of mental relaxation in which mind and memory can operate to the full, unhindered by any sense of strain. The result is peak performance virtually every time.

The circumstances of our first interview were unusual. He had been taking part in the Mid-Wales Festival, and had given a recital in the church of St. Andrew, Presteigne. The BBC, personified by Gareth Walters and the staff who worked from the Outside Broadcasts van, were present to record the occasion. Somehow the audience, walking through the unlit churchyard to their pews, had managed to avoid tripping over the heavy cables that connected van with church.

The following morning we were enjoying coffee at the house of another Gareth, Gareth Rees-Roberts, and his singer wife Lyndon. One of the organizers of the Festival, Gareth is himself an excellent guitarist who had won the Julian Bream prize at the Royal Academy of Music. I was hoping for a chance to interview Manuel, but animated conversation continued without the possibility of interruption.

Interruption there had to be, however, because Manuel had a plane to catch from Gatwick. Since I had volunteered to drive him there, I consoled myself with the thought that there would be plenty of time during the drive of some 200 miles. My first suggestion that it was about time we left met with general agreement, but the conversation continued. Knowing the winding Welsh roads only too well, I finally got him into the car, with, as I thought, plenty of time to spare.

It turned out that Manuel had been under the misapprehension that Presteigne was not far from London, and that there would be time for a little shopping in the capital before making the short trip down to the airport. But though distances in Britain are small compared with those in the United States, there are no motorways in Wales; I knew from experience that the journey was going to take the best part of four hours, an average of 50 mph if we were lucky.

With that in mind, I put my foot down as far as I dared, handing over the microphone of the tape recorder to my passenger so that we could conduct at least some sort of an interview. To be discussing Baroque ornamentation while hurtling round the bends in narrow Welsh roads at the maximum speed compatible with safety was a new experience.

We finished the interview and got to Gatwick in time for the flight, but without any time for shopping. We have met many times since, and I never cease to marvel at the playing of this supremely well-equipped musician.

Photo by Simon Fowler

You seem to have a special feeling for the Baroque. Weiss, Bach, Scarlatti. Can you say something about your approach to it?

Manuel Barrueco: The only thing I can say is that I have worked. I have studied to a certain extent how to play baroque music. Of course, that's only part of it. I guess I feel comfortable with it. It's come to the point with me that, whether it's right or wrong, it feels natural to me. I remember, years ago as a student, trying to understand this music, and it was always a struggle; what you do here, what you do there, not understanding certain passages, not understanding certain concepts. I think for the last few years, I've come to the point where I don't have too many questions. That's not to say that there may not be some other faults in it; I know that. But I've become sort of comfortable, playing in this way.

Spanish music too is something that you play exceptionally well. We in England shall never forget your first appearance at the Wigmore Hall, and the dazzling way you played Albéniz and Granados. Is there any particular music you don't play or don't want to play?

You know, I feel comfortable with many different kinds of music. I am flexible. Not only in music, but in other things too. The only music that I have stayed away from has been the Renaissance. And honestly, the reason why I haven't played it in concert is because I feel that it's a specialized area. I feel that it's something I would like to know more about before I play it in public. So I may play a piece or two from the Renaissance, but I'm not going to make an issue of it at this stage until I'm more familiar with it.

As I said before, I'm flexible. I can play renaissance music and feel comfortable with it, but there I still have questions to which I don't know the answers. That's not to say I don't still have a lot of questions about all the music that I play, but I feel that I have enough answers. With renaissance music, I feel that I don't have enough answers. Also, for a long time I didn't like a lot of renaissance music, but I think a lot of it had to do with the way it was played, which I found to be too mechanical and strict. It was not too long before I heard a couple who were playing renaissance music with a freedom that really opened doors for me.

How much freedom can an artist have? I believe you teach — do you find that helpful, or does it get in the way of your performing? In other words, does it restrict your freedom?

When my concert schedule got too busy, I stopped teaching for a couple of years. I've gone back. I missed it. Years ago, an old teacher at the school where I was teaching told me that it was always good for a player to teach. He didn't go into details. Now I think that it is true.

For me, the answer is that to make music, to make art as well as you can, and to give a performance, are maybe two different things at times. If it's going to be art, I think it's something that has to be able to withstand repeated listening and careful observation.

In a concert situation, I think it's much more the impact of the moment, the impression it's giving at the time. If you examine it later, it may not be as good as that impression. I think my playing had begun to rely on effects a little bit too much. I think by having

students, if you practice what you preach, it sort of puts a responsibility on you to maintain a certain level, not only musically but even technically. If somebody gets a little bit of a name, I think people are sometimes inclined to forgive the bad things that one may do.

There is a Spanish expression of which the translation would be: 'Make yourself famous, and then go to sleep'. You are doing minimal work, really, just patching-up kind of work. It's not as thorough as it should be. But I now realize that one has to do something.

I would like to say something about the freedom you mention. Some people get caught up — I say some people but *I* have got caught up at times, and at times I still get caught up on ideas and thoughts and information and this kind of thing. I think ultimately an artist has to do what he thinks is good — what he likes. And then he hopes that other people will like it. For example, I will not play a piece in a certain way because I think people will like hearing it in that way. It would probably not have any conviction. I have to do it in the way I think is good. I have to go with that. That has to be my game, and I just hope that people like it.

It's sad in a way that you can't please everybody. You just can't. You have to do what you think is right, to be honest with yourself.

Is that the difference between an artist and a performer?

Perhaps. I mean there are many times, especially when one's musicianship is developing, when one is confused, you know. You may feel one way about something, while your intellect tells you something else. This is at the developmental stage. Once you arrive at a conclusion that this is what you think is right, you have to do it. You can't *not* do it, afraid of what somebody will say. That's what makes it interesting to me.

Two or three years ago in this country you had the reputation of being a very fast player. This is a dangerous kind of label to give to a musician, isn't it?

That really doesn't bother me too much. The only way in which it used to bother me was that some years ago I would try to live up to what people said I was. This is not a contradiction to what I was saying before. For example, I would hear people say 'he plays without mistakes'. Then I would try so hard to play without mistakes. The point is, I have never played without mistakes, and from what I can see I never shall! So I tried to be something that people were telling me I was. On the other hand, I'm sure it has helped to keep up a certain standard.

Nobody in their right mind would deny themselves the opportunity of having a good technique. The more technique you have, the more you can do with the music. No question about it. Technique is necessary. People interpret technique differently. Some people think technique is playing fast and loud. Some people may interpret it as not only that but also individual control of notes. Some people, for example, can play really loud. I wouldn't be so interested in that without these other aspects of technique.

People sometimes take a narrow view of it. It doesn't bother me when people say 'he's fast', 'he's slow', 'he's warm', 'he's cold', 'he's musical' or 'he's not musical'. It's human nature. Different people come to concerts for different reasons. If they enjoy it, I think they can enjoy it on any level they want to.

There are always influences. As much as one tries to be as honest as one can, there are still influences. I don't think they can be avoided. I think one has to learn to deal with them as much as possible. I find myself all the time getting off the track somewhere, and then going back in again. Hopefully!

I have come to a certain point now, and I can't even describe to myself what it is. The easiest way for me to describe it is to say that I will do what I think I should do, what I like, what I think is good. I will try to be as honest as I can about it. And then let things happen, let things be the way they want to be. That probably sounds awfully simple...

. . . But of course it isn't. You have arrived at that point by way of a lot of hard work.
You have to work. Of course, I haven't stopped working — that's not the case at all. You know, I think it's very normal to kind of fall asleep. I think if one becomes famous it's easier for one to impress other people. People will tell one perhaps how great one is perhaps more often. One gets a better reaction from the public simply because one has more of a name. One starts believing that one is really something rather special. And I think it's a normal human reaction. Anyone having this happen to them would probably react in the same way. It would take an unusual human being not to be too much affected by that. But I think we all do to some extent or another.

Isn't that why the best artists are unusual people — because they can stand up against that kind of human weakness? They don't believe their own publicity.
That could be a weakness in itself. It may be that a certain kind of temperament is so critical that it doesn't allow one to relax.

There are at least two ways of enjoying one's work. By your own standards as compared to others; and to keep judging yourself by your own standards. That's the important thing.

There are also certain other aspects. Perhaps it's hard for, let's say, guitar students, music fans in general, to understand unless they've gone through it. If one wants to build a career the normal way, meaning from the bottom up, I think there are times when certain risks are taken. And sometimes one is going to fail. Maybe somebody comes to a concert and sees one in a situation where one has failed. They may arrive at all sorts of conclusions without really knowing what's going on behind the scenes. That doesn't mean to say they don't have the right to be critical and to complain. I think they should, and I think this will keep the artist more honest — I hope.

This is related to what I said before, about having come to a point at which I'm comfortable. It's something else I wanted to say, because I know that there are guitarists and guitar students, for example, who many times have asked questions about what they have to do in order to be comfortable.

Also I feel, and I have contributed in part to it, that there's a kind of negative cloud around the guitar world. I don't know if you would agree with me, but I have sensed that kind of being critical, kind of 'I don't want to be a guitarist for this or a guitarist for that' attitude — and this is from a guitarist!

Do you understand what I mean? You know, it would be perhaps funny to have a caricature or a cartoon or something of somebody holding a guitar and saying 'I hate guitarists.'

In a sense I actually love the instrument more than I have in a long time. I understand its beauties a little bit more. It's a really beautiful instrument, but really misunderstood very often. Not only by people outside the guitar, but also by guitarists themselves.

With the guitar, we've gone through an incredible stage which I think is a development of questioning so much about it — you know, is it valid, is the repertoire good? What I'm saying is that after this, I've finally come up with positive answers.

Do guitarists perhaps develop these negative attitudes because they are aware of how other people regard the guitar?
Sometimes. The other day I did a television show in Germany, and one of the pieces I did was the *Chaconne* by Bach. And one question was 'Why did you play this on the guitar?' I could have said, well, you know, Bach transcribed some of his violin music for the harpsichord. But all these kinds of things in the end are just excuses. The only answer is: listen to it! I'm saying this, assuming it's a good performance on the guitar. If you don't like it, then don't listen to it. It's that simple. When I hear good music well played on the guitar, to me it's really a beautiful experience. I think also that there is no doubt that we have a lot to overcome before people can hear the guitar. Some people become very snobbish, you know, and I do believe that snobbishness is a type of ignorance. But then again, one has the right to make certain choices and say 'I don't like this' or 'I don't like that' or 'I won't give this any time'. It's their prerogative. The truth of the matter is that we also have a long way to go in improving the musicianship of our guitar playing in general. How many times people come to the guitar and don't necessarily hear a musical performance! They may think that this is the guitar, when in fact it's not the guitar but only the guitarist. Aside from the fact that some people may not like the guitar, I really do not believe that anybody, given a good performance, could possibly dislike the instrument. It's something I cannot see. I can see them taking a while, perhaps. But I cannot see them disliking it.

On the other hand, I have to admit that when I hear the guitar poorly played, I cannot see anybody liking it. Talk about the violin being a horrible instrument to listen to when it's poorly played — I think the guitar gives it damned good competition. A poorly played guitar is a horrible thing to listen to.

What does one do when one hears the guitar poorly played? Discourage the player — or encourage him in the hope that things will improve?
I believe in being straight and honest about it, and letting things take their own course. If somebody's concerned about the guitar out of love for it, the best thing they can do is to try to do the best job they can in what they do, whether writing, playing or composing, or whatever field they're in. That's what's happening to the guitar at the moment.

The bad players eventually become lost to view, it's true, but meanwhile they can lose audiences for everybody else.
I don't think you can have the good without the bad. To expect there will be only good players is unrealistic.

Do you think that the guitar is still at a stage where there is a higher proportion of bad players than with violin or piano?
I think if somebody feels that it's bad to have so many bad concerts, then they shouldn't go to these concerts. If they don't go to the concerts, then there will not be those concerts. Nature will take care of that! If they go to those concerts, they are supporting them. Besides, you know, ultimately people are human beings, and I find it's very difficult to judge for oneself. I'm sure that the vast majority of people who get up and play a bad concert probably do not realize they're playing a bad concert. They probably think they're doing at least a decent concert — at least I hope that's the case. And they need to learn, they need to know.

I really believe that time takes care of things.

CC

Photo by Jane Hamborsky

JULIAN BREAM

There have been times when Julian Bream has declined an interview, feeling that he has said quite enough about the guitar. He is keenly aware of a truth not always appreciated, that music is not talking about it (or writing about it) but playing it. Fortunately for his multitudinous admirers, he relaxes that opinion from time to time, when he feels that verbal communication can usefully complement his unparalleled musical communication.

Come to think of it, his verbal communication is pretty unparalleled, too. Who else can talk about music and the guitar with so beguiling a blend of humor, passion and down-to-earth common sense?

Classical Guitar magazine has interviewed Julian Bream many times. This particular interview, by Chris Kilvington, found the 60-year-old maestro in a communicative mood, discussing many different topics with the warmth and commitment that characterize his very best guitar playing. **CC**

In a 1985 interview, you said 'guitar music is largely not intellectual music.' What did you mean by that? After all, you are regarded as a champion of new music and one of its greatest interpreters.
About 40 years ago I met the famous Italian composer Gian Francesco Malipiero, had an introduction to him, and played for him on both the lute and the guitar. He said: 'You know, they're two very different instruments, the lute and the guitar; the lute is music from the spheres and the guitar is the music of the streets.' In a sense that conveys exactly what I meant when I said that a lot of guitar music is not intellectual; the guitar is an earthy, sensuous, and ravishingly beautiful sound in the right hands. The music, or the quality of the music, is nearly always on the slight side; it doesn't have any grave intellectual import. I feel the guitar is an instrument of the senses; it has a great charm, and it has half a dozen pieces which could be said to be great, probably not half a dozen even. And the rest of its repertoire is, on the whole, rather light-weight. But that doesn't mean that a fine player cannot invest that music with great meaning. In a sense it's more of a challenge to play the guitar repertory than that of the piano.

I think it was well summed up by Edgar Allan Poe in his short story, *The Fall of the House of Usher*. The anti-hero is a guitarist, and the gist of the idea as it affected Poe was that although the range of the instrument was not great, *because* of those very limitations there was a certain tension created in the performances which made them magical. He said it much more beautifully than that, of course.

The constraints and discipline can be creative as well as sometimes being harmful to the creative process. To play a dozen notes beautifully on the guitar — any notes — can evoke such expressiveness. But it's how you play those notes that is important. And how you link those notes, and how you use the diminuendos of the plucked string that in itself creates

a myriad of silences. But it's those silences, and the tensions between the impact of the next note they create. That is important — that is the poetry.

Why does one get it right, so close to being perfect sometimes, and not at others? That's true, isn't it?
Yes, it's true, but that's the charm of public performance, that it's never the same. Even the instrument itself, because the density of wood is so fine compared to that of a violin for example. It's very finely calibrated, always subject to the prevailing conditions of the air, the humidity, the dryness and so on. Sometimes in a concert hall where it's too humid, the instrument simply won't sing as you want it to. And when it's very dry the guitar can be rather shrill and ungiving. And your nails of course, their condition and length, and the state of your strings, whether they're brand new or three months old — should they have been changed? Then the hall itself and its acoustic, which obviously very much affects the way you play. I always play a little faster in a dry acoustic, and I think that most people do, because you've got no assistance from the hall to help the notes sustain and thereby achieve the phrasing as you want to present it.

Another consideration, and a most important one, is the public. When you go to a concert there's such a wonderful — or can be, shall we say — such a wonderful feeling amongst most of the people, and that feeds back to the performer. And if people are attentive and concentrating and willing to let themselves go into the music, then I think certain things can happen in a recital which make it a memorable, or at least a pleasurable, event.

This business about the audience — why should it not always be excellent? Every audience has surely come to be entertained or involved?
I wonder about that. When I was a student I used to go to concerts in London, and they weren't hugely

Photo by Nick White, EMI

advertised as concerts are today. There was perhaps a little notice on a Wednesday in The Times or The Telegraph, but you had to know where to look. But the fact that you had to search and hunt, to make an effort, meant that you weren't just some ordinary old concertgoer. And that is already a wonderful beginning from the point of view of the public. Nowadays promoters want to get as many egalitarian bums on seats as possible, because it is largely an economic exercise for them. And so the great thing is to find new audiences, and that comes about through advertising, the media, and so forth. They bring in people who wouldn't normally have gone to concerts 40 years ago. They think, 'Hello, I saw him on the box, perhaps it might be a nice idea to go to his concert'. So they go. You get people coming out of curiosity more than anything else.

And sponsorship. I'll give you a typical example of a bit of dead wood in the audience. Nowadays, nearly all my concerts are sponsored, like the one the other night in Bath, sponsored by the gas company. They gave their top employees tickets, with a special bar laid on for themselves and their friends — then they hear the concert and have a slap-up dinner somewhere afterwards. So it's really just an outing for the company, and people are not going to say no to a trip to Bath, with a free concert and a free meal thrown in. It's very hard to get through to dead wood. If you succeed, you've actually achieved something. That's the problem with this modern sponsorship: admirable

when it's working; but, finally, it doesn't always help.

What do you think would be the perfect audience, if such a thing could exist?
I don't think anything is perfect. London can produce a very good audience — in the Wigmore Hall, for example, with just over 500 seats. The one year I couldn't use the Wigmore I went to the Queen Elizabeth, a cold and rather austere hall but not a bad acoustic. And I had one of the best audiences I ever had. Yet the Wigmore is the ideal hall for the guitar. When I was a kid just after the war all the great artists played there, I mean the very greatest. Pierre Fournier, Victoria de los Angeles, Rubinstein — that calibre of artist. And the Segovia evenings there were just as magical. Whereas when he moved across the river to the South Bank into that very dry, large hall, I felt it was only half a musical experience. So I think that halls are very important as far as the quality of audience goes.

How do you go about choosing a new piece — and what are the processes for you between that and performing it?
These days you're asked for your program maybe a year ahead, whereas before it was a couple of months. People want to get everything organized early, and I find that rather sad. I've just been giving my programs for next May, yet now I have the summer pretty much off to learn things and make records. I'll probably learn something that I'd like to play in my next season's concerts, but really I'm stuck.

My programs have a typical and rather conventional shape. I play what I really like to play, and if nobody likes it, well, they can go home. To be able to take that attitude — well, at the age of 60 I feel you've earned that prerogative. I play only music that stimulates me, and I never, ever, get bored with the pieces. But I do rest them, perhaps for a number of years, and then pick them up again, and I see totally new things. I'm doing that now with Lennox Berkeley's *Sonatina*. I found that the old concept I had of the piece wasn't bad but that I just didn't bring out all the beauties which I now feel in the composition. I can tell by the fingerings I used. It's a very well-made piece, and charming music. I remember Britten once saying — and he seldom had a good word for any other composer and was very critical of English composers in particular— 'That is very nearly a great piece'. Coming from him, you can be sure it's a damn good piece anyway.

To what extent is your interpretation planned in your

dynamic and tonal phrasing, and tempo, and to what extent is it intuitive on the night?
Tempo is very spontaneous because, as I mentioned earlier, it is, among other things, to do with the acoustics and how you feel. You know, it's the old heart that sets the rhythm. Tone color — which, as you know, I use rather a lot — I sort of work out, but not always. Sometimes I enjoy experimenting or reversing the colors; a passage taken near the bridge I might try beyond the soundhole, and so forth. And that keeps one on one's toes.

Is that purely for the possibility of discovery?
Yes. And for fun. Dynamics are largely prearranged; but the intensities of those dynamics are not.

And how does that happen?
According to the hall and the audience. If the audience is really concentrating, you make them concentrate even more — well, you don't *make* them, you just do, it happens. Sometimes you can play so quietly, perhaps a tiny, gentle artificial harmonic, but if you can get it to ring exquisitely with some left-hand vibrato added, it has a certain magic.

Such an important thing about the carrying power of the guitar is the actual sound you make on it. If the sound has a real centre, is really focused, then that sound really carries through the air. It doesn't matter about decibels; it gets there. And if the sound is not well focused, a bit angular or thin, that will often not register so much with people. It won't travel. I experiment a great deal when I'm performing, always trying to get the instrument to ring a bit more or to have a little bit more incision in the articulation. I'm always trying things, and sometimes I fall flat on my face. But it's worth a try.

Tightrope walking?
A little bit. But audiences like that. The ones that know, they know what you're doing and they're saying 'No, no, he's not going to get away with that one.' And you do or you don't.

It keeps it live, doesn't it?
That's it! I was doing a concert recently somewhere in Germany, and finished with Falla's *Miller's Dance*. And that fantastic last A minor chord right at the top of the instrument — I missed it by a semitone! Except, of course, for the open A; the rest was A flat minor — the very last chord of the concert. They're very serious in Germany, but the whole audience collapsed with laughter. I was so annoyed with myself, but I have to say the audience enjoyed it.

I just shrugged my arms and walked off. I can see that it was amusing and I was grateful that they laughed, but for me it wrecked the whole evening. I felt I'd let the composer down. But that happens from time to time, and it does liven things up a bit. I'm always looking for the very best out of every phrase.

Do you think you're changing?
At the moment I sense I'm improving, somehow. It's a wonderful feeling. Something has happened. I'm enjoying the whole business of making music so much now — I mean, I always have, but in some ways even more now. As you get older — and this is not just to do with music — you begin to get rid of things that are a waste of time. You say 'I don't want to do this', or 'I'm getting rid of that'. I want to simplify life. Because since the beginning of time life has got more complicated, and there comes a time when you want to concentrate on what's truly worthwhile. And all the rest of the stuff — chuck it! I've cut out a lot of the waste of energy and time. You're not going to live for ever, you know time's limited and you suddenly realize that it goes at a hell of a lick. It seems only yesterday that I was 50. The great thing is to get rid of all the unnecessary stuff.

Do you do exactly what you want to do?
I've always been idealistic about music. I suppose. One of the things I remember as a student at the College after the war was that we were an idealistic generation. It was a rough time coming through the war, but we had ideals. And I miss that now. There weren't so many people doing things; there weren't so many people, period. And there was space, and there wasn't this sort of competition and this sort of elbowing.

You're talking about the musical world?
You bet — but also the world in general. There weren't the pressures, particularly on young people. Today they race into these competitions, and if they win they maybe get a prize of half a dozen concerts and a recording contract if they're lucky. That's a lot of pressure on a young person. My generation, we sort of matured into our profession slowly, and I think we were very lucky to be able to do that. Now it's very different. It's the commercialization of life and the competition of it all which has caused a lot of unhappiness for people in general.

Do you think there's any value in music competitions?
I think they can sort out the good players. Let's face it, in the old Communist ethic there was no such thing as

competition, everybody had the same. But the Russians also had their music competitions; they had to have something to sort out the great from the not so great. Even the Bolshevik Russians had that. They treat music very seriously; it's a genuine part of their system of education. Look what wonderful artists come out of Russia — and they're trained at a very early age. It's terrific, it's wonderful. They become so deeply involved with the music itself.

In the same way as an actor can become his role, should a musician attempt to become the music, or maybe the composer?
Sometimes one should think about the music deeply without the instrument, with only the score. We must certainly find out a bit about the composer and the environment in which he worked. It all helps. The important thing for a performing musician is that he must be the servant of the composer. And that would be very difficult if you've got a big ego, if you think you're just the greatest. Those people tend not to be the best interpreters, although they can be flamboyantly brilliant and good value. But as I see it, one's role is in the service of the music. And then to be able to convey that music in such a way that it's wholly, utterly and totally convincing. That is a very great responsibility for a performer.

What do you actually think about when you're away from the guitar and working with the score?
The shape of the piece, and sometimes the fingering. It's getting to know the first note so that paradoxically you can almost hear the last note, you can feel the whole sweep of it. It's hard to achieve. Two works of Bach ideally employ that idea, both in variation form: the *Goldberg Variations* and the *Chaconne*. And then you go through an experience which transcends time. I use the word paradoxical because the transcendental quality of the music means that it is always stretching out, and yet the relationship between the variations always brings it back. So you've got this inhale/exhale situation, and it's that tension which can be so moving and so wonderful in a variation piece of that quality. Much better to look at that sort of thing away from the instrument.

Can music sometimes express what words can't?
That's an interesting proposition. There is an abstract purity about instrumental music, whereas words can give a fixed emotional framework to the work. Instrumental music conveys a dimension that is abstract and mystical and also engages the intellect. And those three things are, above all, intercepted by the heart.

But that doesn't mean to say I don't like songs. I love songs, the French songs of Fauré, Debussy and Ravel, and the German Lieder. It's a different concept of music.

I wasn't thinking of songs so much. Everyone in this life must, at one time or another, have been, as we say, 'lost for words', incapable of expressing linguistically something that was within themselves. Maybe music can sometimes offer that expression.
The music is obviously saying it for you, not any words. That's it! And that's why writing about music is in some way a complete waste of time. And yet, even so, a person's thoughts on music can be very revealing. I think you've got to read musical criticism with the foreknowledge that it is a waste of time basically. Yet it can be a highly entertaining business. I read a wonderful book recently about the critics in Beethoven's time and what they said about his music. It's amazing what you can learn about the society of 170 years ago. We tend to class music into categories, and contemporary or avant-garde music is said to be something difficult to understand for many people, and often stretches the medium which is being used to its utmost breaking point. But this is a natural corollary to how things evolve.

One must remember that in the 18th century nearly every new work was an avant-garde piece. Audiences were hearing nothing other than avant-garde music. Take Mozart's clarinet concerto: when that was written it was way out, and the G minor symphony too. People weren't listening to Palestrina; they listened to the music of the day. Maybe one or two people sang a few Bach chorales, but it was generally a totally different situation. I think musical life was much livelier because of that, and the fact that the musical language was in a wonderful state of evolution at that point in history.

Do you think, then, that it's a backwards step to play works of the past?
No, I don't think so. But it's rather hard luck on contemporary composers that they have to hear a masterpiece by Bach before they hear the first performance of their new work. It's unfair for them to be compared with the beauties of an age which had a totally different aesthetic. I do admire someone like Pierre Boulez or Harrison Birtwistle; their music is continuously evolving. And most music of the last 15 years has become so-called 'melodic', or you could say harmonic in the quasi-traditional way. And I think most of it is pretty mediocre stuff.

I hardly know of a person I want to commission a piece from now. I think the two composers alive with the greatest musical ears are Takemitsu and Lutosławski. *(Both composers died a few years after this interview took place — Ed).*

You know, there was always a time when I felt I must commission so-and-so, I must get a new work. Maybe it's because I'm getting older, but I'm not so very enthusiastic about what I hear now. I don't go to many concerts but I regularly listen to the radio specifically to hear certain works and get the feel of a new composer — there may be a Beethoven in our midst that we don't know about. It's very easy to make great sweeping statements about things, but that's my general feeling at the moment.

You wouldn't say no to another Nocturnal or Bagatelles, quality-wise, would you?
Well, there's nobody who can write that music any more. They're period pieces, they're of their time.

I notice that guitar programs, when I see them, are rather more conservative than they used to be. And architecture, and painting....

Is that wrapped up with the political scene, the extremely functional politics we've seen in the last ten years or so?

I think it's the way the world is. I believe there's always a spirit moving through the world, always has been. And today I feel it's so unhappy. The violence of it all! It's a terrible time. I feel that it's hard to compose beautiful things in a world which is killing itself, killing itself in more ways than one. I don't think it's a pretty picture. Do you?

On composition again: the critic Edward Greenfield once wrote 'with the "wrong" notes written, the player is prevented from bringing out the instrument's proper resonance.' Any thoughts on this?
I would say that certain keys have specific moods, and one of the unfortunate things about the guitar is that it's limited in the ways it can transpose. This is very indicative in the 19th-century sonatas. I can hardly think of a guitar sonata that has a development section. And key relationships do play such an important part of classical sonata form; they create part of the tension of the music. A thematic idea in one key sounds so different in another, and the guitar finds it difficult to cope with that in terms of musical development. Yet sometimes a remote key can give a covered feeling to

the music. Takemitsu's *All in Twilight* has lots of G Flat, A Flat, D Flat, yet it sounds very well. The reason is that he's worked it all out very carefully on the fingerboard. It gives the piece a rather muted feeling, which I believe he wants.

A change of tack: what sort of practice are you doing nowadays?
About three or four hours a day. I start off quite early in the morning and work through until midday. I don't practice in the afternoon. In the morning I'll start about 8, do an hour, have a breather, another 45 minutes, a breather, and so do about three hours playing in a four-hour session. I'll do a bit more between 5 and 6.30, and then I put the old box to bed and have a glass of gin. Down here my days are very simple. I might go out and do a bit of gardening in the afternoon or walk the dog; it's such a negative time, whereas the mornings and evenings are great. That's the thing about being a performer, you tend to move towards the evening.

You're a late-night person?
No. I used to go to bed very late, but not now.

Are you still having to do lots of practice on technique since the accident to your arm, or have you got all that back again?
It's pretty much sorted out. But I had to do a fantastic lot of practice initially. And then I carried that on because I really enjoyed it. I had to change my hand position slightly because of the accident, and then the left hand, I changed that too. I did a double change.

What sort of things?
I tended to play with rather flat fingers on my left hand, and I didn't notice it until I saw the scenes from the films on the Guitar in Spain. I looked at my left hand and asked myself, do I really play like that? It was terrible. It sort of sounded all right, but I thought I'd never develop my left hand if I continued to play like that. So I had to change, and that was very hard to achieve at my age. But I'm glad I did it; I really had to slave, but I'm so pleased that I did it. I hadn't actually seen myself playing for a long time, which you don't in the normal course of events. The palm of my hand was too far away from the fingerboard. And what a hell of a job it was to rectify it, too.

Being virtually self-taught, I have always had to approach these things a bit like that; trial and error — and a lot of trial specifically.
I had to start from the very beginning. About a month

17

after the accident, I did I5 minutes just moving the fingers, then half an hour, then 40, 50 minutes, then an hour. Diatonic and chromatic scales, arpeggios. I worked in front of a mirror and I would watch what was going on and I gradually built my technique up again. It was interesting. I wouldn't recommend it to anybody, but you do learn more that way.

With your right hand, did you just reconstitute what you had before or did you change things?
I changed things a little bit. The position of my thumb. And I'm quite happy to have changed my wrist position also. Whereas previously I kept it more or less the same throughout a performance — although I moved it up and down the strings — now I'm quite ready to change the angle, to move it as I feel. It's not a very pure outlook to technique, but it's one that suits me now.

I also notice that guitar players in general don't fuss with their right hands anything like they used to in terms of the old Tárrega bent wrist. And I'm not at all sure that's a good thing either; the thing with the Tárrega bend is that you didn't have to support the wrist, it just fell that way. But with this flatter method, you have to consciously support the wrist.

When you had the accident, did you feel like packing it in? Did it ever seem that bad?
It was certainly a pretty traumatic experience. It does have an effect on your life and your outlook upon things. It was terribly bad luck being involved in such a catastrophic accident, but I also feel I somehow had great fortune; really, I'm lucky to be alive. It gave me another dimension of feeling to have gone through an experience of that kind. It did change my life.

I stopped for a month, and maybe that was good too. The initial thought was 'Maybe I'll never play again.' I don't know what effect that would have had on me. I would have missed the playing terribly, I must say, because I love playing. Maybe I'd have done a bit of teaching — yes, I'd have done that. But as soon as I felt I could move my fingers I knew I'd play again. That was why I had the operation done on a local anaesthetic, so I could talk with the surgeon. I really wanted to know what he was doing.

Is it set in a particular way?
Yes. When they do these operations they're limited by the amount of bone that's there, and I wanted to know just what was destroyed and what was fixable before he set it up. He might have said 'I can do it this way,

but your little finger won't work.' And I'd have said 'OK, I'll have no little finger working.' And I'll tell you what else — it crossed my mind that I'd take up the old plectrum guitar again, because, as you know, I used to be a jazz player.

Les Paul had a similar accident, and his arm was fixed, but fixed just for playing; that was it.

Which jazz guitar players do you like?
I'm not really up on the moderns. Wes Montgomery was a phenomenal player. I admired him tremendously.

Joe Pass?
Joe Pass I think is a lovely player. It's very unusual playing. The way he conceives his harmonies cries out for fingerstyle. Wouldn't you say that? And of course Tal Farlow, Charlie Christian and, the best of the lot, Django. Without a shadow of a doubt.

You said, in A Life on the Road, *'One day I will teach.' What would you get involved with?*
I don't know. I reckon that will be when I'm not doing so much concert playing. Playing and teaching is not a good combination. I think to teach institutionally could be rather boring for my temperament.

More masterclasses — that type of thing?
Well, I enjoy doing classes. I do one at the Royal Academy of Music every term, and I learn a lot myself. I sometimes trade someone else's ideas with my own. I have been known to misread notes, and I can find that it's in a class that I get those notes right. I enjoy a class because I can talk about other things than music. Music is a way of life, music has fashioned the way you think about things.

Some students are a little bit intense. I'm all for seriousness, I absolutely approve of that. But I think there's an intensity where they're not looking at themselves from any vantage point and preparing what they're doing. I can talk about other things, which can yet relate to the music and help them to relax a bit more. Because it is a hard thing for students to get up there and go through their pieces in front of each other.

I get a little bit melancholy about the prospects for some of these players. The standard has improved tremendously in the last ten or 15 years, and I don't know where we're all going to earn our bread — to put it in a nutshell. There are some very fine players about and it's sad that at some point they'll realize they can't realize their ambitions professionally. At least they'll have had a go, and there's fulfillment in that. It's a hard life, a hard profession. You've got to be tough, particularly now when there's so much competition in a rather small fishpond.

Are you giving any masterclasses now as you travel around the world?
Not many, just the odd one. I want to wait some years yet before I start teaching in any serious way. Yet I know it's a good thing to impart what experience you've had, particularly towards the end of a life. Because I've had a marvellous life and I do want to convey things, and I will. But I'm still learning, still experiencing, and I want to keep that, to keep playing.

What changes do you observe in the guitar scene as you've known it? How was it when you were a boy, then a young man, then at 40, and how is it now?
When I was a boy there was no possibility, professionally speaking, to make a career with the classical guitar. When I was 20 there was a distinct possibility; when I was 30 the possibility had become an actuality, and when I was 40 my career had taken off and I was making a lot of records. I would say that at 50 my career had reached its zenith, professionally speaking. Nowadays there's not so much interest in the guitar among the general musical public. But at 60 I would say that my career is flourishing as well as ever.

What do you think are the reasons for the present decline of the guitar in terms of audience numbers?
I think a lot of younger players' programs are, not exactly boring, just not very well planned as musical entities. I also think there's a higher priority given to

technical brilliance than to musical evocation. And I think that what moves people is the interiorization of music that is distilled and then projected. This age is not exactly a poetic one in any case, so you can't blame these artists; they are of their generation and made by the environment in which they live. They work very hard and their technical achievements are important and can sometimes be exciting. But finally technical achievement must be the servant to the musical achievement, and that is a very hard thing to manage in this climate. People still require that certain spirituality of music from their performers. And I just think it's in short supply.

Countries that have been deprived of the technological society and the mass hysterical materialism that we've indulged in — I refer to those countries that were formerly communist — actually produce better musicians by and large because they're not cluttered up with the coldness of materials and the calculated business of owning things. Our whole thing is geared to 'achievers', but when you're a musician you're not an achiever. You have to have a sense of humanity, and humility. Because you know you're never going to achieve 'it'.

We've got to 60. What about the rest of your time? What are you looking for? Where are you headed?
Oh, I should think for the grave! *(laughter).*

CK

Photo by Colin Cooper

LEO BROUWER

Creative musicians do not, on the whole, like critics. And with good reason, because generally the critic has spent less time on the music than the composer has in composing it and the player has in rehearsing and practising it. When critics spend at least an equal amount of time on a work before writing about it, then their status might improve. Comment, of course, will continue to be made, much of it the uninformed or at least ill-informed product of an imperfectly digested consumption.

It can be a little unnerving to meet someone whose work you have known and written about for a long time. Some composers — Benjamin Britten was one — have an almost pathological hatred of critics and regard their work as unnecessary. At the highest creative levels, perhaps they are.

But then, I am not happy with the critic label, preferring to write about music that I either admire or enjoy. Leo Brouwer's music comes into both categories, and I was therefore delighted to be summoned to the BBC studios in Maida Vale, London, to meet him.

The composer Gareth Walters was doing fine work for the guitar at that time, hosting a half-hour weekly broadcast on Radio 3, attending guitar festivals around the world, engaging the best guitarists to play for the BBC, and generally doing a wonderful job in bringing the classical guitar to the radio audience while encouraging it in many other ways. Bringing Leo Brouwer to England was one of his most obvious successes. Out of it came numerous conducting engagements for Leo, the Concerto Elegiaco (Brouwer's third guitar concerto) which Julian Bream played and recorded, and a radio recording of the Toronto Concerto (the fourth guitar concerto) with John Williams as the soloist. All this made as British airwaves. Gareth Walters decided to direct his musical and organizational skills elsewhere, and a general apathy crept into the BBC, so far as the guitar was concerned, from which it has never recovered. The guitar has been left to the discretion of individual producers, who appear to prefer a second-rate piece for the piano to a first-rate piece for the guitar.

At that first interview Leo explained his 'conversion' from avant-garde to nouveau romantique. Time to take another look at Vaughan Williams? That seemed to be his message. We did not know then how his new style would develop, but after most of the music that was being fabricated in considerable quantities by the serialists and post-serialists, we were willing to listen to almost any alternative, even minimalism.

Leo Brouwer's excursions into the strange and barren landscape of minimalism have managed to avoid tedium, which is not surprising when you consider the resourcefulness of the man himself. The Cuban landscapes he depicts are anything but barren, and are perceived in the glow of Brouwer's own creative vision. It demonstrates that it is not the form that matters so much as the skill of the composer who works in it.

My second interview with Leo Brouwer was in Rome, where he was conducting a performance of his Concerto Elegiaco, with Leonardo De Angelis the soloist. Before the performance Leo held a press conference, attended by several Italian journalists as well as myself. Leo chose to talk about the binary nature of the universe: night and day, hot and cold, north and south. He mentioned the Italian writer Italo Calvino, who was also born in Cuba, and whose novels included the remarkably binary manifestation of The Cloven Viscount, the unfortunate man who was split into two halves during a battle. One half was good, the other bad. Brouwer had just composed the Helsinki Concerto, which contains these ideas.

Then Leo chose to talk about the significance of numbers. Also in the evening concert was his From Yesterday to Penny Lane, a reworking for guitar and orchestra of seven celebrated Lennon and McCartney numbers done with other composers in mind. Bach was one of them, described by Leo as 'A sonata in five movements, on a ten-note theme.' It was, naturally, assigned the number 5 in the series. For similar reasons, the Falla-flavored piece was given the number 7, because of his Seven Spanish Popular Songs.

Then Leo pointed out that his own personal number was 3, because he had been born on the 1st day of the 3rd month of the year 39 — 1939. An Italian journalist said excitedly that his own number was 6, because he had been born in the 6th month of 1966. Everyone began to examine their own birth dates to see if they contained numerical significance.

It was the end of any serious discussion, and the press conference degenerated into a cheerful free-for-all as every journalist present competed for attention. Leo surveyed the scene benevolently, and announced: 'We are all crazy — fortunately.' It brought a semblance of order, but it was too late: Leo had to leave to prepare for the concert, and it was clear that I had nothing on tape that could legitimately be called an interview.

Instead, I wrote an article on binary rhythms, bringing in Leo Brouwer, Italo Calvino, the Rule of Opposites, and the Manichean principles that see a primordial conflict between each pair of extremes. It filled the space and met the deadline, and in some ways I was quite pleased with it; but it is not an interview, it does not reveal much about Leo Brouwer the musician or the man, and for that reason I prefer to rely on that first interview, in June 1985, which is printed here with some editing.

What are we to make of Leo Brouwer's astonishing shift in direction? Announcing that the avant-garde is dead, he turns back to melody and tonality of the kind that we tend to associate with the nationalistic and romantic composers such as Dvořák, Martinů, Janáček and even Tchaikovsky and the other Russians.

It is rather as if Schoenberg, after half a lifetime of writing serial music, had suddenly come up with *Verklärte Nacht*, the post-romantic work he wrote at the outset of his career. But there are many other parallels. Perhaps the most obvious is Stravinsky who, despite the uncompromising starkness of *The Rite of Spring*, went on to compose a large amount of music that by no stretch of the imagination can be said to carry on where *Rite* left off. This music is generally referred to as 'neo-classicism', and its composer as the first neo-classicist.

Walton went through a neo-classicist phase before developing the warmer style that we associate with his later music. Bartók, too, was a neo-classicist before Hungarian folk music claimed his attention. Prokofiev's early, lively and rhythmically very strong music can be described as neo-classical — but his change to a warmer and more lyrical style was, as we know, 'encouraged' by a government clearly unaware or uncaring that it constitutes an assault on an artist's integrity to attempt to impose a style from outside. Hindemith was one neo-classicist whose music does not appear to have undergone any fundamental change (musicologists may argue), but it seems to be the rule rather than the exception for a composer to make one or more somewhat drastic changes during his or her career.

If neo-classicism is now dead, so, according to Brouwer, is the avant-garde. He calls his latest music 'hyper-romantic or 'neo-romantic', and the tag will do as well as any other. After 30 years of atonality and aleatory, he feels that it is time to relax a little as we approach the end of the 20th century (possibly the most disturbed century in human history) and to enjoy music to the full. If you argue that you already enjoy Leo Brouwer's music (and most guitarists do), he would no doubt reply that *he* no longer does — at least, not in that particular form — and that it is time he composed something along different lines. It is an essential condition of the creative urge that you write what you believe in. If an artist doesn't believe in what he is doing, how can anyone else?

It is necessary to say this, because already there are critics who suspect a seeking after the kind of popularity that the *Aranjuez* Concerto has been accorded, especially in the fourth concerto, the *Concierto de Toronto*. I don't think this analysis holds much water. Rodrigo was not seeking that kind of popularity when he wrote his concerto. If he had sought it, he probably wouldn't have got it. Besides, Brouwer has managed very well without such popularity in some 30 years of professional musicianship, during which time he has achieved a level of eminence given to few guitarists. And he has achieved it by composing and playing the music that he wanted to compose and play.

Naturally, Leo Brouwer will not escape criticism. Neither will he lack praise. Both reactions should be regarded with caution. It is impossible to assess new music accurately, whatever the pundits say, except in terms of technical competence — and even that is a matter for argument. Time is necessary for assess-

Photo by Colin Cooper

ment. Will listeners ultimately become bored with the 'accessibility' of the fourth guitar concerto and ultimately return to the 'difficulties' of the first? Time alone will tell. Meanwhile, we might as well sit back and enjoy the new forms in which Leo Brouwer's compositional skills choose to express themselves.

Leo Brouwer himself denies that his new music constitutes in any way a return to his roots. He insists that the roots have been in his music all along, even in the most difficult of his atonal and/or aleatoric work. The implication is that his composition is not a path leading to a destination, but a growth, a large tree, perhaps; we have been considering the branches and the foliage, but now we are being invited to contemplate the roots which have been there all the time. The composer has shovelled away a little of the loose earth that covered them, so that we may the better observe the massive strength. Our perception of the whole tree is thus enhanced.

There is another, and possibly more fundamental, way to look at what some observers may feel to be a severe case of compositional schizophrenia. Brouwer himself provides the clue: 'There has been too much brain', he said in reply to a question about the nature of recent contemporary music. He feels it is time to appeal to other and equally valid human attributes, of which the heart and its basic rhythm is obviously one but not the only one.

Those of us who have become accustomed to the cerebration now have to come to terms with a kind of celebration — of warmth, of romance, of melody, of the approaching end of a century about which most intelligent people must have mixed feelings. Have we much to celebrate? Leo Brouwer thinks so.

He came to London in April 1985, to conduct the BBC Concert Orchestra and the Langham Chamber Orchestra, which is also a BBC organization — and, incidentally, just celebrating its second anniversary. He chose all the music himself. It was his first conducting engagement with the BBC, and he wanted to provide a good variety of music — some well known, some new or not so well known. With the Concert Orchestra he did Falla's *El Amor Brujo* with mezzo-soprano Mary King, Schubert's *Rosamunde* and his own *Canción de Gesta* (the *chanson de geste* or *cantus gestualis* was a medieval verse-chronicle of heroic exploits). This is a work for wind ensemble, written for and commissioned by the Pittsburgh Wind Symphony three or four years ago. The PWS have a summer course, spent cruising down rivers on a boat, suitably acknowledged

by a quotation from Handel's *Water Music*.

For the Langham Chamber Orchestra, he wrote *Canciones Remotas*, a four-movement work for strings. It is dedicated to the Langham, whose qualities he much appreciated. 'I am so happy with these musicians', he said, and they seemed to enjoy the experience too. He had taken care in the choice of other music — *Homenaje a Federico Lorca*, by the Mexican composer Silvestre Revueltas (1899-1940), Gershwin's *Preludes* for piano (1926), arranged by Brouwer himself, Samuel Barber's *Adagio for strings*, Henze's *Der Junge Törless* , and *Three Pieces in Olden Style* by the Polish composer Henryk Gorecki (b.1933).

The three-movement work by Revueltas was being rehearsed. Piano, harp, exposed trumpet (rather like the trumpet in a mariachi band), piccolo, clarinet, percussion. A lively, Mexican feel about the texture and rhythm. Extrovert coloring, huge chords, a double-bass open-string tremolo. Xylophone, tam-tam, a tuba like a foghorn, muted trombone like a breaking wave, all making a strong effect. The third movement could almost be an extract from *Façade*, if Walton had decided to put in a Mexican episode. Leo liked the sound of the brass: 'The London sound', he said.

He had arranged two of Gershwin's three piano preludes for strings. The first has a 'Summertime' mood, cellos playing over plucked violins. It goes well, but at the end Leo turns to the control room and asks if Gareth Walters wants a second take. 'What for, Leo?' comes Gareth's voice. Leo blows a kiss into the air and says thank you. He launches into the next prelude with renewed zest, moving energetically on the podium, no baton, but fluent arms.

By the time the orchestra come to his *Canciones Remotas* they are playing as if they had been rehearsing for a week instead of only half a day. Their professionalism is exemplary. One of Leo Brouwer's fingerprints in this work is the quiet, rising arpeggio, with echoes of — could it be Vaughan Williams? Delius? Tchaikovsky? But the strong violin syncopation is pure Brouwer. It so happens that Leo admires Vaughan Williams, praising the *Suite for Brass,* the *Fourth Symphony* and the *Fantasia on a Theme of Thomas Tallis*. Other English composers also appealed to him. Gustav Holst (for *The Planets* in 1915) was one of them.

'Your composers know all the instruments so well', he said. 'Because I play them myself — I studied cello, clarinet, trombone, double-bass, percussion and piano.

So that when I compose, I can put in the fingering. I don't do crazy things that are impossible to play. This is something that you English people have. Britten, Walton, Vaughan Williams — the Fourth Symphony is incredible! Clean designs which are as basic as Bach's *Inventions* or the first movement of Beethoven's *Pastoral* Symphony. Magic squares! Beethoven took a four-bar theme and built up the whole structure with it.'

To explain what he was driving at, Leo drew a version of Paul Klee's Bauhaus tree design. There were two very basic trees, with leafless branches. In the middle, an identical tree but inverted. The branches have become roots. And the third tree, with an outline added, becomes a leaf. Thus are the forms of nature interconnected. The leaf becomes the tree; the brick becomes the building. And Beethoven's four-bar theme becomes the first movement of the *Pastoral* Symphony.

Samuel Barber's *Adagio for strings* was immensely popular during the second world war, many people finding in its slow unfolding of string counterpoint a reflection of their own fortitude implicit in the underlying tragedy. Nearly half a century later, only its musical qualities remain, but they are considerable. The LCO got the point quickly, efficiently dispatching the music to the master tape file, and turned their attention to Henze's *Der Junge Törless*, which was originally written for a film in 1965. Elegiac and energetic by turns, it contains plenty of movement. some spikiness,

a serene violin tune — good, well-contrasted writing that exploits the form and avoids monotony.

Gorecki's three pieces elicit a wonderful surge of tone, effortlessly reaching the heights of string band sonority. And so to Mozart's String Serenade K525, invariably known under the name which helped to seal its popularity, *Eine Kleine Nachtmusik*. Leo steps away from the rostrum, humorously indicating that the orchestra know the piece so well they can play it without him. He steps back, of course, and introduces several nice touches, giving one passage a series of little pushes to create a fractional tension, omitted in the repeat. Subtle gradings of dynamic demonstrate a keen musical intelligence at work. He asks for a diminuendo at bar 14 in place of the more common crescendo. It makes sense. Every phrase comes alive. It is clear that it is not the piece itself that is well worn but the minds of the people who listen to it — and very often of those who play it.

This is what creative music making was about, even if it was taking place in a recording studio rather than a concert hall. But thousands of people would be listening to the broadcast eventually, and it had to begin its existence as a live performance. Nevertheless, the concept of the importance of live performance was not one that was automatically held within the hallowed halls of the BBC. As manager Peter Holt put it, 'Some people's idea of music in the BBC is a piece of plastic with a hole in the middle'.

Photo by DG Winkler

On this evidence at least, the creation of the Langham Chamber Orchestra two years earlier was more than justified; a creative act in an environment where cutback and recession and budgetary limitation were words of common currency.

It was clear that Leo Brouwer is a very good conductor. Did he enjoy conducting more than playing or composing for the guitar?

'No. For me, the guitar is total communication. But conducting — I've learned how to do it. I enjoy the ability to produce the colors, the dynamics.'

So no career change was contemplated. What obviously was interesting as a topic of discussion was the form of his latest compositions. 'That avant-garde epoch of mine is a little bit gone', said Leo. 'A little bit too old, maybe. I think in this part of the century we need to relax and enjoy it. I think that in the near future music is going to get very romantic once more. It has been too brainy, too cold, too mathematical — too *mastermind*.'

He feels strongly the lack of communication for which the music of 15 or 20 years ago is in his opinion responsible. 'I did it also', he admits. 'I did everything! I scratched the guitar, I cut, I broke the strings. Whatever was done, I did also.

'Guitar music should change. It will go back to romantic, national music, I think. Scottish folk songs, Welsh, Irish, some French, Canadian, Indian folk song — all coming back in a kind of reconsideration. In a way. it's like the turn of the last century and the nationalistic school.'

He saw no future for the avant-garde as we knew it. 'It is a moment for opening doors, for alerting people, for cleansing music. Since 1971 I've started to introduce the old universe of sound once more. Quotations, allusions, E major chords, cadences, Bach chorales — keeping the attention on the heritage. No more Boulez! No more Stockhausen! It's finished!'

The *Nutcracker* instead of *Le Marteau*? 'Nutcracker — why not? I love it. The most simple and the most beautiful music. Now we are going to have hyper-realism or -romanticism. It will become the new expressionism. 20-century music *has* to go somewhere other than the avant-garde. All the things I did 15 years ago were necessary; but, as everything in history has done, things have reached a turning point.'

It was, said Leo Brouwer. the turning point of an upward spiral — an eternal spiral, if you like. 'So we are continually encountering the same point, but developed. We are once more taking up 19th-century music but on a higher level of expression. I don't mean that we are going to surpass Mahler or Brahms. I repeat, I'm not talking about quality. It is one step further in remodelling the whole thing.'

Neo-classicism had flourished in the 1920s and 1930s, with Stravinsky the main figure and with Hindemith and Britten (whom Brouwer feels to be one of the greatest) also playing prominent parts. But that was not going to return. The names that Leo mentions now are Copland, Vaughan Williams, Shostakovich, Rachmaninov, Walton and Holst. He speaks with utter conviction. He does not say that these things *might* happen, but that they *will* happen, or are already happening. In 50 years' time, perhaps, some composer will be heralding the arrival of the neo-avant-garde or hyper-aleatoric movement, and speaking of Stockhausen as a great communicator. Meanwhile, we have Leo Brouwer's music to enjoy — and one feels that neo-romanticism is by no means the end of it

By way of a postscript, it is worth noting that it is only by pure chance that we have the *Tres danzas concertantes*, *Tres apuntes*, *Elogio de la danza* and many other pieces, because he had thrown them away with a lot of what he calls 'garbage'. It was a friend, Jesús Ortega, who happened to have copies and was thus able to restore the music to a now grateful guitar world.

An extract from another interview (with Gareth Walters, CG September 1984) deserves to be quoted, since it underlines Leo Brouwer's philosophy and helps to explain further what appears to many as a baffling change of direction:

'The heritage of Schoenberg was so strong that the entire world was influenced by this challenge to transform the language — the code of communication. But once this language is absorbed into you, and you try to present it as a piece of art, you discover after a certain period that you need to create and to express in many, many other languages.'

To keep up with the old Brouwer we had to learn a new language. This time we are relearning an old one, but if Brouwer's past record is anything to go by, it will have more than a few new words in it.

CC

ROLAND DYENS

There is a touch of the magician in Roland Dyens. In performance, this ability enables him to follow one of his own jazz-influenced compositions with music by Fernando Sor, and it does not seem incongruous. At least, it does not seem incongruous to those who are able to keep their minds open to relationships between not merely notes but also pieces and the periods in which they were created.

Unfortunately, a kind of rigidity has become the norm, fuelled by the Early Music movement, in which only the boldest spirits dare step out of line. Roland is one of those spirits, and he incurs criticism among those who have made up their minds in advance: about, for instance, the place of jazz, or the way an ornament not only should be played but must be played. These are the people who believe that there is only one way to play Sor. They have contributed a lot to knowledge, but they are not so expert when it comes to evaluating a living individual's creative talent. Thus one or two individuals shook their heads in a worried fashion when Roland Dyens played for the first time in England, muttering that Sor should not be played like that. All I can say is that he was played like that, and it was wonderful. The only golden rule is that music must be created during a performance; if it is, then departures from received wisdom can be accepted; if it is not, all the 'authenticity' in the world will not save it.

When I asked Roland — no doubt impertinently, because one should be careful about asking a magician questions — he replied, somewhat enigmatically, that he 'listened to the silence'. In other words, the space around the notes is as important as the notes themselves. It is an approach that would probably not get you very far in some music — Bach, for instance, who was more interested in the structured intricacy of the notes themselves than in the spaces around them — but it can show other composers in a new light, as Roland Dyens demonstrated brilliantly.

Roland Dyens is one of a small handful of composer-guitarists whose work seems to me to be reaching beyond the confines of 'classical' guitar. Through their knowledge of the fingerboard, through their understanding of what the guitar is capable of, through their essential creativity, these artists are composing guitar music that is new in every sense. It is difficult to classify it, but that is our problem, not theirs. Their work reasserts the supremacy of the guitar as an individual's instrument above all other instruments.

Our interview was conducted in the back of a swaying, lurching minibus in Poland one autumn afternoon, and was printed in Classical Guitar in March 1995 with the title 'The Sound and the Silence'.

Photo by Jacques Vangansbeke

Roland Dyens was born in Tunisia, North Africa, in 1955. He won the Palestrina International Competition in Porto Alegre, Brazil, in 1979, and in the same year won the Special Prize in the Alessandria Competition, Italy. He studied composition with Raymond Weber and Desire Dondoyne, and is currently Professor of Guitar at the Conservatoire de Chaville (Hauts-de-Seine). He was later appointed professor of guitar at the Conservatoire National Supérieur de Musique of Paris. He spends most of his year in France, but is much in demand at international guitar festivals around the world.

'My first teacher was one of these very rare teachers that came to your home. In this period, in the 60s, there were no real teachers in Paris. He was one of the last of these people, very old, coming on a motorcycle. It gave me the taste for the guitar. His name was Maison. In my records, when I have the opportunity to mention him, I do: "Roland Dyens, élève de Robert Maison et Alberto Ponce" — but nobody knows about Maison. It's a gesture to him.

Everybody asks me, who is Robert Maison?
It's an opportunity to explain who he was." Roland Dyens began to compose very early. 'When I got my first guitar, my first wish was to create something, some songs, to improvise. It was my own feeling. I don't remember when I decided to become a composer. At the same time as the interpretation and the technique, there were always the two aspects in my life. I never separated interpretation from creation. It was like a recreation. While I was studying Villa-Lobos or Pujol, sometimes there was an overdose of working, so I improvised on a phrase of Villa-Lobos or a bar of Pujol. I took it and made some re-recreation, then came back to the music.'

Sor's *Bagatelles Op.43 'Mes Ennuis'* ('My troubles') is a work that does not often find its way into the concert hall. Roland told me how he came to find it — for this was before the days of Brian Jeffery's Complete Facsimile Edition for Tecla. It makes a nice little story:

'In Marseilles there was a very old teacher, Louis Davalle, a bit like the French Segovia, not very well known but a good teacher who had a number of students, among whom was René Bartoli. I'd heard about Davalle, and one day I decided to meet him. I was in the south of France, and I had to give a concert near Marseilles. I got his phone number, and he invited me to his home. He was a docker who had fallen in love with the guitar one day in the 30s. I went to his house, and he told me about his life, which was rich in anecdotes and stories — you can imagine. He showed me his very old Ramirez, from 1924, and pictures. Incredible. And he showed me some of his favorite music, among which was *Mes Ennuis*. And he asked me to play it by sight. I played it — and fell in love. I said to him — because I love challenges — "I have my concert tomorrow, and I want to play it." And I played it one day later, by heart. Six months later he died. So I had the good luck to meet him. He was very old, over 90. Every time I play this music I think of him.'

Like all free spirits, Roland Dyens has had his share of criticism from people who would prefer that so-called 'classical' music is kept rigidly within a certain mold. He, like Sérgio and Odair Assad, has never had the slightest hesitation in superimposing his own strong creative impulses. It is what great interpreters have done throughout the ages. Only recently have we become obsessed with 'what the composer wanted', as though the composer were still around and able to influence events. Such an obsession places music firmly on the shelves of a museum, rather than making it the living, breathing thing that living people love and revere. There are only two kinds of music: good and bad; and if Sor would not have been entranced by what Roland Dyens did with *Mes Ennuis* last October in Poland, then Sor wasn't the man I take him to be.

It is an unfashionable view, not held by the scholars and musicologists (Roland Dyens calls them 'integrists') who insist on classical music being played strictly in accordance with a classical tradition, with little or no possibility of new light being shed. Imagine Shakespeare being performed in this stifling way! The Royal Shakespeare Company would have to sack all its actresses and engage a bunch of adolescent boys. It would lose its audience overnight, and deservedly.

'They come to a concert only to look for faults and mistakes,' said Roland about his 'integrists'. 'They never have the idea of bringing something fresh. The people who today interest me, in the guitar, are those who bring something — a little stone, a little dust, even, but something, something new and fresh. I don't really understand the way of playing the same repertoire in the same way. What's new, pussycat? What's new? *Rien de nouveau*! That's why the Assad brothers are really the musicians I feel closest too — because we have the same chemistry.'

Now, this question of silence. Good painters often perceive not the objects in front of them but the space around them. The result is often an unsuspected freshness. Is Roland's perception of silence something of the same sort?

'For me, the silence is one of my favorite things in the music. It's something I learned only quite recently. It's something that comes with age. When you speak about silence to students of 20 years old, they understand, but only with the brain, mentally. To them, music must be sound. What is silence? Silence is when it's finished? No! It's like the air in painting, you know. The silence between two notes. The last note you play, you can even see this note falling down. Like a tennis player hitting the ball at the very last moment. That's a great feeling.'

Roland has mastered the art of persuading an audience to listen to these perfectly timed silences. Is it something that anyone can learn?

Courtesy Classical Guitar Magazine

'I'm not a demagogue about music. I think, for example, that a-rhythmical people can never be rhythmical people. Music is not an obligatory, democratic thing. To think that everybody can be an artist, or a great artist, is wrong. It's something you have. You can spend, hours, years, trying to teach this idea to some people, but it is impossible. It will remain an intellectual idea, but the most important thing about music is that it is felt in your body, in a very natural way. I may appear to be an abnormal musician, an atypical musician, but I feel normal; I'm improvising, composing and playing, I'm an interpreter, I joke with the music, I'm ready with music. What else? I'm a musician at the end of the 20th century, nothing else. An active, living musician.

'I can't understand the divorce between composers and interpreters. I fight against that. The divorce was more or less declared in the middle of the 19th century by the first composer who wrote a cadenza. For me that's the date of the crime. It was the death of improvisation in classical music. And therefore the interpreters play what is written by the composer — and nothing else! When I play a concerto I always improvise the cadenza. I would like others to do the same. I'm not seeking loneliness on my planet, but it's a fact. And it's a pity.'

One knows exactly what he means. During the last round of the competition in Tychy, Giuliani's A major Concerto was played four times — and each time with the same cadenzas. There can't have been a musical intelligence in that hall that did not long for something different. But the players did not dare to do it, Roland said, '— because they don't know how. It is assumed that the composers of the last century were always very serious people. But they were also very happy people, sometimes jokers, you know? We are making religious people out of them, very serious classical people. I think music in the classical world is getting very serious. It was the contrary at the time, I think. Because the composers who played their own music improvised. What is a prelude etymologically? It is "before playing". What I do at the beginning of a recital is the same. I'm connected to these people, yet I'm thought of as some special guy. I feel really normal, you know. And I feel lonely. I would like others to do what I am doing.

'A journalist once wrote that I was "a classical musician in the hands, and a jazz musician in the head". For me, that is the best definition. But classical music is my house, my family. I love to travel and I love to come back. That's why I always play Sor in my concerts. I have always been in love with Sor's music, and this is my way of saying to people "I'm a classical guitarist like you". But I have *un peu de gourmandise. Je suis gourmand! J'ai beaucoup d'appetit.*

'I am a classical player visiting jazz music, re-reading jazz in his own conception. I bring it to the classical guitar. If I were a jazz player, I would have bought a Stratocaster or a Les Paul electric guitar. But I'm not a jazz player. I'm classical — and curious! I do some travelling, I go to the market, then I return to my house, the classical guitar.

'I feel really flexible. I love every discipline of music. Everything interests me in music. Accompanying a popular singer with my guitar — for the first time — as well as playing a suite by Bach, playing in Sweden for the Arvika Festival, one of the oldest festivals. They were celebrating their Jubilee. Jazz and classical guitar at the same time. Every night I played with jazz players. The Swedish school of jazz is very good. And I played in the pub every night, with the jazz musicians. And in Arvika the classical teachers told me that never before had an invited classical guitarist played with the jazz musicians. For me it was normal. I never felt forced to do these things. Jekyll and Hyde! During the day I'm playing classical — and at night, the jam sessions! I feel very good in each situation.'

The world of Roland Dyens has opened up so widely now that the possibilities seem almost infinite. Yet in his teens he was advised to make a choice: one thing or the other.

'I was 18 or so, in France, where music is very traditional, very conventional. I'd already heard this sentence: "My dear, one day you will have to choose which camp you are going to join". Classical or jazz, you had to choose. But I never made the choice. And it's too late now! But I'm happy never to have made that choice, because my public in France is so mixed. I have all the bourgeois people, with the rockers as well. And rock players do like my attitude towards the classics. My best souvenir of a masterclass is paradoxical. It was in Cannes, a class in a classical guitar festival for rockers, hard rockers. And the organizer said to me: "Roland, I've got a crazy idea. Could you come to Cannes and teach a masterclass for rock players?" I was a bit afraid, but it was incredible: I've never got such silence, such attention. I was explaining the different colors on only one string. It was amazing, when you think of their materials, the wah-wah pedal and everything, and I'm just playing in a primitive way with a wooden guitar, from the bridge to the fingerboard, and making different sounds, harpsichord sounds, lute sounds, baby sounds. It was crazy, surrealistic! He asked me because he knew I was open to this kind of thing. Someone who spoke rigidly in classical language would not have connected. They would feel themselves almost to be assaulted by him.'

Roland's masterclasses in Tychy were given to classical students, of course, and were highly successful. Did he in any way find it difficult to communicate?

'No. I loved it. My language is more implicit than intellectual or analytical or musicological. I'm speaking so that an old man or an old woman not in the guitar world could understand what I'm saying. It's full of examples, jokes, examples from jazz, from songs, from Sor, something from what the student is playing. For example, I stop him during the third bar of Sor and say "If Charlie Parker had played this...." You know? It's really open. My masterclasses are the reverse of something rigid and boring — at least I hope so.'

Like the creative artist he is, Roland Dyens has any number of irons in the fire. One current 'baby' is his concerto for guitar and string orchestra, which he would like to be better known. As for the future, he says he has no premeditated ideas.

'I'm open. I don't want to plan two years in advance. You know what I mean: in two years I will do this kind of concert, and in three years maybe this kind of record. I don't have this feeling.'

'I'm open. I don't want to plan two years in advance. You know what I mean: in two years I will do this kind of concert, and in three years maybe this kind of record. I don't have this feeling.'

EVANGELOS AND LIZA

Courtesy Classical Guitar Magazine

The original title of this article was 'Greek Meets Greek'. It was borrowed, with acknowledgments, from John Duarte, who used it to subtitle his *Greek Suite*, written for Evangelos and Liza in 1968. Nathaniel Lee's original line, some three hundred years earlier, began 'When Greeks joined Greeks', and went on: 'then was the tug of war!'

Nothing could be less warlike and more harmonious than the partnership formed in 1963 by Evangelos Assimakopoulos and Liza Zoe. After graduating from the National Conservatoire of Athens (each taking First Prize with honors), they were soloists for a time — 'competitors', says Evangelos — but found a duo partnership more to their taste. They married in 1965, went to study in France with Presti and Lagoya and also in Spain with Andrés Segovia. Segovia said 'I felt entire satisfaction and enjoyment. They have rhythm, good taste, emotion, technique and vital dedication to music'. He encouraged composers such as Castelnuovo-Tedesco to write for them.

Since their arrival on the international music scene in 1967, Evangelos and Liza have toured extensively in Europe and North America. At first they were known as the Athenian Guitar Duo, but American impresario Sol Hurok persuaded them to adopt the form they now use. It's certainly more personal, but the original name

had a nice classical ring to it.

We talked first about the wide range of music available for two guitars, and what worked best for the combination.

'And what kind of music,' said Evangelos. 'There is no limit. You can make transcriptions from baroque music, from Bach, from Vivaldi — you can arrange for two guitars what you are unable to arrange for one, what Bach wrote for instruments other than the lute, for example, such as the harpsichord and violin, and so on. Then there is Spanish music. But original works, unfortunately, are very few.'

'Except in contemporary music,' said Liza. Many composers were writing for two guitars now. Castelnuovo-Tedesco had written a concerto for two guitars, Rodrigo had written the *Madrigal* Concerto. Pierre Petit had written for two guitars, and Pierre Jouvin had dedicated pieces to the Duo. And John Duarte had written his *Greek Suite* for them in 1968.

'Before this Jack Duarte had written several pieces for Presti and Lagoya,' said Evangelos. 'Unfortunately, Ida Presti died, and some of those pieces were not played. He wrote *Sans Cesse* (Op. 34, 1967) for them, but they never played it. So Jack sent it to us and said: "You can play it now". And of course we played it. It's a nice piece, very nice.'

The repertoire was improving all the time, and with a number of other duos now performing, the field was beginning to be enriched. Evangelos and Liza had done their share of enriching; among the original compositions they played were a number of arrangements of works written for the piano, by Albéniz and Granados, for instance, that they feel are certainly a better fit with two guitars than with one, and possibly even better than with the piano. But what did they find was the most popular with their audience?

'It depends on where you play,' said Evangelos. 'And the standard of the audience. If you play in London the audience is demanding — very demanding. They like to hear all kinds of music, even contemporary music. But in smaller cities they like mostly Spanish pieces or other pieces that are easy to assimilate. In the bigger cities, like New York, Paris and London, people like to hear suites by Bach, and contemporary music.'

Did that mean that they chose their programs according to where they were playing? Evangelos said that sometimes they played their London program in a small town, but Liza put it firmly in an artistic context: 'First of all we create a program that we feel is good.' After that, it would be modified if necessary, according to circumstances. But sometimes they simply got tired of one program and wanted to play something else. Evangelos said: 'Some years ago we were playing only baroque music. Three-quarters of our program was music from the Baroque. The following year we got tired of baroque music and did classical and contemporary instead. This year we're playing Spanish music. We're coming back in November, and I think it's going to be different again.'

'Perhaps we'll play the concerto by Castelnuovo,' Liza added. It could have been a tantalizing hint, but it was not enlarged upon.

The Duo divide their time between touring and teaching, not wanting to spend too much time doing either the one or the other. They may decide in any one year to do a tour in Europe and another in the United States — about two months of giving concerts — after which they return to Athens to teach. For about three months every year they simply relax and practise — 'renewing the program', Evangelos called it. For four or five months they give lessons at the National Conservatoire in Athens, where they are both professors of guitar. There was a lot of interest in the guitar in Greece at present. And there were, said Evangelos, very many guitarists in Athens, professional and amateur, of a very high standard. Some of his own graduates were ready to give a recital at the Wigmore Hall.

This interest extended over Greece, to Thessalonika, Crete, Patras — all the big cities. And composers in Greece were beginning to write for two guitars: Dragatakis had written a three-part work and a concerto for the Duo, and Giorginakis and Haliasas were also becoming well known.

Prominent composers like Theodorakis and Hajdidakis had used the guitar in their compositions many times. But it was not easy to persuade composers in general to write for two guitars. As Evangelos said, 'A composer is not easily inspired unless he knows his work is going to be performed' — a remark of realism more than cynicism. 'So, since there are not many guitar duos in the world, composers tend to be a little bit careful. Because they want their work to be performed

not only by one artist or two, but internationally. But we try to get composers to write for us, because I think that the future lies in that direction.'

Unlike many other countries, Greece had no organization that could help with the commissioning of new work. This was a source of considerable disappointment to the Duo, who could not help noticing the support given to the artists of other countries. Evangelos mentioned the support the British Council in Athens had given the several English guitarists who had played there: Julian Bream, David Russell, Julian Byzantine and many others. Liza mentioned the Goethe Institute in Germany as another source of valuable support. However, in the 14 or 15 times the Duo had played in London, not once had anyone come from the Greek Embassy.

Such official indifference made their work harder, but at least they had the consolation of knowing that their success was entirely due to their own efforts. Nevertheless, they had some help, and from an influential quarter. 'The person who really helped us,' Evangelos said, 'was Andrés Segovia. We met him in 1967 at Santiago de Compostela, and again in '68 and '69. He was impressed by our playing, I think, and helped us to find agents. We shall never forget that.'

When they started playing, the classical guitar was practically unknown in Greece. There were a few of Segovia's 78rpm records around, but they were not easy to find. Occasionally Greek radio would play a Segovia record. Both Evangelos and Liza were excited when they heard the sound of the guitar.

Seeking tuition, they knocked at the door of a teacher, Dmitri Fampas. He happened to be the best teacher in Greece.

'It was a matter of luck', Liza said. 'We didn't know who was a good teacher and who was not.' They went to the Conservatoire and studied with Fampas who, they both agree, had a lot of knowledge and a lot of inspiration. Fampas had been a pupil of Segovia. Another Greek student of Segovia, one of his original six at Siena, was Miliaresis. Both he and Fampas brought Segovia's methods to Greece and began to teach. It helps to explain why the guitar was officially established in the National Conservatoire of Music as early as 1953, and why it has attained so high a standard.

Evangelos and Liza feel that the guitar is more popular

in the Mediterranean countries than in more northerly countries. They have yet to visit some Scandinavian countries, though they are aware of the rapidly growing interest in the guitar there. I asked them which were their favorite places to visit. Evangelos replied with great courtesy that London was the centre of the arts, and it was most important to play here, and they liked to be here. Paris, New York and all the other big cities in the United States — they enjoyed playing in all of them, but London was the most important. 'But,' said Liza, 'the most demanding audiences are in Athens.'

Athens receives a good share of visiting guitarists from abroad, recent performers including Roberto Aussel, Gabriel Estarellas, Martin Myslivecek, Oscar Ghiglia, David Russell and Manuel Barrueco. 'And there is going to be an international competition,' Liza said. 'You must mention that.'

This took place during the following November, in Athens. It is in fact the Callas Competition and has been in existence for several years, but this was the first time the guitar had been included. Why had the guitar suddenly found itself in what hitherto has been a voice and piano competition? 'Because', said Evangelos, 'everybody can see that the guitar has made so much progress. There are hundreds and thousands of guitarists everywhere'.

Basically, the Duo teach the methods of Pujol, Carcassi, Aguado, Coste and Giuliani, with of course the studies of Sor and Villa-Lobos. But, Evangelos emphasized, it was not the methods that made good pupils: 'Every player is a different personality, so we must solve his or her individual problems'. Duets are given to all pupils, because it helps so much with keeping time and rhythm. As Liza put it, 'They can listen to one another, and that is very important'.

Playing as a duo imparts the sense that the music must be built, whereas a solo guitarist sometimes listens to a record and tries to imitate it. The duo form was thus useful for teaching players to think for themselves in the matter of interpretation.

It so happens that the latest recording to be issued by this experienced duo was of solo performances, Liza playing music by Weiss, and Evangelos music by Albéniz. Yet they seldom if ever play solos in their concerts. Liza laughed, and said 'We miss playing solos, so we thought it was a good idea to record some'.

'It was only to see what we could do,' Evangelos affirmed. He felt it might be dangerous to mix solos in with their duo performances on the platform, because people have come to accept them as a very fine duo. 'It could become something like a circus. We think it's more important for people to listen to the music.' It is an attitude with which all musicians and, it is to be hoped, most audiences would agree.

They make a record every year, under their contract with EMI. They play Ramirez guitars in all their duo work, matched as far as possible to give what Evangelos calls a 'total result'. Liza says they are very steady, very stable: 'You can travel anywhere with a Ramirez. No problem.' But the guitar she plays on her solo recording is by Paul Gypas, one of a number of very good Greek guitar makers now operating. In fact, the first prize in the guitar section of the Callas Competition will include a guitar by Gypas. And, the Duo add mischievously, the second prize will include a guitar by Ramirez.

CC

Courtesy Classical Guitar Magazine

ELIOT FISK

I first heard Eliot Fisk play at the Wigmore Hall in the mid-1980s. I had long admired his fluent playing, his extraordinary technique, the seeming ease with which he overcame technical problems that most guitarists would not even have attempted to solve. I was not prepared for the almost physical excitement of hearing him in the flesh, magisterial, authoritative, sweeping all obstacles before him as he proceeded on his imperious way. There was a warmth, an immediacy of communication that I had not heard in his recordings, impressive though they are in their own way. Only when that particular warmth can be captured on disc will the recording super-sede the concert hall and the live performance. Until then, there is no substitute for a concert of music during which the communication between artist and audience suddenly crystallizes into a realization that here is something very special. There was a touch of greatness in the Wigmore Hall that night.

Eliot had agreed to an interview the following day. After the excitements of Sunday evening, Monday morning was anticlimactic. My questions sounded labored, Eliot's replies sounded perfunctory. There was a danger that it was going to develop into one of those occasions, every interviewer's nightmare, when, in his efforts to make his questions more interesting, the hapless interviewer makes them longer and longer, while the interviewee's replies become shorter and shorter. The ultimate is a question lasting a minute and a half, to which the answer is monosyllable, usually No.

Then people began to arrive. I had not invited them. Perhaps Eliot had issued a casual invitation the previous evening. Perhaps they came uninvited. Whatever the reason, all of a sudden there were five or six people in the room where there had been only two. Normally I might have resented such an intrusion into my professional work, but on this occasion it worked like a charm. Eliot, responding to the presence of an audience like the great performer he is, revealed himself to be an impassioned supporter of musical truth, an equally passionate denouncer of apathy and indifference, and an eloquent crusader on behalf of what he felt to be right. The excitement was infectious, and soon we were all involved in what turned out to be one of CG's liveliest interviews ever.

Eliot Fisk: I started to play when I was seven. My mother thought it would be a nice thing to have a little bit of music in the house so she sent my father out to buy a banjo. He'd played banjo in college, and the idea was that we could sing songs at home with my brother, who is handicapped by Down's Syndrome.

My father came back with not just a banjo but a six-dollar steel-stringed Gibson guitar, and that's how it began. I started first on the banjo and played it for about a month. It was an awfully bad banjo, and I also got a little bit tired of that pinging quality. So I started to play the guitar. We had this record and booklet that went with the record, showing how to play all the different chords. I remember playing *Home on the Range* in A major.

I taught myself the chords, and after three months, as I was still fooling around on the thing, my parents offered me lessons. Roger Scott, first double-bass player in the Philadelphia Symphony Orchestra, was an old family friend and he said I should study classi-cal guitar, so I went to Peter Colonna, a student of Segovia.

I was never serious in the beginning. I wasn't pushed

Photo by Allen Bloomfield

by my parents. I just started to play for myself, for fun. I really preferred running around outside, play-ing sports. I was very athletic, and played a lot of sports. As a kid, I practised guitar only about half an hour a week.

Then we went to Sweden, where my father had a sabbatical from 1965 to 1966, and there at first I was a bit lonely because I was going to a Swedish school and I didn't yet speak the language. That's when I started to practice more, about two hours a day. Then I went back to America. I had learned Swedish by that time, but I'd also got more involved with the guitar. And then I had my first really important teacher, William Viola.

He was a very important influence on me. Among other things, he would say 'You'll never be satisfied'. How prophetic that was! He was a very demanding teacher, which was good for me because it was just what I needed at that time. It was really then that I built the foundations of all the guitar technique I ever developed, from this one man who had mostly taught himself from the records of Segovia.

I had two years of weekly lessons with him, from the age of twelve to 14, then we moved. For a number of years I studied, in the summers only, with Oscar Ghiglia at Aspen. One summer I had the good fortune to study with Alirio Diaz at Banff. Soon after that I met Segovia, who was always my inspiration, always my great idol. I had the chance to play for Segovia. Every year, when he came to New York, I'd go to see him a couple of times and play for him at his hotel.

Meanwhile I had become old enough to go to college. I went to Yale. By good fortune — again — it happened that Ralph Kirkpatrick was teaching there, and I studied with him. I would say that my first important teachers in the long term were William Viola, Oscar Ghiglia and then Ralph Kirkpatrick, who helped me to lay the basis for all my subsequent musical development.

I don't know what I would have done if I hadn't met Ralph Kirkpatrick. What was so great about his teaching was that he didn't deliver fiats but would always proceed in a Socratic way by asking questions. Or he would just draw your attention to something and let you stumble around there for a while. Then he'd drop another clue and you'd stumble a bit more. If you really got off the track, he'd drop another clue. This was probably the greatest teaching I ever had.

But I don't think I would have been able to understand it if l hadn't had all those years of studying with Oscar Ghiglia at Aspen. Oscar always thinks in terms of the music first. I never really studied *guitar* with Oscar, I studied *music* with him. I remember one lesson that was devoted to producing the sound with the right hand — Oscar always had such a beautiful sound — but basically it was about music, and that was a great source of stimulation for me.

I had very little time with Segovia, though all in all I would say that he has been my greatest inspiration. I still go back to his records as an inexhaustible source of new insights — even from the same record. New insights and new learning always take place when I hear Segovia in person or listen to his records.

I know you have firm ideas about teaching. How far are they based on your own early experiences?
I probably teach most similarly to Oscar, of all the people I've studied with, although I don't know if I've got as much patience as he has. I like to teach through the personality of the student. I don't like to impose. In that way I follow the example of Ralph Kirkpatrick. I like the student to do the seeking.

I think the duty of the teacher is to supply the student with a method of thinking, a method in inquiry, more than it is to supply the student with the nuts and bolts of how to play. That presumes, of course, a basic level of technique. Obviously in the early stages there are ways to use the hands efficiently and ways to use the hands inefficiently, and you've got to have some very definite guidelines. But the further you go, the less definite the guidelines become.

The more advanced the student, the more it becomes an exchange of ideas. I find that I learn enormously from that. I have a great range of students. I have some who are just about professional level, and some who are beginners, and just about everything in between. And sometimes I learn more from the beginners than I do from the ones who play very well.

It's very nice to have an ongoing contact with a number of students. You get to observe how a personality develops over a time, how it flowers.
I don't think of myself as educating future great virtuosos. I don't think I have anybody who is necessarily going to revolutionize the guitar world. At the same time I think that exactly what the guitar needs is more depth in the echelons just below those of the touring virtuosos. There can never be too rich a supporting culture.

I like a student who doesn't agree with me. It challenges me. It forces me to reassess a lot of assumptions I may have made. It's very productive. It shakes you up. And that's maybe the thing I value most about teaching. I would like to see more of this in the guitar world in general, this spirit of inquiry, this Socratic method of going about things where you say that *the only thing we know is that we don't know anything*. And the only thing that we are doing is seeking. So let's at least make our seeking interesting and engaging and maybe even entertaining. In our seeking we might find something for a moment. But the next moment we're a different person and that won't satisfy us any more. We've got to find something else.

This is a frightening thing, because if the only reality is change, you can't fix it, you can't grab hold of any moment. There is always past, and there is always future; the present continually eludes your grasp. And that's also true in terms of artistic development. You can't say 'I am this' or 'I am that', because the next minute you'll change. And with the guitar it's a challenge to get your technique flexible enough: a flexible *Weltanschauung*, a world view flexible enough so that you can change with each moment, so that you can reflect what you are experiencing. I love those stories about Django Reinhardt. Sometimes he had an important performance, and he would just become lost in a daydream and go off wandering around in the streets. There was no barrier between feeling, sentiment, emotion and the expression; it was a wonderful, spontaneous unity.

Or, for example, take the tragic stories of Dinu Lipatti. Listening to his records is always a humbling experience. He takes about two measures — and you're in a transfigured mode. Now you can't study how to play like that physically; it's a communication of mood, of sentiment, of being; it's a transference, a reflection of a state of being, and I think that is what we all have to bear in mind — and what we have to treasure.

This again relates to teaching. Each one of my students has something special, maybe not whole big areas but something that he or she does really well, and something that only he or she can do. That's what I try to bring out in a pupil.

Getting back to Lipatti: he hadn't been able to practice for his famous last concert, but had just been lying in bed with a temperature of 104, trying to control the fever. And all these people had come miles and miles to hear him play. His friends and family said, 'Dinu,

you must cancel the concert', but he said 'No, these people have come, I have to play'. And he hauled himself out of bed and went to play.

There's a record of the concert. First of all, it's technically perfect. It's just as if the man had taken flight. You want to resort to religious terminology, because there doesn't seem to be any other way to describe what happened there. He plays the Chopin waltzes, and at the end of the concert he hasn't got the strength to play the last one. But you still hear this desperate desire to communicate. To me, that is the highest level. We can't hope to attain it, but I hold it to be a model of achievement.

It is not achieved through physical means. Lipatti hadn't been sitting in his room practicing that day. But he had built a technique from the age of four, so flexible and so perfect that he could just get out of bed, go to the concert hall and play this breathtaking, tragic, moving, unbelievable recital.

A few months later he was actually dying. He was listening to a Beethoven String Quartet — Opus 95, if I remember right. He got out of bed and played two pieces, the last one of which was the Siciliana from Bach's Flute Sonata in E flat. He'd made a transcription for piano. He played that, and died very soon afterwards.

This immediate connection between being and expressing — that's a real goal that each person can strive for in his or her own way. No two people can achieve it in the same way. Everybody supplies part of the whole; everybody contributes. In Dante's *Purgatorio*, when one soul makes an advance, all the others are jubilant, they jump for joy. And that's what I think about playing the guitar — or anything else you do in life; when an advance is made, it's a spiritual advance. Everyone is the richer for it. We should all jump for joy, not turn green with envy, when we hear someone else play well.

Of course technique has to be studied too. We have a lot of focus on technique in the guitar world, and because of that the technical level — even in the last ten years — has risen to a height I would never have believed possible. And it's thrilling, it's wonderful. Now we're at the point where we can begin to focus on the deeper issues.

Is your first approach to a piece of music a technical one? Or do you consider the entire piece from the

beginning?
How you approach each piece varies with the piece. You need a different approach for each ethic. It's important to enter the *Zeitgeist* of each ethic. If possible, one ought to try to get to know the literature, the art of that time. Imagine yourself as a human being alive at that time. You need to have as much information as you can get in the way of general historical background which is available in books and libraries, but I also think it's helpful — if you're fortunate enough to have the chance — to go to the countries where these people flourished.

Sometimes hearing the language is helpful. Of course, many things have changed, but some have stayed the same. There is still something that distinguishes English culture from German culture, Italian culture from Spanish. Regional accents still play a part in the understanding of music produced by these various cultures.

In my own case, it also helps me physically to play the pieces better, instead of beating them into the ground with repetitious practice. Of course you have to practice well, you have to study. But I love creating an ambience around the piece; so many more ideas come to you than if you're just working out of your own imagination.

Do you feel that, generally, there is too much emphasis on playing the guitar as a physical process?
I think there is a danger, because the guitar is so complex physically. To manipulate the guitar is a nightmare. As Segovia liked to say, for composers it's like writing for the piano with one hand, or for a violin with six strings. And it is a tremendously cumbersome instrument, so it's easy to become focused on the physical problems involved in trying to manipulate it. But at the same time, what is increasingly going to become interesting for guitar audiences, as a superior technique becomes more and more taken for granted, is: what has somebody got to say?

Often, if somebody has something to say, it completely overwhelms technical barriers. If somebody doesn't have anything burning inside, doesn't have a passion burning, doesn't have a fire inside that has to come out, to make contact with other people, I don't really see why they're trying to make an international career. I see what they're doing as loving the guitar, playing it in their spare time, teaching the guitar, maybe playing it for their friends. But who said everybody has to become Julian Bream? There's only one of those.

Who knows why we need to communicate? You can find a whole lot of philosophical reasons and sociological reasons and psychological reasons. But most of the people in art who have captivated me have had that burning desire to say something, to communicate.

I feel, especially in the guitar world, that there's a conservatism and a great fear of innovation — and also, conversely, a tendency to accept without question anything that comes from a well-established source. At the same time people tend not to accept very fine things that come from unknown sources. This is true not just of the guitar world but of human nature. I'd like to see more people thinking for themselves.

This relates to teaching, because it's one of the things I try to encourage in my students. It also leads on to something else I wanted to say, about factionalism and in-fighting. We need to come together now as a community and try to interest more people in the guitar, to expand our audience. And that's why new talent is always welcome. In America we have an effective program called Affiliate Artists, funded partly by the government and partly by private industry. What happens is that you go into an area where there's very little culture, and you live there for a period, usually staying with a family. Years ago, in Illinois, I gave 40 performances in 21 days.

It was an effective way of reaching out to people. I think of people sitting around in institutions. Not every institution is going to want the classical guitar, but I think this kind of reaching out is greatly needed.

The guitar world needs an organizer of genius to figure out how to expand the audience. Because we have the base now; good players, magazines like yours and others, an increasingly high level of writing, of criticism — of everything. The infrastructure's already in place; now we need an organizational genius to bring it all together for the good of all of us

There is a widely held view that a guitarist acquires a technique at first, then looks around for something to play with it. In your philosophy, the music comes first....
You hear this so often. 'First I'm going to learn the notes, and then I'll put the expression in'! From my earliest days I have never, ever, learned a piece that way, and I don't know anyone who can play beauti-

fully who ever has. My God, if you don't react to the music, it *can't* be good.

It's one thing if you want sometimes to practise a difficult passage for the right hand. Some people like to practise only the open strings, then they put the left hand back on. I can understand that in certain isolated instances, but after a while you're going to be able to hear nothing but the open strings. You're going to deaden your ear.

It cannot be good to induce this *tin-earedness*. I don't care if your technique runs along like a little machine afterwards, it's not going to have a good effect on your playing in the long term. I think you work technique at the same time as you work music; always one in conjunction with the other, because they help each other. That makes the process go faster, not slower. That's the way I have always learned — always, always, always.

I'm in a state now where the technique comes pretty fast. I know how to fix technique. I practise very small groups of notes and I string them together. I don't think of groups of 24 notes; I think of six groups of four notes. Anybody can play four notes fast. Then you just do it six times — and you've got 24 notes. But if you think of 24 notes — *aaagh*! You won't be able to play one of them well.

So many times people ask me, 'What do you do about nerves?' They're going to play one concert a year, and they expect they're not going to be nervous! Before a concert I play for friends. And if I don't have enough concerts, I play for friends. If I only had one concert, I'd play the programs for friends at least once, and hopefully twice. And it's much harder to play for friends in a small room than it is to play in public. Then when I go to the hall, the audience is just an extension of my friends.

You have to realize that the audience is just like you; just human beings. They've got their insecurities, their fears, their loves, their hates, they're just like you are.

There is an element of the unpredictable in your performance. Is that one of the secrets of your success?
Of everything in life! You can't predict that you're going to fall in love with someone. And if you do fall in love, you can't predict that you're going to have a beautiful time on a certain day. Everything in life is like that.

Some things have to be reliable. It's nice when the bus comes on time. But the really great things hardly ever come like that.

But despite the unpredictability and the need for it, you still have to plan a concert.
You simply react to the unpredictable when it comes along. In a macabre way, it's the cornered beast theory: necessity makes you very resourceful. Improvising around a cough — sometimes you can space a note around a cough, you know. Or maybe you played one part too fast, so you play the next part too slow. Improvising the balance of art work.

It's as if Leonardo had to paint the Mona Lisa in front of an audience instead of in the studio. This is what my generation wants to do; they want to paint the Mona Lisa in the studio. But performance isn't like that. You've got to improvise a new one every time. Maybe this time some of the brush strokes don't look so good. But, you know, those are the breaks.

This really is the difference between the performer and the good musician. The good musician need not be a performer, but the performer must be a good musician — and something else as well.
That's a very good point, because many people, teaching in universities, perhaps, are better musicians than people making very big international careers — not just in guitar, but in piano and violin. But they don't seem to have that performance spark, whatever it is. They don't have that ability to improvise with the unpredictable.

Then there are people who do have the ability, but who decide that they just don't want the lifestyle of an international artist. This is a very sane decision, I can only say. But there are not so many guitar concerts, and no matter how big your career is, I don't think you're in danger of burning out. So guitarists have it about right, I'd say. People in my generation who are doing comparable things, like Manuel Barrueco, Vladimir Mikulka, David Russell. Göran Söllscher and others, travel a lot, but not too much. We get a lot of very nice support from the audiences, but not so much that it puts your head out of line.

As you get older, you want more and more for each minute to have meaning. You get to look for things that aren't so superficial, that aren't so glib; you get to understand the difference between entertainment and art. I can think of a couple of very big careers that are based more on entertainment than on art, and to me that wouldn't be worth it. I love entertainment; you can't go around being serious the whole time. But most of all I want to understand, to seek and comprehend and try to be an artist.

There's a big record store in the States that has a little magazine. They had a big article on Julian Bream, and then they did something about me, so it was a sort of 'younger virtuoso—older virtuoso'. The guy was trying to say 'Well, what do you think about Julian Bream?'— as if he was saying 'He's all washed up'. So I said I think he's wonderful. I like him because he plays with a lot of guts and takes every risk in the book.

My generation has gotten so *serious*! So *humorless*! Where's the *joie de vivre*? You find young players coming out and playing like stiffs. Young players who are so boring, so dull and so timid. Towards the end of

Photo by Johan Fjellstrom

his life, Rubinstein used to say: 'All these younger pianists, you know, they play a hell of a lot better than me, but when they walk out on the stage they look like old insurance salesmen.' Those may not be his actual words. But these players exude no charisma. And this is what's going to kill the guitar if it keeps up, this tendency to be so careful and so god-awful bloody boring and take no risks and no chances, everybody trying to be correct and trying not to offend anybody with anything that might be just a little bit unusual.

And young players — this is the ridiculous thing — young players are no longer allowed to develop. They're expected to drop out of the forehead of Zeus, fully formed. You're not allowed to be a young player, bursting with piss and vinegar and maybe it sometimes comes out right and sometimes it doesn't — you've got to be perfectly formed, mature. Mature, you know! Boredom passes for maturity in the guitar world. It makes me sick.

I've shot my mouth off on that one, but that's what I think.

This kind of communication with an audience is not taught in the colleges. Ought it to be? Can it be? If you play like that for an entrance exam, you get into trouble.

The worst problem for the guitar is that it's so quiet. If it's going to be so quiet, you'd better do something interesting. The future of the guitar is not in being a too-quiet instrument.

The man who is most misunderstood is Segovia. 'Oh, the old man,' people say, 'It's amazing that he can still play concerts at the age of 92.' This is the great left-handed compliment that gets dished out to Segovia.

I think these people must have wool in their ears. In my book, Segovia still *plays* the guitar. In his prime he played it better than any of us younger people. Much better, because he made more meaning with it, he had more expression. He made the guitar bigger than it had ever been. Maybe we play faster, we play more notes per measure — so what? We are barking up the wrong tree — the tree of accuracy. We're trying to do with the guitar the things a machine does well, not the things a guitar does well.

The guitar is an instrument of suggestion, of implication. When you try to make the guitar sound like a piano, you're going the wrong way. I'm the first to say independence of parts; know all the parts, sing the parts, hear all the intervals. That goes without saying. But the great thing about Segovia is that he makes the guitar sound like the voice, not like the piano. Nobody else has come close to it. And nobody's even trying to do it any more.

That's the amazing thing. I go back to Segovia, I go back to those old records, and I get knocked out. You hear that passion, that expressivity, that daring. And the way he *changes* the music is so fantastic. He rewrites things. What comes out is what the composer *wanted* to say but didn't know *how* to say with the guitar.

I heard him play Torroba's *Sonatina* not long ago in Cologne. After the concert I got the music and wrote out all the changes that Segovia had made, and they were fantastic. Here he is at 92, and his musical mind and his musical sensibility are so superior. We aren't even at the bottom of purgatory, you know; we're still climbing up from the bottom of the Inferno, while he's up there in Paradise somewhere, to take a Danteesque metaphor.

It's been said that all philosophy is a footnote to Plato. The longer I work on the guitar, the more it seems to me that all classical guitar playing is a footnote to Segovia. It would be a horrible loss if people forgot just how revolutionary he was, how daring.

This burning fire, this need to communicate being impelled outwards by his personality — that's what we're missing in the guitar world, and that's why, to me, he's always the model.

It makes me so angry that people are forgetting his wisdom. It makes you see how little understood he probably was. That people can have come to that point of condescension towards him — it enrages me. 'Of course, the tone!', they say — but it's *beyond* tone. If it's tone you want, there are plenty of imitation Segovias who produce a beautiful tone. But they don't sound like Segovia. Not every tone that Segovia produces is beautiful. The tones that *have* to be beautiful, *are* beautiful, often because they come next to something that isn't so beautiful. Truth isn't all beauty. You have to have a little bit of evil in you too; you're not going to be interesting if you're just sweet and good all the time. Segovia has got a little devil in there.

But the younger players of my generation scare me. So when this interviewer asked me about Julian Bream, I said 'Thank God he's there'. Because that's what I would like to aspire to. That direction, rather than the direction of my own generation.

CC

OSCAR GHIGLIA

Born in Livorno, Italy, in 1938, Oscar Ghiglia nearly became a painter. But the guitar took precedence, and he enrolled at Santa Cecilia Conservatory in Rome. Masterclasses with Segovia in Siena followed, and his professional debut was made in the Spoleto Festival, where so many young musicians have begun successful careers. Segovia invited him to be his assistant at the University of California, and since then he has been in continuous demand, both as a performer and as a teacher.

In late middle age, Oscar Ghiglia has become perhaps more of a teacher than a player, but when he plays you are aware of a supreme sense of style. The accretion of decades has brought an understanding of music that few people under 50 can appreciate.

As rich in anecdote and humor as he is in music, Oscar Ghiglia is excellent company. His powerful but benign authority makes him welcome at innumerable guitar competitions, and it was at one of these — the first Philippos Nakas Guitar Competition, in Athens — that we met for this interview.

Oscar Ghiglia: My father, who was an artist, had been taught guitar first by his father and then by a very famous Roman actor from the time of Fascism, Ettore Petrolini. He was a comic actor who played the guitar. They had a friend in common from Sardinia, a well-known musician called Gabriel, who had found all these ethnic musics in the island. He and my grandfather had met while my grandfather was there as a tourist, painting — he was also a painter. He happened to be adopted by some brigands there; they apparently didn't think he was a dangerous fellow, for they kept him in their place for as long as he would, and he settled there and painted as much as he wanted. That's how he met Gabriel, who was a very nice guitarist who could play in the tradition of the Sardinian people. My father learned through this combination of people. I always heard him singing songs and playing. Whereas my mother, a pianist, would lead me in quite a different direction. But I didn't particularly care for the piano; I thought it was too loud, for one thing, or too square, or too black, or too white — anyway, something too much. My father used to play the piano, very badly: I probably followed his example, and my mother shooed me away from it.

During the War, we were in Rome, my older brother and I; there were German raids, and Allied raids against the Germans, and the bombs would fall all around our home, but fortunately none of them hit where we were staying. During the time when the alarm was on, when the sirens rang all over the city, my mother would sit at the piano and play, and we would sing Schubert's Lieder. It made us forget the danger. Then, when they were very close and we heard the first bombs fall, we all ran down into the shelter. Music was always something connected with some impending doom.

Courtesy Classical Guitar Magazine

Before I was a teenager I never thought of playing the guitar. I was a painter, as my father was. Painting kind of took me away from people. I was already solitary, and I needed the company of others. Painting was something you did by yourself. I loved to be by myself, but then I figured that I could do the same thing with the guitar. It was an easy step when I quit the painting; there was no harm, no pain, no sorrow, no regret.

Do you still paint?
Sometimes. But I stayed at the same level as when I was about 13, when I picked up the guitar. I entered the Conservatory of Rome when I was 16. I played and sang songs for a couple of years, after which my

mother thought that was enough playing around and that I needed a solid classical education in music. That year the Conservatoire of Santa Cecilia, the first conservatoire in Italy, had opened a guitar class. You could not get a diploma for many years; it was just a certificate, it wasn't valid, it wasn't worth anything. But it was very good, because I studied all the repertoire, especially the didactic repertoire, all the etudes.

Not all became guitarists. The class was made up of 16 at the beginning, and only about ten stayed. And only about five remained in the guitar world. Some stayed in music, and one became a conductor, Gianluigi Gelmetti. He and I entered in the same year; he was eight years old and I was 16. He was very little: a prodigy. He decided after his diploma that he wanted to continue with composition and conducting. He came to Siena as a guitarist, but he also followed Celibidache's classes.

1957 was the first year I went to Siena, but Segovia was absent that year, having an eye operation. He came the following year, and the year after, when Alirio Diaz was holding the class. Alirio was a very good teacher who opened a lot of doors, especially concerning tone, sound. They would never tell us how to do any one thing, you know. It was just take it or leave it; it was there, a display of certain things. If you were able to get them, they were yours for the taking. But the problem was that sometimes it was very difficult to do this. How do shape your nails? — 'Well, not too much this way, not too much that way.' How do you hold your guitar? — 'Not too much this way, not too much that way.' How do you touch the string? — 'Not too much this way, not too much that way.'

Segovia taught by example?
Yes. Alirio also; he would mention sometimes that his left hand had been a problem which he had resolved, whereas the right hand had been quite natural. So we were all looking at his right hand — but it was a hand of a different kind. His right hand is not like mine. So I tried to copy his right hand in front of a mirror, trying to put it in the same position — and I couldn't! There was no way I could move my thumb as he moved his. South Americans, especially Colombians and Venezuelans, have a hand made in such a way, with fingers that go into that position naturally.

Nobody else was able to do it like that. Whereas it was much easier for me to imitate Segovia's position of the right hand. I also have large hands, although my fingers are not as fat or as long as Segovia's. Segovia had very long fingers. His thumb extended to such a length that he hid it when he was in front of a lady. He put his thumbs inside his cuffs. He was somehow modest. People used to look for his thumb when he was playing. They couldn't see it. It never came out, like John Williams's.

Segovia always took care to keep his nails out of the way when he shook hands. And such a soft hand he had! Cool and soft. You never had the impression that he would perspire or that he would squeeze anything in his hands.

Alirio was more influential the first year, because I fell in love with his sound. The following year Segovia was there and Alirio was there, so there were those two poles. Segovia was teaching Alirio every day, so when Alirio played you could hear him at his best. He played Sor's Sonata opus 25, the Allegro: when the chords came, they sounded like an orchestra. Incredible, the huge amount of sound. Beautiful. And so strong and rhythmic. It took me the whole year afterwards to try and figure out that sound.

I came back the next year with a great sound. Alirio was sitting next to Segovia, and Segovia heard me play. I played a short piece with that great fat sound I was so proud of, and Segovia, instead of saying 'Bravo! Beautiful!', turned towards Alirio and said: 'I don't understand why they try to get such a useless amount of sound' — and he played the same thing with the tiniest sound I've ever heard. Why? All that work— 'useless'! I had spent hours and hours at it.

Segovia thought I was a nightmare for him. I had long hair and a beard that had started to crop. During the night he would see an image that he wouldn't recognize, a black mask or something, somebody who would take his head off his neck and keep it in his hands. And then he would realize that it was me, in his dreams. I never really liked this. I was a pupil, and he never told me. Other people kept telling me these stories. He made fun of me because I made faces, you know, grimaces, when I performed Bach. I played this Gavotte by Bach and I made such grimaces that he imitated me. I felt so humiliated. He said, 'Look, you're holding the guitar like a lightning conductor. Don't hold your guitar like that!'. So I tied a bottle of water at the end of the guitar to pull it down, so that it wouldn't go up like that. It took some time to get used to that position. It was very uncomfortable. I had to learn to bend my whole back Now, finally, I can hold it any way I want. I don't like to hold it too high because then it's like an archlute. I sometimes look at a cellist, and there's quite an uncomfortable bend in the elbow there where they hit the low strings.

Anyway, it took a long time to learn how to hold the guitar and how to sit. I'm still learning. Then came Alexander Technique in the 60s and the 70s. I read a few chapters of Alexander's book, and it seemed to be a way to help towards this quest for the right approach to the guitar. Because it seemed that the greatest successes I've had were due to a lot of work, so that afterwards I felt it as a heavy load. Every time I saw John (Williams), it was such an inspiration because it seems it just came from heaven, you know; his nervous system had no heavy particles, just motion, action.

So, it was a very good experience when John came to Siena. For one thing, I thought that Eliot Fisk should have studied with him. But John didn't particularly like teaching at the time. I think he has probably changed his mind now. Once John told me that he had finally found a reason to teach, and that was to teach people to do what they want, not what they are expected to do. He felt that he been expected to do things for too many years. That's when he took up with Sky. It was a reaction.

All the same, he is very grateful to his father for putting him through that experience, of making him do what was expected of him and giving him a remarkable technique in the process.
Absolutely. And he was such a good psychologist, his father, because he never made John tired of what he was doing. Christopher Nupen told me that John had to sit and play for 20 minutes before he could go out to play. But in 20 minutes he had to do so much. He was given a whole list of pieces and he went through all of them. If he didn't do them in 20 minutes, he would have to stay as long as it took. It was a very nice strategy. John was very sharp, and probably did it in less than that time.

Would you say that, in a sense, John was also an influence on your own playing, in addition to Segovia and Alirio Diaz?
Everyone I've met has been an influence. John, Julian Bream — I'm sure that you cannot really rule out anyone. Even people I didn't like were an influence. For instance, as a guitarist and a student of Segovia and in the class of Segovia, we tended to dislike everything else. It's some kind of sectarianism that

takes place — I hate that word, but somehow it takes place. So, when we heard all those beautiful *rubati* that Presti and Lagoya did, our blood would curdle. We would never do those things! They were absolutely forbidden. Yet when I went to visit Presti and Lagoya in their home, they were so nice and hospitable, and we had a big dinner together and we met their friends. Evangelos and Liza were there — I probably wouldn't have met them and become friends if it weren't for Presti and Lagoya. They had just recorded a new LP, and they played it for me. I really liked the piece that Rodrigo had written for them, *Tonadilla*. They told me they were giving a class the following week at the Schola Cantorum in Paris. I went to study there when I won the competition in Paris; it was among the prizes. I had decided to take a course with Jacques Chailley, the French musicologist who now teaches at the Sorbonne. He taught just a small group of students. He would sit there and speak about music and make us write music 'in the style of' after he spoke about it.

I asked Presti and Lagoya if I could just drop in during their class. I dropped in with my then wife, who was not a guitarist — she had a doctorate in urban geography — but we found out that we were both registered as players. She played 'God Save the King' on the guitar; it was all she did. We had big fights with Alexandre (Lagoya). He didn't like the fingering Segovia was doing, etcetera. I felt defensive, and I resisted. Ida Presti was very nice, because she tried to calm me down and she tried to see my point of view. However, I think I learned a lot from that week, even though it wasn't my cup of tea, so to speak. I learnt that, first of all, I was opinionated to the core, and that there were many things that I should have known that I didn't know. I found out that Segovia did allow things that were never put into words — but they knew how to put them into words. So it was another influence. Today I'm putting into words, for my pupils, what I think are the transcendental artistic grounds behind Segovia's so-called 'transgressions'.

The Aspen Festival must have been a considerable influence.
Aspen was very influential because of the very much alive ambience, chamber-music making, the concerts, the rehearsals, the people. It was started by Albert Schweitzer right after the war, actually as a cultural event that had nothing to do with music: it was a literary institute, and it had some music just to keep company there. Then the music part bloomed, and the rest stayed as it had been in the beginning. It's still

there, but the music is the main thing. The chamber music has always been very important. All the greatest quartets have played there.

So it was really instructive to discuss it with my students, to bring them along to hear Isaac Stern, to hear Itzhak Perlman, Pinchas Zukerman, all these up-and-coming musicians as well as the old ones, and to discuss the performances with them. Some were discouraged.

There was something of that at Siena too, wasn't there?
Yes, but not in such an open way. In Siena it was one-to-one; you went to a concert, but you didn't talk about it afterwards. Because, simply, you don't walk in the mountains for an hour and then walk back in the cottonwoods, talking. That's why you talked. In Siena you went out and had a pizza, and then you talked about different things.

I remember talking with a student who said that she didn't think she would ever be able to play the guitar in the way a violinist had just done. This was Stern, who had just performed a Mozart concerto, conducting and playing. And it was so beautiful. I told her, 'Why did you think in such a negative way? Did you like it?' 'Of course I liked it. But I know that I will never be able to do it and that I should stop'. And I said, 'But if you really liked it, then whatever you really liked in this playing, it's something that is already yours. It's in you. All you have to do is to take it out. But it's there. I'm sure that all the things you didn't notice in his playing, probably 95 per cent of the things he lives for you didn't notice, you don't even know they exist. But what you know, what you liked about his playing, is what is already in your pocket. So you can take it out and cash it!'

I had always been warned against outside influences. My father used to say 'You must not study with Segovia, because you will become a small Segovia. Stay by yourself, so that you'll be yourself.' I felt guilty when I went to study with Segovia. I felt guilty when I liked something that somebody else did, because I thought that it belonged to him. Then I realized that what I saw was not what he saw; it was what *I* saw. It was my own.

I try first to open my students' ears. Once somebody can hear, then his creativity is already under way. He's not trying to make a phrase the way he's been taught; he's trying to make a phrase the way he hears it. Of course he knows there are many laws he has to learn. But the hearing is his own. Sometimes in the examinations in Basel some teachers who have examined my students have told me that one common thing among my students is that they can hear. I thought that was the best compliment I could have.

You go to a lot of festivals and competitions. How do you feel about the level of playing in this competition (Philippos Nakos, Athens)? How do you feel about competitions generally?
I was very pleased with the reaction of a student of mine who was not admitted to the final, whereas my other two students were. She took it very well, but she knows that her work is still under development. She's discovering a second personality growing inside her.

Unfortunately, sometimes you see a player who is so much in love with his sound that he will not do anything else but follow that sound of his fingers on the strings, so everything will be pervaded by that. Whereas I try to teach students to be in love with the music, with the score, to look at the score like a magic ball and see all the truths coming out of it, coming directly through the mind, through the senses, rather than impose a certain shape of playing to the kind of sound, the kind of approach. The approach comes with the score. The score tells you what kind of approach to make.

Competitions are the most important things now for the young kids who need to get out, to play, to do things. They cannot undertake a career without winning competitions, because there's nothing else. Festivals with competitions! Competitions with festivals!

How far does your decision not to impose go? Aren't there times when you have to impose something better than what is there?
I take responsibility for what I'm doing. I will never touch a thing that I know is good; I care too much about the individual's personality. I think it is the main thing that he has. All I try to do is just open their eyes and their ears and to stop them from doing certain things that they do without really wishing to. If they think those things are good, they can always go back to them.

I'm now sharing students with Hoppy Smith (Hopkinson Smith, lutenist), when he's away, or when I'm away. It's very interesting. I took four of his students for one class, and he took four of mine. This was last month. I don't know what he did to them. I'm going to see them when I go back to Basel.

I'm sure it's good for them. You know, you see these persons and they're quite different. Because the people who go to the Schola Cantorum to study old music are a special breed. They belong to a different time sphere. Those who play renaissance lute do not mingle with those who play baroque. They are quite different. When they go and hear Bach, they think it's Stravinsky. Such modern music — 'Oh, it's too much!' Those who are with medieval music, when they play the lute, they cut old combs to get the right pick — they import combs from Brazil.

The students I found were all people I had talked with in the cafeteria, South Americans mainly, and I liked them very much. One was baroque guitar, another was archlute, and another one was theorbo. Every time it was a different approach. I don't read tablature like they do, so I just listen and try to shape up various things, telling them what it is they're missing. Sometimes their attitude is more towards a certain idea of style regardless of what the score says.

It's a different approach. Not so much related to the instrument as to the style of playing. So I was saying 'Your sound is very sweet, it's very beautiful, it's very alive, it's perfect, but the piece you're playing is not that. This is a bourrée. A bourrée needs some more guts. You can't have sweetness so much when you play a bourrée. You have to have heavy feet, so to speak. A bourrée was made for stamping on the grapes, to make wine. If the music calls for that, you've got to indulge in that.' They said: 'What? With a baroque guitar?' Find a way! Do it! Maybe use a different stroke. Then it sounds different. They wouldn't go for that by themselves.

But there's no direct line back, so we can't really tell how they did it in the 19th century. We can only tell from the instrument. The instrument itself is already a proof that it existed. The score is another proof. And the fact that the players had five fingers. We put all this evidence together and something comes out that is very close to what might have been. The rest has to come from the culture and the imagination.

CC

Courtesy Classical Guitar Magazine

43

SHARON ISBIN

As head of the guitar department at Juilliard, Sharon Isbin is the first ever guitar professor to have an official post in that august establishment. She follows, in somewhat grander style, a tradition begun more than one hundred years earlier, when Giulia Pelzer (born in 1837, sister of the more celebrated Madame Sydney Pratten) became professor of guitar at London's Guildhall School of Music.

She is an extremely able solo performer who delights to play in various mixed ensembles (her frequent collaborations with the Brazilians Carlos Barbosa-Lima and Gaudencio Thiago de Mello are outstanding), in addition to which she is a teacher of formidable powers.   Sharon Isbin has also been a director of the guitar department of the Tureck-Bath Institute, and has taught at Yale University, the Manhattan School of Music, Mannes College of Music and the Aspen Music Festival. She has recorded a wide range of music, and her list of CDs is highly impressive. Its importance may be judged by the inclusion of many substantial contemporary works, brought into existence through her enthusiasm for American music and her ambition to expand the repertory.

One important aspect of her development as a musician was her association with Rosalyn Tureck, the pianist and harpsichordist who once played Bach on the Moog synthesiser in order to demonstrate the universality of his keyboard techniques. But fingerboard techniques are different, and I asked Sharon Isbin if she saw anything at all incongruous in a keyboard player editing a work such as the Suite in E minor for guitar.

Photo by Michael Lavine

Sharon Isbin: There is nothing incongruous about working with a keyboard player in editing the Bach Suites for guitar, provided one's goal is not to imitate another instrument but rather to achieve a deeper understanding of the music. When Rosalyn Tureck agreed to edit the lute suites with me, I realized my fortune in being able to learn from her lifetime devotion to studying and performing Bach's music. It is that depth and clarity we bring to the music - the years of analytic thought, hard work and experience.

I try to explore the guitar's potential as a distinct, unique instrument. Though it may bear similarities to other instruments, it is certainly not a harpsichord or a lute or a violin. The sustaining quality of a bass note on the guitar, for example, is quite different from that of the above instruments. Therefore, one has to consider each individual case about whether to stop the ringing if there is a rest, or to allow the note to sustain (such as in the opening of the Prelude of Suite BWV997 or the Prelude of the Prelude, Fugue and Allegro).

One advantage, I might add, to working with a non-guitarist is that I was not influenced by preconceived notions of what was possible technically or musically, and what was not. In our work, so many ideas were explored and achieved that the realm of 'possibility' expanded considerably.

We hear a lot about authenticity nowadays. How far does this passion for authenticity work against musical communication? Why can't we enjoy Bach on our own terms?

First of all, there is no such thing as an 'authentic' performance of Bach, because the man is dead and we have no recordings. We have only educated guesswork, based upon treatises, score markings and other sources of historical information. That material, combined with musical sensitivity and understanding, with luck creates a synthesis that may come very close to something Bach might have envisioned. To deliberately ignore, however, the knowledge that is available about performance practices of the time, because these practices are not in accordance with 20th-century attitudes, is bound to do an injustice to the music. If I go to see a performance of Shakespeare, and the actors haven't a clue as to the meaning and pronunciation of 16th-century English, I would be appalled. Worse yet, if they chose to deliver the text in colloquial 20th-century style and vocabulary because of their lack of skill and understanding, I would feel cheated of the writer's great art (it's almost as much fun as hearing Schubert Lieder sung in English!).

If, however, a fine jazz musician takes a theme from Bach, improvises, changes the rhythm and structure and creates something entirely new, that is another story. This new creation does not then purport to be Bach on its own terms, but another medium, another art form. Transmutations of this sort vary in their degrees of success. The best ones spark off challenging creativity and inner continuity. Back to theatre, if a director or playwright takes a Shakespearian theme and successfully transforms it into an avant-garde surrealist production, it would succeed (if it's good) as an avant-garde surrealist production, not as an attempt to faithfully reproduce Shakespeare. Non-interest in historical perspective, its structural and spiritual components, is a far cry from creatively veering into totally different mediums.

Many early music people believe that it is misguided to want to play Bach on the piano. By the same token, they would argue against playing baroque music on a modern guitar. But nearly all guitarists do. Is any defence needed?
Bach is one of the few composers from the 18th century onward whose music is not based upon individual instrument sonority but upon structure. That is one reason why Bach works on the Moog synthesiser and Chopin does not. Since Bach himself often transcribed from one instrument to another, and sometimes did not even designate specific instruments, there is a clear precedent for transcription. Much of what is 'appropriate' is determined by context. Can you imagine going to a clavichord recital at the Barbican?

Leo Brouwer, a towering figure in contemporary guitar composition, wrote the Tres baladas *('El Decameron Negro') for you. Did you ask him for them? What was the story?*
I received the score of Brouwer's *Tres baladas* in the mail one day with no advance warning. You can imagine my delight. I think these are some of his finest pieces and I've been performing them everywhere. They are based on old erotic love stories from Africa, and volumes of these charming vignettes were collected in the 19th century by the German anthropologist Leon Frobenius. I love the colorful programmatic nature of the music, which also makes considerable use of Afro-Cuban rhythmic elements. I've always had an affinity for Brouwer's music, and looking back I can think of few recital programs in which I did not play at least one of his works.

Segovia is supposed to have changed a piece according to 'the needs of the moment'. Is this improvisatory element ever present in your own playing?
I have been performing extensively with my trio Guitarjam, which features myself, Larry Coryell and Laurindo Almeida. In working with these outstanding musicians, I've come to appreciate even more the great skill and control inherent in spontaneity and improvisation. Their art is much like composing on the spot, a tradition dating back to earliest forms of music. Playing precomposed music, we classical players don't have quite the same liberties, but it is a joy to participate in styles and venues which do permit that kind of creative expansiveness.

Why is there still a great preponderance of male professional guitarists over female?
When you consider that it takes a good 20 years to become proficient on an instrument, it is not surprising that it takes time for new generations of guitarists to emerge, including guitarists who are women. In another 20 years, it is likely that men and women in more equal numbers will be professional guitarists. It is interesting to note that in France, many more women than men attend guitar masterclasses. One reason may be the everlasting and powerful musical heritage left by Ida Presti, who continues to be a strong role model.

I think we are all agreed that the guitar needs to be accepted more into the general world of music. Is it easier in America than in Britain for a guitarist such as yourself to achieve this level of acceptance?
One of my goals in presenting the guitar on such a grand scale in the two festivals I recently directed, Guitarsteam '85 in Carnegie Hall, and Guitarfest in St Paul's new Ordway Music Theatre, was to bring together many kinds of performers and audiences. During the seven concerts of the Carnegie Festival I featured over 40 performers and an orchestra. Musical styles included classical, jazz, Brazilian, African, flamenco, Middle Eastern Sephardic, Elizabethan and folk music. The chamber music combinations included flute, violin, string quartet, voice and percussion, all

45

with guitar or guitar-related instruments (such as the 3rd-century Persian oud). I watched with great joy as the punkers with green hair who came to hear jazz guitarist Stanley Jordan sat next to Bill Kanengiser's three-piece-suited Long Island relatives for an evening of half classical/half jazz, a new experience for most in the sold-out recital hall that night. The week was truly a celebration - of the guitar, of all music, of humanity.

The next time I met Sharon Isbin, she was on her way to Holland to do a tour that included a recital at the Concertgebouw, Amsterdam. She had just made a recording of Spanish and Latin American music for Virgin Classics, who also produced successful record of Bach's music. Titled 'Road to the sun — Estrada do Sol, Latin Romances' (VC 79 11 28), the CD included Leo Brouwer's El Decameron Negro, *a work that had been written for her in 1981. She was delighted to be able to record it, along with Rodrigo's impressionistic* Invocación y Danza, *in a program of more traditional Latin music. Contemporary music, she said, was not something to be afraid of. Julian Bream had shown the way in that respect, and Sharon Isbin paid due tribute to his efforts. Virgin Classics were taking another step in the same direction.*

Virgin had high artistic standards, said Sharon, and moreover were wonderful to work with. Of her recording of Bach's four lute suites in Rosalyn Tureck's edition, she said: 'Other companies might have shied away from something they might have considered too sophisticated for the mainstream. But Bach has such an international appeal that he transcends all those kinds of boundaries.' Public response had been good. The record had excellent reviews in the New York Times, CD Review, Billboard, American Record Guide, many newspapers, and all the guitar magazines. In Germany it sold out in the first month. It was chosen in Gramophone as a Critics' Choice Recording of the Year and in CD Review as an Editors' Choice Best Recording of 1989.

'It seems to be of interest to non-guitarists as well as guitarists, and I'm pleased by that, because the more we can take the guitar out of its own little world and bring it to others, the more they will appreciate it and realize that there is guitar music that's serious and meaningful, and that isn't stereotyped in one way or another, with the usual associations for guitar.'

The collaboration with Rosalyn Tureck had undoubtedly brought Bach's guitar music to the attention of a wider musical listening field. 'It's funny, you know, because the kind of collaboration we're doing strikes non-guitarists as so perfectly natural. Occasionally you encounter approaches to guitar from someone who's steeped in the 19th-century tradition, with 19th-century fingering and ornamentation, and who has difficulty freeing themselves from that anachronistic mould. But most welcome the guitar as a modern, 20th-century instrument with tremendous capabilities of expression — dynamically, rhythmically, lyrically and sonically. My whole purpose in presenting this music was to draw on the guitar's vast resources and to make Bach's music really flourish. One can't merely imitate another instrument, such as the lute, violin, harpsichord or piano. Once you think in terms of imitation you lock your mind into a frame of reference that denies the grand panorama of what is really there and all that is available to you.

'It's so important to recognize the instrument's individual and unique qualities. For example, the overlapping string sound that you can have naturally on a six-stringed instrument can translate into a more microcosmic sensibility as well. When you do trills on the harpsichord, you've got that undamped resonance. The guitar has that too, but the capability of damping as well. We can control that to an even greater degree, so that when you finish a trill or mordent, you stop the vibration of the penultimate note and you don't have that non-harmonic ringing. That beautiful blend gives an opportunity in the course of the embellishment for great musical expression.

'But if I wanted to copy the harpsichord, for example, then I wouldn't damp the string at the end, and we'd be left with a situation that was musically undesirable in most circumstances. And if I wanted to copy the lute, then I would do strictly left-hand trills, and then I'd be denying the greater volume and lyrical possibilities of the modern guitar. If I were trying to imitate the violin, then I'd have to use a bow.'

The manner of the expression, fingering as well as embellishment, has to come from the musical structure. 'Bach continually wrote for one instrument and then set the result for another. In this manner, he transcribed hundreds of his own works. He sometimes did not even specify instrumentation. With regard to the lute suites, we only know with any certainty that one was written for the lute, and even that takes transcribing in order to be done on the lute. Bach arranged BWV1006a from his E major Violin Partita, and BWV995 from his G minor Cello Suite. BWV996 may have been written for the *Lautenwerk*. But they all have textures that relate very much to the lute. 'It would be absurd in this day and age to think of a keyboard player playing Bach's music without embellishment, but that's what had been done for so long on the guitar and on bowed instruments as well. Yet if you go to the manuscripts of something like BWV996, it's filled with embellishment: the Prelude and the Courante, the Sarabande - and there's a lot that can be gleaned from that. In that suite, much of the embellishment I play comes from original manuscripts. I think too that when people are working with the editions of BWV996 and 997 which Tureck and I have published with Schirmer, they should take them as models, but ones which can be altered so long as the music's structural integrity is preserved. As performance editions, they are the first of their kind with extraordinary attention devoted to phrasing, embellishment, dynamics, articulation and fingering.'

Bach himself, in transcribing from one instrument to another, would make changes that were necessary. Structure had to be the guide. His own transcriptions were never mere imitations; he expected each instrument, in Sharon's phrase, 'to flower and flourish with its own integrity.'

Unlike many modern exponents of Bach on the guitar, Sharon Isbin seemed content with six strings, though clearly extra basses would open up many new possibilities. But she is happy with her Tom Humphrey 'Millennium' guitar, with its steeper neck angle (designed to create a greater impact on the soundboard, much like a harp). 'I'd been playing one of his other instruments for six years before I bought this one, and I'm really pleased with how it sounds. But there are many guitar makers, and it's a very personal thing. You have to choose what you sound good on.'

Her reasons for not having extra strings were practical more than anything else. She needs six strings for Spanish, classical and contemporary music; more than six, and resonance starts to interfere with the sound. 'A large number of strings may sound beautiful in some baroque music, but it's not essential musically. And I don't want to travel with three guitars. It's hard enough travelling with one.'

Sharon Isbin commissions many new works. In November 1989 she performed a new concerto, the fifth to be written for her. By Lukas Foss, it is based on American folk themes and is called *American Land-scapes*. 'The last movement is Bluegrass, with a Fossian twist, and the second movement is in variation form based on a white spiritual called "Wayfaring Stranger". The first movement uses a couple of old colonial period American folk tunes, which Foss fragments and develops contrapuntally. It's an unusual and clever kind of approach. Each movement is very different, but they're all held together by that common strand of celebrating an American cultural heritage, which really hasn't been done before in the context of a guitar concerto.'

And, of course, the guitar plays an important part in that heritage. A fairly recent study, said Sharon Isbin, discovered that roughly half of American households have a musical instrument, with the guitar the most popular, followed by the piano. 'You're talking about over 15 million amateur and professional guitar players in the United States. That's a tremendous number. With all the bellyaching that goes on these days about older audiences dying off and presenters wondering where the young people are to replenish them — because many are so blasted out on rock music and rap — I really feel that it's important to cultivate the familiarity of the guitar in a way that can be attractive to young people and draw them into classical music.' She has used this philosophy in a number of her own projects, including her five-part series 'Guitarjam' for American Public Radio, a big national radio network, in 1989. Each of the one-hour shows, which she conceived, wrote, directed and played in, had its own theme, but was nevertheless united with the others.

'For example, the first one had to do with Brazilian music, and was called "Brazilian Journey". On that program Carlos Barbosa-Lima, myself and a Brazilian percussionist did a number of works by composers such as Nazareth and Pixinguinha. It was very interesting to examine some of those popular styles and how they influenced a writer like Villa-Lobos. How the modinha form, for example, would creep into a work like the *Etude no.8*. The show gave people a better idea of the origins of Brazilian music, from jungle sounds to classical traditions. On another show, I included Odetta, a well-known black folk singer in the United States who does blues as well as more traditional folk music. In the same program I played the music of Brouwer, in particular the third Balada from *The Black Decameron*, because it uses a lot of Afro-Cuban rhythmic and lyrical elements, including antiphonal call-and-response that goes way back to more traditional African chant styles. I also demonstrated some of the folk music of Barrios and Lauro as a way of showing how our classical repertoire has early folk roots as well, the guitar being so much an instrument of the people and of popular culture.'

There was also a banjo group playing hot jazz of the 20s and 30s, along with Cuban rhythms and the South American tango. All interconnect, said Sharon Isbin, even Scott Joplin and Ernesto Nazareth, who shared similarities of style and syncopation at the same time. A sort of cosmic unity, she suggested.

'In a more traditional vein, another show focused upon early music: Paul O'Dette came and demonstrated on the renaissance lute and on the baroque lute - that was fascinating, because I asked him to take a theme and show us how embellishment would change it, not only from period to period but from country to country. It was also quite wonderful to hear a movement from one of the lute suites on the baroque lute and then on the guitar. In another program, a Sephardic trio, Paco Peña, and music of Albéniz and Falla provided fascinating insight into the development of Spanish music.'

Creating the series was a lot of hard but satisfying work, but it did bring the classical guitar to an audience that might not otherwise have been exposed to it. Commissioning the concertos also represents a step away from the traditional guitar audience, for the simple reason that symphony orchestras attract large audiences who know little about the guitar. And getting well-known composers to write for the instrument results in its being taken more seriously.

In 1989 Sharon Isbin gave the first performance of a work for guitar and orchestra by the Pulitzer Prize-winning composer Joseph Schwantner, with the St Louis Symphony in Carnegie Hall and in St Louis. It was done again in Utah, and she was amused and delighted to see the headline in the local newspaper: 'New Sexy Savage Guitar Concerto'.

Salt Lake City is Mormon country, and very traditional. 'I thought, great! This piece has really reached people on a visceral level. And I felt I understood the piece for the first time. Those two words sum it up — I'd never thought of it that way before.'

The Schwantner work was 'beautifully orchestrated', eliminating problems of balance. Schwantner was a guitarist himself, which clearly helps. 'He doesn't perform any more, but when he was a teenager the guitar was his first instrument. He really knows the

instrument, and what he did was very unusual: he used the guitar as a kind of central control board for the orchestra. It's hard to describe without hearing it, but he realizes that, this being his first major guitar piece since he was a teenager — he's in his late forties now — all of his writing has been using guitar as a model subconsciously in terms of the sharply articulated attacks and the pitch register distribution in a lot of the chording. So for him to write this piece finally for the instrument that has for so long inspired him meant returning to his early origins. And that's why he titled the work "From Afar . ... A Fantasy for Guitar and Orchestra". The orchestra complements the guitar's sonority, and the cadenza of course allows the guitar to do even more.'

Photo by Stuart O'Shields

People often forget that virtually any instrument that competes with the orchestra is going to lose. If you write any concerto, you have to watch that aspect. With the guitar, and despite the care taken by composers, the problems seem exacerbated .

'For so many years we've had to deal with the idiosyncrasies of the amplification technology. I've come up with a solution that really works. I place a couple of speakers mounted on poles about ten feet high at the back of the stage, centered so the orchestra can hear what's going on. If they can't hear what you're doing, there's not going to be much co-ordination. The sound reaches out to the audience, and the soloist can hear it as well. Sometimes one might need a small monitor, just for enhancement. It sounds natural for the audience too, because they're hearing it from where you're sitting, and by the time it reaches that front row it's not on top of them, it's already been filtered through a good 30 feet.

'It's important to have a good engineer who's sensitive to EQ and that you have time beforehand to set it all up. The other problem these days is rehearsal time. When I came here and played with the London Symphony Orchestra at the Barbican a few years back, we only had one rehearsal in the morning, and that was it, a 45-minute run-through. Fortunately, the piece that they requested was the *Aranjuez* Concerto. My thought was, had it been a less familiar work or a premiere, there simply would not have been enough time to rehearse. Can you imagine preparing a new work in 45 minutes? And then giving a performance?

'I mean, they know the *Aranjuez* beautifully, and they play it wonderfully; and for 45 minutes that was a good choice to make. But I think it's really important that, as programming complexities become an even greater morass to sift through, we do not abandon contemporary music. Allotting enough rehearsal time to develop and create new works is still going to be important.'

Among Sharon Isbin's many achievements are the New York premiere of *Clocks,* written for her by the 1990 Grawenmeyer Award winner, Joan Tower. Another is the concerto written for her by the American composer John Corigliano. In 1997 the Concerto for Violin, Guitar and Orchestra, with Sharon Isbin and Nadja Salerno-Sonnenberg the soloists, was performed in New York. The process continues. Her latest plans include, as ever, new commissions, recordings, and lots of concerts.

'My focus is solo recitals and concerti, but my work with the Guitarjam Trio, with Larry Coryell and Laurindo Almeida, was certainly an eye-opener in terms of drawing in an entirely new audience for the guitar. It's been a lot of fun. And I find it has loosened me up with music that can be flexible with that kind of freedom. And in terms of concerts it's been very successful. For example, in 1989 we played at the Kennedy Centre in Washington, D.C., which seats about 2800 people; it was a four-concert guitar series, and that program sold the best. It's exciting to know that you're bringing in a mixture of people, many of

whom are hearing classical guitar or Brazilian style for the first time. But the Trio was always an adjunct to each of our solo careers.'

In September 1989 The Juilliard School of Music, New York, started a graduate program in classical guitar - one of the last major schools of music to give credibility to the instrument in this way. It is also one of the most prestigious. Sharon Isbin, a holder of Bachelor and Master of Music degrees from Yale University, is its Department Head and Principal Faculty Member. Announcing the program, the Juilliard President, Joseph W. Polisi, referred to the guitar's unique position in Western musical tradition. He said: 'We look to Ms Isbin's dedication and artistry to help us achieve the goal of enhancing that great tradition in the years ahead. It is Juilliard's hope that we can nurture the finest classical guitar performers as well as encourage more composers to create new music for the instrument.'

In the light of such clear-headed dedication, it is hard not to feel optimistic about the future of the classical guitar.

CC

NIKITA KOSHKIN

There was a time when the Russian guitarist-composer Nikita Koshkin found it difficult to travel abroad. The restrictions imposed on him lent even more glamor to the shadowy figure that had composed the startlingly brilliant The Prince's Toys; so much so that a kind of competition began to see who would who would be the first to succeed in bringing him to Britain. Chris Kilvington won that particular event, and Koshkin duly appeared at the 1992 Cambridge International Guitar Festival. This interview by Chris is a direct result of that occasion.

Nikita Koshkin's subsequent appearances outside his own country have been numerous, and invariably the result of efforts by individuals who believe in him and his work. It was Frank Koonce who brought him to the USA, arranged concerts for him and set up the process whereby his first recordings were made and issued. Thus it is no longer difficult to meet Nikita Koshkin. Instead of the myth we have the man; and it is more than a fair exchange. His expansive presence, his capacity for hard work and his demanding musical standards make him a prominent figure at international guitar festivals and competitions everywhere. He has taken his rightful place among the outstanding composer-guitarists of history, a line generated by Sor and Giuliani and continuing to our day in musicians like Leo Brouwer and Roland Dyens. CC

Chris Kilvington: *You have never repeated the formula of The Prince's Toys, thus avoiding a tempting trap to which others have been more susceptible. Later works have all had their own particular identity; yet, in spite of all the different personalities of Three Stations on one Road, Usher Waltz, The Elves Suite and much more, your compositions still retain your own distinctive voice. How closely is that connected with your harmonic language?*

Nikita Koshkin: My harmony is quite traditional, a tonal language which derives from Prokofiev and Shostakovich. Inside the tonal language you are very free, not confined. If you think that tonality represents chains, then by all means cut them to be free — but you will not have real freedom because you are already not able to use something. Tonality can go in all possible directions.

As far as the architecture of the piece is concerned, I need a big solid foundation to keep the house in order. Tonality is that bedrock. I notice that many composers today are coming back to tonality, but I never went away from it. Take the tonality of C major. It does not mean you have only seven steps; you have twelve, all with equal weight. Every step is independent. My harmony is based more on intonation than on classical rules, founded on the melody and the feeling of the harmony.

Chromatic moves give a sense of drama, development and movement. It makes all the ingredients such as melody, harmony and rhythm very mobile. If you use chromatic steps quite infrequently, then this occasional intrusion gives more tension to the piece. It's the same with my 10-string guitar; I employ the basses economically, and then there is the possibility that every appearance of a bass note will be beautiful. I don't want a chromatic salad. The use of chromatic movement, its rate and quantity, depend entirely on the piece.

I cannot feel harmony as something that is independent of melody — they are a single unity. I never write a melody and then harmonize it; always the two come together. Never once have I done otherwise.

You need aesthetic proportion. If you go beyond it, then it stops being art. Forte, double forte, fortissimo, all prolonged — where next? After a while it's just a noise, and the logical conclusion is the breaking of strings. It's a question of discipline. If you shout perpetually, the other person will not hear you. It starts to be boring.

Photo by Al Abrams

Your work seems to bear out in architectural form what you say about proportion. What do you feel about musical shape?

It's very easy to make a sculpture, or so it is said. You take a piece of basic stone and cut away what is not necessary. It's a little bit like this in composition. When a composer is confronted by a problem of shape, it's best to cut away rather than add. When I have some problems I let the music run in my head many times until I feel whether it's correct or not. It's not mathematics, but musical sensitivity. Every piece of music is a sort of life which you are creating, and each one has specific forces unique to itself and its development.

When I begin a piece I have no idea how it will end. Often I find that in fact I have started in the middle. Various details arrive, I start to feel how it will conclude, and from where it will arrive. I might feel that three balanced movements would be right, only to discover that one is enough, that the work is complete. So why say more? I'm not a complete slave to an original idea. Science makes us think, life makes us feel and art allows both things to happen simultaneously. In composition this just happens, and I cannot find an exact frontier between the two things. I do believe that my music is a very sincere work.

We spent some time previously discussing ensemble music. Might this be a future development for you? It seem to me that your sense of line, harmony and rhythm could offer the ideal components for a quartet, for example.

Well, certainly, for me ensemble music is a very attractive and promising possibility. It's a sort of geometric progression. Two guitars do not literally double the possibilities of one, but they do represent a dramatic widening of opportunities.

I will take up your suggestion. I will make a quartet, especially with my ideas for students. Students are not stupid. If they are to grow well, they must start with excellent examples of music. I am far from saying that I am excellent, but at least I can do my best. If they see someone trying, and also try themselves, then we play a part and something will come of it. Beginners must not start with silly music. Your idea is a very provocative one. I can see that it is vital to get a good balance across the parts; not difficult, but not empty. Students, according to my experience, like to have interesting music where they can feel the results, so the separate parts must be as interesting as possible.

Guitar ensembles usually have short pieces or transcriptions. A string quartet finds it perfectly possible to have just three pieces in their concert program. Two or more guitars can surely stand very important music.

Do you feel your writing to be orchestral in nature?
Certainly. My musical education in Russia was anything but specifically centered on guitar. The composers I really appreciate are not guitar composers. I particularly enjoy the symphony orchestra, which can produce virtually anything. Nevertheless, the guitar is a rich instrument, with so many colors — a really diverse palette. Some of my own pieces, such as *The Prince's Toys, Piece with Clocks, Usher Waltz,* have an orchestral flavor in their sound, but transcription would be impossible. They are for guitar only, for specific use of guitar colors.

What I think helps me is that I also perform on the guitar. I think that those who do not are often incapable of treating various lines with equal importance, and the result is that the guitar sounds like a not very nice instrument. Castelnuovo-Tedesco, Rodrigo, Ponce, all produced good guitar sounds without being players, but they are fairly rare examples.

You mentioned the impossibility of transcribing your works. What about transcription generally?
I do prefer original works for the instrument, because so often when we transcribe music we lose so much. There are exceptions; Albéniz found a second life for his music through the guitar. And Bach; his work lies in musical meaning rather than orientation towards a specific instrument. Ultimately, it lies in how it is made, in its excellence.

You have stated a preference for non-guitarist composers. Which ones do you most appreciate?
I admire Tchaikovsky for his fantastic melodies, which are built upon excellent orchestration. There is a great mastery here, which is hidden within the score; great mastery of development, of the ability to create real drama. Prokofiev has a very fresh harmonic language. Shostakovich has excellent feeling of shape. Stravinsky's fine rhythms are marvellous; his approach to music was unusual in his time, and is still fresh. He could have achieved a more traditional melodic development, but chose not to do so. I love his music, it's absolutely great. And Mussorgsky too. I also very much appreciate the French impressionists, Ravel and Debussy, for their colorful scores; beautiful, aesthetic music. They certainly influenced me. Charles Ives I was shocked by, but I enjoyed his original ideas,

so different from what I was used to.

Which guitar composers do you like?
Well, Giuliani and Sor, naturally, and Villa-Lobos. And I love Britten's *Nocturnal* and the *Bagatelles* of William Walton. What a pity that he wrote nothing else; those Bagatelles are beautiful.

What about guitar music composed more recently?
Shostakovich said that a composer must not be afraid of being not modern, of using clear melody. He must believe in himself, in his ideas and work. If I need clear harmonies, I use them. I am not afraid of not using a so-called modern style. Some people are afraid of working directly; they work in a mist, and the result is hidden in a cloud of false notes, many of them completely unnecessary.

Your opinions are generally strongly formed. Can I assume that your musical education provided you with a foundation upon which to build them?
Well, certainly the Russian conservatories are of a very high level. The approach is wide, but not at the expense of quality. In the secondary schools it is absolutely obligatory for anyone studying music to study conducting as a specific discipline. The guitar can belong in the tradition of instruments such as the balalaika and domra, and our players of these instruments are excellent, but it is necessary to follow other

courses. Certainly, not every guitarist will become a conductor, but you are teaching how to work with music without touching an instrument. This is very important. Also in the Institute you must continue to develop your conducting skills for a further two years. Conducting really helps you to think properly as a soloist.

You appear to have a liking for the waltz form. Can you say something about that?
At first I was surprised myself. I didn't realize how much I was using it. The waltz is very attractive, not simply for dancing. In a traditional Russian waltz it is customary to present something deeper than simple dancing music. Tchaikovsky and Rachmaninov can provide you with examples. We have a tradition of the concert waltz; there is the possibility for great expression with this rhythm. 3/4 is much softer and smoother than 4/4, which is square in movement, strong and strict. 3/4 is less exact and fixed, more sensitive. But to be honest, for me it just arrived naturally along with melody and harmony. Rhythm has an exact musical meaning; it's not merely a pulse, but also contains an image within it. When we hear it, just a beat, we also hear music arriving. Melody, harmony, rhythm, all arrive together. And I might also add that the changing of time signatures within a piece of otherwise strict rhythm makes for a promising conflict, and can create a lot of tension.

In Voronezh during February 1992 I heard many young guitarists from your country. What did you think of them?
This was the first real opportunity to see the young players from all over the ex-USSR. We did have some competition, but only between players from secondary schools, and only Russians. And the guitar was only part of the whole business, along with all the folk instruments. Frankly, I was very surprised and delighted — as I think you were yourself — at the high level of performance. It was an occasion that revealed not only fine students but also fine teachers.

As readers of this magazine will know, a favorite subject of mine is teaching the early learning of the upper fingerboard. Have you any thoughts about that?
It is an excellent idea. I have always been meeting the problems of wide frets, distorted left elbow, undue pressure, and so on. The only thing is that we do not yet have the pieces, and I will start now and support your idea. We can collaborate if you wish, and begin to make a new repertoire for a new school of tuition. According to my experience, it looks a very attractive

idea. It is so hard for little children to start in first position. Now we must stop talking, and I must write music.

...And he did. Within hours he had composed four cleverly written pieces. The following day he wrote the first short movement of a work for my guitar duo. He was rarely without a guitar in his hand, and with several days free in Cambridge after the Festival he also finished for me a solo piece that had first seen the light of day in a hotel room in Voronezh. He works very quickly. He has a mercurial character which spans more than the usual emotional extremities, and as a Gemini myself I can understand this. Whether motivated by sparkling sunny inspiration or by a dark melancholy, he appears capable of writing music of high quality virtually at will. Is this the 'Russian soul' he speaks of? The artistic nature of a descendant of Turgenev? Or simply Nikita Koshkin himself?

CK

LOS ANGELES GUITAR QUARTET

No guitar quartet in the world has a higher profile than the Los Angeles Guitar Quartet. Formed in 1980 by four young guitarists from the University of Southern California, it achieved prominence almost from the beginning. After ten years Anisa Angarola left, and Andrew York came in to join John Dearman, William Kanengeiser and Scott Tennant. The brilliant style of the ensemble remained unchanged, continuing to be highly successful, both in concerts and in their many recordings.

All four members are distinguished soloists in their own right, and Andrew York has made a considerable reputation as a composer of originality. Classical Guitar magazine's Reviews Editor Chris Kilvington heard them in 1995 and, as one always willing to stray from established routes, lost no time in going to interview them. His first question concerned their arrangements and compositions: how they did them, why they did them, and whether or not the arranger had individual members of the ensemble in mind.

Andrew York: First I just get the musical ideas I want to express down on paper. Though I may come up with an idea that is tailor-made for one of the four of us, it's mostly in the final construction of the parts that I allocate the material to take advantage of each of our individual strengths and also to make the parts at least somewhat democratic. I dislike pieces where all the action is in the first one or two parts. There's no need to give all the action to the first chair in a guitar quartet which has four homogeneous instruments. Playing third guitar myself, I hope for more than a boom-chic accompaniment pattern to play. However, when I'm asked to write for other quartets I'm sometimes told to give all the hard stuff to a certain player. In that case I'll try to accommodate their needs while still making the other parts tolerably interesting.

Photo by Blake Little

William Kanengiser: We've become pretty picky about arrangements, and we've found that most of the commercially available ones don't meet our needs. It's a bit of an 'if you want something done right' attitude, I suppose, but it's also because there are some specific requirements that we look for. Obviously, it must be a good piece that lends itself to transcription, done with some understanding of the particular resonance and voicing that works for four guitars. But we also try to play arrangements that make use of John's extended bass range, as well as other voicing possibilities — I frequently tune the sixth string to C and the fifth to G.

Even more important, we always want to play reasonably democratic arrangements. So many published ones have first guitar playing the high stuff, fourth always playing the bass, etcetera, so that things aren't passed around or shared. Well, the other guys simply wouldn't abide me getting all the juicy melodies all of the time! My arrangement of *Capriccio Espagnol* and John's *Barber of Seville* Overture are good examples of this equal-voiced writing. This approach not only makes it more interesting for us, but for audiences as well. Since we're not a 'family' group like a string quartet, the real strength of our configuration is the possibility for any one of us to play first fiddle.

What does the group feel about the value of the bass guitar in guitar ensemble playing and composing?
John Dearman: I play a seven-string guitar. The seventh is a low A with a 2-fret bass extension for that string — there is a notch of fingerboard which continues behind the nut under the seventh string. It's hard to imagine how we got along without it before. Transcriptions are so much easier with the ability to open up voicings and contrapuntal textures, and it also adds an extra element of color to orchestral arrangements. My guitar also has 22 frets under the first and second strings (up to high D), and while these aren't the most

attractive sounding notes they are nevertheless useful for doublings, orchestral color and so on. I use them in almost all of our transcriptions.

One of the important things in any guitar ensemble playing is choice of fingerings, as these naturally affect timbres and mechanics greatly. Achieving this in duo is one thing, but how do four players manage to achieve a satisfying answer to this most interesting challenge?

Scott Tennant: Well, first of all, by the time we get around to fingering the music we've usually read through the piece and know what it sounds like. This helps a lot. I personally proceed to finger my part based on comfort and ease first. Then I see if I'm playing in duo with anybody somewhere and usually consult with that person to try and match fingerings based on the phrasing or whatever. This is a tough question, really, because no matter what we do fingerings are constantly being changed as we work on the piece.

Any instrumental ensemble needs to practice regularly together, and I was naturally interested to know how the quartet worked in this respect, whether they subdivided, how they discussed all the various points of interpretation which inevitably arise, and so forth.

John Dearman: When we first began playing together, we did so on a fairly casual basis, meeting about once a week — just often enough to get things together for our next ensemble class meeting. Within a short time we started getting real offers for concerts and gradually made more time for rehearsals, probably peaking at about five or six days a week leading up to our first appearance in New York in 1984.

As our separate lives and careers have become more busy and complex, we normally find it best to meet for an all-day session once per week. Practices begin with espresso drinks all round, followed by discussions of business matters, followed by more espresso. When we finally do get to practising we usually try to begin with something that takes a fair amount of concentration or discipline. Brushing up old repertoire is a good example; if we put that off till the end of the rehearsal everyone's a bit loopy and before you know it the *Brandenburg Concerto* becomes a polka and Falla turns into reggae or bluegrass.

Metronome work, incidentally, is often helpful in correcting problems in tempo that always seem to creep into more familiar repertoire. That out of the way, the rest of the rehearsal is given over to a combi-nation of recent or new repertoire, the reading of new scores, and of course more espresso. When dealing with the pieces in progress, we usually work as a four. We sit around a table in order to be able to hear the other parts equally, though before the first performance it's a good idea to sit in line order so as to simulate the concert situation, where of course you can't actually hear what anyone is doing. We're actually not very systematic. We generally play along at tempo until a problem arises. If it's a rhythmic issue, we go through the parts solo, in pairs, subdividing, with metronome etc. This is the easy part. It's tempo, dynamics, articulations, colors, rubatos, ritardandos, use of ligados and all the rest that take up most of our time in rehearsal, as these are by nature much more subjective and therefore subject to often endless negotiation.

It seems to me that in any ensemble the discussions about interpretations, choice of repertoire, etc. can surely develop musical thinking, in that nobody can simply operate subjectively but must organize his or her thoughts in such a way as to justify them. What does the quartet feel about this?

Andrew York: We each certainly have different ideas, not only in musical interpretation, but also in choice of repertoire. As you say, the advantage in discussing a musical approach to a phrase is that you get exposed to other viewpoints, which can be enlightening and make your own thinking less static. We try to reach compromises when there are noticeably different ideas on a musical strategy. It can be helpful and personally clarifying to have to articulate your thoughts about something as abstract as music and the performance itself can benefit from the pooling of our musical thoughts. The danger in interpretation by committee is becoming stubborn and arguing a point just to get your own way. In terms of repertoire, my preference is to expand our selection of works stylistically to move us out of a strictly 'classical' interpretation.

Who sits far left? Does he cue everything?

Bill Kanengiser: I sit far left, as seen looking out from the stage. We've experimented with a lot of different seating arrangements. We even used to switch seats, depending on the piece, but decided that playing musical chairs was too confusing for everyone. Ultimately we settled on a standard configuration, with me on the left, then Scott, Andy and John. It works out in our arrangements to be 1st, 2nd, 3rd and 4th parts respectively. We're so used to this that we frequently find ourselves sitting in restaurants and queuing up for planes in score order — a nasty habit, but we're trying to break it!

Anyway, we have found that it's quite convenient for the far left player to give most of the cues, for the simple reason that it's easier to catch a cue coming from the fretboards side of your peripheral vision. Obviously, I don't give all the cues because it depends on the musical situation as well, but I do begin a large percentage of the tunes with a quick nod of the skull. Cuing is an acquired skill, but it only hints at feel and tempo; we already have to have a pretty unified sense of how a piece is going to go after I nod.

How does the group manage precise rubato, especially those not planned and drilled in rehearsal?
John Dearman: The key to improvised rubato is to be aware of, or even to assign in rehearsal, a leader for a given .passage. Then in performance everyone simply follows that person's lead. This is a neat trick for ensembles as it accomplishes two very important things — we have the ability to play like a 'soloist', in that we can play a piece with more rhythmic spontaneity, and we can also avoid a huge argument in rehearsal about how to plan out the rubato as a group.

A quartet of the standing of the LAGQ obviously has a lot to offer in teaching others. Do you ever teach as a group, and what weaknesses have you found in ensemble students? And do you find that teaching helps in any way to clarify your own playing?
Scott Tennant: Many guitarists play in ensembles as if they were driving their car and only focusing on the ground ten feet in front of them. In ensemble playing, like driving, what the others around you are doing helps to determine what your next move will be.

Bill Kanengiser: I teach ensemble at the University of Southern California as an individual, so with my students there I can call the shots. When the quartet is on tour we sometimes teach ensemble masterclasses, 'tagteam' style, and the proceedings can border on anarchy — screaming, ranting, endless headbutting over whether an entrance should be *p* or *mp*, or if a cut-off should be on or just after the third beat — a lot like rehearsals! Well, it's not really that bad and we obviously do share many opinions about musical aesthetics and practice strategies. Sometimes, besides the basics of ensemble mechanics, we try to impart to the students that an ensemble doesn't start to mature until it has had its first big musical argument.

Guitar ensembles are such an important development

tool for students, for so many reasons — working on solid rhythm, strong projection, how to listen, how to work effectively with other musicians. The biggest problem as I see it in student groups is a tendency not to prepare an ensemble part with nearly the attention and detail that would be given to a solo piece. I try to emphasize that rehearsals shouldn't be sightreading or part-practice sessions; everyone should have their part down so that full attention can be given to listening and playing together. Sometimes we even follow this advice . . .

I know that as players you have all had a strong relationship with Pepe Romero, from USC. In addition to being an internationally renowned soloist, he is also a member of the famous Los Romeros family guitar quartet and is known as a fine teacher. Will you tell us more about him?
John Dearman: What I've always found remarkable and inspiring about Pepe is his ability to project his personality in performance. He so obviously enjoys what he's doing, has so much confidence and to my mind strikes a perfect balance between artistry and entertainment. His teaching can be very abstract. He talks a lot about things like visualization, perception and the awareness of the actual vibrations we create while playing. See what living in California does to you? Really, it makes a lot of sense and covers some different territory from the usual. As for quartet work, I think he once said 'It's the most difficult thing. Without Papa, we would fight all the time!'

Bill Kanengiser: I have such deep feelings for Pepe. He really is my guitar 'guru'. Obviously, he's transcended the technical boundaries of the instrument, but he also has such a profound sense of the poetry of music and the artist's role in the musical world. He's an amazing teacher — sometimes very specific and technical, sometimes inspirational and mystical. The funny thing is that, despite his vital impact on me as a player and his role in putting the quartet together when we were his students, he didn't directly work with us as an ensemble coach more than four or five times. The model that he and Los Romeros gave us to follow was the real impetus that inspired us, even though we evolved to be a pretty different kind of group. We've stayed very close and Pepe, and his family did us a great honor by playing at the fund-raiser in 1993 for Andy's wife Barbie after her accident. I also thank Pepe for making me an espresso addict.

I was fascinated by Scott's 'hidden thumb' technique, which I had heard of somewhere. Which thumb? I

mean, how do you hide a thumb? And why?
Scott Tennant: Actually, I believe the complete title is 'The Secret Hidden Ninja Thumb Technique'. Someone heard me do this tremolando effect with my thumb in Falla's *El Amor Brujo*, in the movement titled 'The Cave'. All it entails is skimming rapidly back and forth over a bass string with the thumbnail to create an eerie, creepy effect. In order to do this well I've got to plant down my three fingers on the first three strings for stability and then turn my hand slightly to where it looks like a lute player's hand with the thumb under. So I guess this person couldn't see my thumb moving and therefore the sound seemed to be coming from nowhere. Like a Ninja-in-the-night, eh?

What are you looking forward to in England?
Scott Tennant: Finally getting a chance to sample some Tennent's ale on tap. It's our family name, which, through the research of an uncle, became Tennant some time about a century ago in Canada.

John Dearman: One word — Chunnel! You know, we angelenos are obsessed with our fair city's inadequate public transport, so I'll probably just ride around on the Tube and those double-decker buses for a couple of days. Seriously though, I'd like to get out in the countryside, see the sights and sample every kind of ale I can find.

Andrew York: As you know, I love to come over whenever I can. I want to have some real ale and enjoy the green countryside. Time permitting, I'd like a visit to Hampstead Heath to pay respects to some of my favorite trees there.

Bill Kanengiser: Unfortunately, we have such a tight schedule that our sight-seeing might be limited to a roadside blur and the top ten from 'Michelin's Guide to the Green Rooms of Rural Britain'. If there is any time, though, I sure would like to hang out at Stonehenge.

A last question — where do you feel you are headed as a group? What do you want to lay down as your mark?
Andrew York: I'd like to see the group move away from transcriptions of traditional pieces and towards newer music that explores the unique potential of guitar quartet. I feel that is essential not only for our ultimate success, but for the medium of four guitars in general.

Bill Kanengiser: Well, I don't know for sure, but I do know that since Andy's arrival the group has gotten more in touch with our American musical roots and that we're having a ball playing together. I guess we could claim to be on a quest to make the guitar quartet as viable a concert medium as the string quartet by expanding the repertoire, popularizing the genre and charming the pants off audiences around the globe. Or it might just be a gig. Honestly, we don't usually think so long term about what we're doing, about how posterity will view us. We're just trying to create something that we like, have fun doing it and hope that other folks like it too.

Scott Tennant: My view of it is simple: to play music that we love, as best we can.

CK

Photo by Blake Little

57

VLADIMIR MIKULKA

I first met Vladimir Mikulka in 1981 when he was the special guest artist at the Cannington Summer School. Like everyone else present, I was amazed by his brilliant array of technical skills allied to a most refined musicality. Of particular interest was his inclusion in the program of Nikita Koshkin's The Prince's Toys, *a remarkable piece demanding virtuosity from the performer. Since then Mikulka has introduced several other excellent items from Eastern Europe, with the name of Štěpán Rak outstanding as a composer of vital and expressive works. On subsequent visits to this country he has also demonstrated his familiarity with traditional compositions; that old favorite, the Bach* Chaconne, *is still a wonderful test of a guitarist's technique and musicianship, and Mikulka's 1983 rendering was a model of clarity and beauty. He has established himself as one of the very finest players in the world today, with an awesome control over his prodigious gifts, yet unlike some others he does not feel the need to be constantly alone with his guitar; he becomes very much involved in the society around him, and is sensitive to the motivations and needs of other people. He enjoys company, and revels in animated conversation.*

Earlier this year (1984) I visited Vladimir Mikulka in Paris, and there was certainly much discussion. Topics ranged far and wide, and during their course I found myself wondering just what it was that provided the foundation for this virtuoso performer's artistry, over and beyond mere juxtaposition of remarkable dexterity and fine concern for sound and phrasing. What lay behind this?

'I wondered the same thing in listening to Segovia or Bream, for example; it seemed almost mystical. But now that I am performing myself I can see that it's much simpler than when I did not see behind the curtain, so to speak. I would say that, as in many professions, much of it is concerned with a sense of responsibility. This is to myself as an artist. You must be very honest with yourself, search through yourself for your true ideas about what's happening around us in the world, and your opinions about these things. Because this is what music is for, a language — as in any art — through which you express your ideas about the world. It's obvious, if there's no world there's no art; and art exists as a philosophy of being. If there was a definite answer as to why we are here, if it were mathematically or logically possible to explain, then there would be no art. Art touches hearts in a strange and unexplained way, almost a little irrationally. It expresses people's desires for something better, for the realization of dreams and wishes.'

It has already become apparent that any curtain that Vladimir had lifted was an individual one. Highly individual talents have obviously unique ways of being arrived at; one could hardly expect the same route for all, and would certainly not wish it.

Vladimir agreed. 'It is sometimes said that everything can be achieved through work, work, work; far more of this than talent. But you cannot make art without talent. You get inspired, you react in certain situations without knowing why. Personally speaking, I am very happy that I found the guitar, that I discovered my talent. Was this chance? If you are a fatalist you will not think so. But, chance or not, it is lucky, almost like winning at the lottery. But then — what are you going to do with your prize, what will you make with your talent? We must learn how to handle it. You must, of course, have a musical talent in your head which you can indulge, and then the physical talent for the realization of expression; ideally one must contain both to an ideal degree. Maybe you have the ideas but your fingers may be, well, disadvantaged. Again, in other musicians you feel that someone really does possess talent and yet does not work equally to it.

'Connected with this, as far as I'm concerned, is what music has become for me in the last decade or so. When I won the Paris competition at 19 I didn't have the same conscious pleasure I do now; it was more a game with tunes. I was not conscious of messages then, although I may have been delivering them unconsciously. It was not that I wanted to play particularly fast, or anything of that sort — I never actually cared about this for itself — I just wanted to play as near to perfection as I could. I was young and all of a sudden there were many important professional engagements as a result of my success, so I wanted to try to best assemble my talents for the public. Now I am much more aware of what I am doing, I try to go to the primary existence of the music. It has become a necessity as much as food, something which belongs absolutely to life and which I can never forget because it expresses completely my feelings.'

What Vladimir had said about responsibility was now apparent. It occurred to me that many other musicians would also like to sincerely convey their thoughts about life but for some reason can't manage it; what did he think?

'Yes, it may not work. It's a skill of developing and clearing your thoughts and then directing them so that they are communicable with as many people as possible. It's difficult to formulate yourself, to search for the most precise and exact definition of your feelings. And if you can't achieve this you can't have true clarity of idea about the piece you're playing and will probably perform it in a way different from that which you would wish, and also different from what the composer would wish. You must serve both so clearly and in unity.'

Two composers Vladimir Mikulka has served well and very clearly indeed are Štěpán Rak and Nikita Koshkin; they are now his personal friends, but I wondered what he felt when he first met them and their music.

'Things all began with this strange and interesting personality Štěpán Rak. There was a playing room for guitarists in the Prague Conservatory, where we both studied. Rak was sitting there most of the time and producing the craziest sounds on the guitar I ever heard, compositions or ideas which came at times to his mind. This stuff was supposed, by all my guitar colleagues, to be unplayable; nobody ever dared to try some of his techniques, or even ask him for some of his pieces. For myself, I loved to hear him but thought, as did the others, that his music was so highly personal that perhaps no-one else would ever play it. Nevertheless, one day I asked him for the score of one of his pieces (*Andante and Toccata*) and proceeded to learn it. *Toccata* is not the easiest of his pieces, but I probably managed well, as I could immediately see how it functions. If I spoke about "craziest sounds" before, I meant an unusual dynamic scale, different tremolo rasgueados, many different techniques, and a striking expressiveness which he could produce on the instrument — although the sound was not always the most clear and polished, it was emotional. Here was a composer-guitarist with a fascinating and varied approach to the guitar. Every time when playing he has some different ideas, so that he cannot keep the same fingering but keeps moving to adventurous areas. Later I understood that this continuing process is important for him, the constant performing of a piece which is thus in the process of birth — and therefore the correcting and balancing of its form. Incidentally, this way of approaching the final shape of a guitar composition by constant performing and balancing all elements is unfortunately very rare in the case of contemporary composers. There are not many at this level and if there were I think it would be only for the sake of communication of their works with the public.'

Did Vladimir think that he had developed his technique in the sense of broadening it by playing so much of Rak's music?

'Certainly, because each piece has a strong sense for instrumental playing and a strong individuality. I eventually premiered 22 of his compositions, either on records or on the stage. Naturally I had to work much to get my fingers around all those peculiar inventions in his music, but I love it.'

And what of Koshkin, and *The Prince's Toys* in particular?

'Well, that's a bag full of tricks and anecdotes. But good ones. It is good humor; I saw it immediately when I met Koshkin in Moscow. We became friends in two seconds and I invited him to visit me in Prague. Later he told me that he liked the previous concerts I had given in the USSR when he did not know me so well, and that he did not have the courage to come backstage. How sorry I was that he did not like the concerts a little less!

'After I had learnt some works of his, the next thing was that he recomposed for me the skeleton of *The Prince's Toys*, enlarging it and adding ideas and movements. After spending time studying and learning it to get it in my fingers, I premiered it.'

Vladimir Mikulka's recording of this work on BIS, together with works by Rak, impressed several reviewers — including myself, tremendously — to the extent where it might be regarded as a milestone in the history of the guitar.

'Well, if this were to be so, then I would only be happy. You see, it is so much more difficult to present the music of unknown composers when you are working on getting your own name known. The promoter will say "Mr Mikulka, what are you going to play in the program?", and I will say "Bach, Giuliani, Rak...". "Who is Rak? Could you play some Albéniz?"

'You understand? The guitar is in constant trouble with repertory. As I said before, you must first like something very much. If you do, then it is your luck, your lottery ticket. When I started playing guitar at 13, I loved it so much that I could not do anything else and in time I learnt a big part of the classical guitar repertoire. That was my chance. As my musical education evolved I had some difficult times when comparing Giuliani with Mozart, or Weiss (though for lute) with Bach. And I still have. Of course, it is easily possible to disregard a big part of the guitar repertory and find many bad points about it. But why use those negative points? The repertory simply belongs to the history of guitar culture, and guitar culture belongs to musical culture. The guitar has its discreet, direct, internal, and personal charm, and if you do not want to see its values it is a pity. Besides, everything becomes history, but today we make new pages of it and that is exciting — we have a chance.'

We spoke for a while about instruments, their various individual qualities and points of comparison, and I asked Vladimir what guitar he used. Now that he was performing *The Prince's Toys* so regularly, I wondered if one instrument more than another seemed especially suited to the various percussive and other effects going through its body, sometimes seeming quite violent.

'Well, indeed, the fact that I now permanently include in my programs music with such effects also influences the choice of instrument. I was playing a Fleta for some time and, though a beautiful instrument, it appeared that the front table, with its style of French polish, was too fragile for this music — also some other parts of the instrument. So I returned to my beautiful and oldest Kohno model 20. I realized that Kohno is a pioneer of modern instruments with regard to many important characteristics of the guitar — tone quality and clarity, increased dynamic, and so on; and, for me at this stage — very important — the firm construction of the body, which resists well the expressive needs of the music I play, and is not oversensitive for travelling.

'You may say, how can this be a really personal instrument when seeming to be all this? Perhaps it might be a bit lacking the personality of guitars such as Romanillos, but does that necessarily mean that you cannot express yourself personally on it? I even think that the guitar with too much personality can sometimes negatively influence your own personality. So nowadays, although I always try to find something good, I think the fact that one does a good job on some piece of wood is more important than the contrary.'

In Paris I had the opportunity of seeing and playing several 'pieces of wood' when we paid a visit to La Guitarreria in Rue d'Edimbourg, a centre for guitarists run by Isabel Gomez from Spain. Stylishly arranged, the premises not only boast some fine instruments for sale - Bernabe, Corbellari and Kappeler, Hopf, Fischer, Ramírez, Contreras were all there — but also act as a focal point for many players both living in Paris and also just passing through. Apparently Angel Romero had visited quite recently, and Roberto Aussel had called in only the previous day. Vladimir made every instrument sound good and gave especial pleasure to Isabel when trying her favorite Pappalardo guitar. He showed me some new things by Rak and I was struck by some visually peculiar fingerings he used, either dictated by necessity or chosen by him for a particular reason. It was something I mentioned to him later.

'If you want to play the guitar well you must not try to play it as a guitar. Technically, it has the big disadvantage when compared with the piano of not having a pedal. We must not think in apparently guitaristic fashion as far as fingering goes. For someone who wishes to express himself well through the instrument, it is necessary to make almost a masochistic search of the guitar to be able to purify the thought absolutely; there may be some totally strange things on occasions but the sound must be clean. To play guitar unguitaristically requires the highest knowledge of the instrument. The first thing is the sound, the tone, for this is why we play. There must be no problem of articulation and we must research all the possibilities of fingering. Thus we think not of playing the guitar but of playing only a thing which is a medium — to think of it as a sound in a general. It is terribly difficult to play the guitar unguitaristically, so to speak, to achieve a free phrase which is breathing freely and calmly and is not cut here and there, offering the most perfect and liberated sound.'

Remembering Vladimir's very practical and direct teaching in his Cambridge masterclass the previous year, I asked him what aspect of technique might be most stressed when instructing a student.

'Economy and efficiency of fingering and hand movements must be taught to a guitarist right from the beginning. This applies to many special individual factors. I could give you an example: the thing in the left hand which I call "finger-preparation", or, if you like, "counterpoint-fingering", when each finger prepares itself to function while the others are still occupied. This applies in many ways; one could take as an instance an arpeggio in which (if musically appropriate) it can suitably economize the change of left-hand fingering from one difficult chord to another by replacing each finger from one chord to another in the order of tones in the second. This saves a lot of energy, is much more accurate, and the system can be applied to anything you do on the fingerboard in the left hand. We could call it "chaining"; chaining the functions of the fingers is like chaining the functions of phrases in a piece.'

Our conversation moved naturally on from a consideration of technical matters in themselves towards the goal for all this dedication; the public performance, and what it entails. One aspect which I thought interesting to touch upon was Vladimir's preparation for each concert. Unlike people in many other walks of life, international music artists are expected, rightly or wrongly, to be able to reproduce unfailingly their best performance on each occasion, an almost superhuman task; yet at each of the several concerts I have heard him Vladimir seems to have achieved just exactly this. There are surely times when all performers feel less inclined towards performing, although contracted to do so. How did he concentrate

to try to give of his best?

'Simply, I try to prepare myself well. Practice, eat, sleep, concentration, practice — of course, one must know in what way it is best to practice, it can apply to personal needs as well as other things connected with concentration. If you do not prepare yourself, you may fail once or perhaps twice, but if you should fail more it is not good for you as a professional. It is like any other occupation; if you open a bakery and are always late in making your bread you will lose customers. Once something becomes your profession and you earn your money by it, you start to risk your own skin, so you had better pay attention to each occasion. The amateur plays whenever he likes, whatever he likes, and however he manages. The amateur *can* prepare himself; the professional *has* to prepare himself.'

How he would prepare an individual concert item? To what extent would he consider the various component details as opposed to its overall length — perhaps the *Chaconne* of Bach, for example, which I had so enjoyed?

'I think that everything must be measured so carefully that the final result becomes very natural, appearing to be easy. This applies exactly to a small detail in

Courtesy Classical Guitar Magazine

61

contrast with the whole thing. First I get inspired by a piece, so that I take it and play it through many times — just sightread it with all its accidental mistakes — to feel its instrumental character and its difficulty, to be able to measure its studying time before my next program. In this studying time I measure the weight of big sections and imagine the ideal performance. After that I start to work in detail; fingerings must function according to phrasing, color, dynamics, and overall expressiveness. It is a very complex apparatus of questions to be asked and decisions to be made. This is in fact the way you construct the piece, brick by brick, but having in mind, of course, the final design. This is for me always a very exciting stage of learning, developing the sections, observing how everything becomes real. The main question is: how well can you construct? This is the profession. If a musician has made an exciting construction that holds together, you will excuse mistakes in execution, supposing that they do not overshadow the construction itself.

'Love for detail is a feminine element; feeling for construction, masculine. If you fall in love with a small section (although probably very attractive) and exaggerate it, make it transparent without measuring all the other surroundings of the piece, then the piece will fall apart. The two elements are absolutely necessary, and when they are made I slightly start to give preference in my performance to the masculine one. I thus have in mind the reason why I play the piece at all, while the work I spent on detail is still present and supports the form. If the detail is symbiotically related to the form in an ideal way and it is confirmed in execution, then everything is in order.

'Unfortunately, we guitarists have less pleasure than other instrumentalists in constructing, and the reason is that we do not have many big, long works, for example in sonata form. Can you compare anything to a pianist who will play two Schubert Sonatas in one evening, one in the first half and another in the second? I would like at least once in my life to experience the excitement of constructing something such as Schubert or Beethoven. Sadly, it will probably never be possible. This is certainly one of the reasons why critics sometimes underestimate the guitar.'

CK

CHRISTOPHER PARKENING

The American guitarist Christopher Parkening has the reputation of having made more money out of his recordings than any other guitarist in history. I do know how true that is, nor does it seem very important when we are talking about music. He has certainly been playing for a long time, coming to the notice of audiences back in the 1960s, when he was still in his teens.

His talent was noticed by Segovia, whose masterclasses he attended. That certainly helped in the launching of his conspicuously successful career. Another important influence was Gregor Piatigorsky, the cellist, with whom he studied interpretation.

Christopher Parkening's association with Mario Castelnuovo-Tedesco was also fruitful. He studied the Concerto in D with the composer, and Castelnuovo-Tedesco was so impressed that he dedicated his second guitar concerto to him. He also wrote one of his 'greetings cards' for the young guitarist: Ballatella, like others in the series, is based on the letters of the dedicatee's name.

We met at a hotel in the West End of London. Christopher Parkening was friendly and courteous, and I only wish I had been able to talk with him about fly fishing, which is his passion. He learned the art on the waters of the rivers Test and Itchen, in Hampshire, two of the great trout rivers in Europe when they are not being polluted by some industrial organization.

His concert on the South Bank was clearly designed to please the large numbers of record-buying fans who flocked into the Queen Elizabeth Hall. They knew him through his recordings; they had helped to pay for the ranch in Montana, the ample time devoted to fly fishing, the lifestyle of a millionaire of refined tastes, and it was only right that they should be rewarded. The fact remains that more than 30 times that evening the audience put its hands together and applauded. Nice work if a guitarist can get it! With an average of less than three minutes for each piece followed by sustained applause, the workload can scarcely be said to be onerous.

There was, of course, much to applaud; Parkening is a very good and a very serious guitarist when he is not handing out lollipops to his admirers, and many of his recordings prove it. Interestingly, there was a time when he more or less gave up giving concerts; he did not need the money, and fly fishing was demanding most of his attention and effort. Why he changed his mind and came back to the concert platform formed one of the topics of our discussion.

Two of the most important influences in your career have been Andrés Segovia and Castelnuovo-Tedesco. Did you study composition with Castelnuovo, or was it interpretation only?

Christopher Parkening: I studied the interpretation of his first Guitar Concerto with him, and was able to premiere his second guitar concerto (*dedicated to Parkening*) in Los Angeles. We formed a long-time friendship, so I was very grateful for being able to know such a fine composer. Through that friendship I met Segovia, and was able to study with him on scholarship at the University of California at Berkeley in 1964, at his first United States masterclass.

The second concerto is the C major, isn't it? How is it we never seem to hear it these days?

The first concerto is probably the more popular of the two. The second is a very lovely piece, however, especially the second movement, which is a set of variations. Of course, the Rodrigo concertos are perhaps the most well known and more often played. I've just played, this last Thursday night, the *Fantasia para un Gentilhombre* by Rodrigo, with the Los

Photo by Christian Steiner

Angeles Philharmonic in the Hollywood Bowl. That's a large place to play the guitar outside!

I have over 70 concerts this season. From here I'll go to Berlin and several other places in Germany, to Vienna and then to Madrid. But principally my tour will take me around the United States and Canada. My European tour begins on Saturday at Windsor, then I play on Monday night at the Queen Elizabeth Hall. I'm enjoying being over here; it's been such a long time.

Have you noticed many changes?
It's probably a little more crowded than I remember it. But that seems to be the case in most cities. I was born and raised in southern California, and I've gradually noticed the increase in population there. It's a rare day when you drive on the freeway there and you don't have to stop because of the traffic. You used to be able to sail through, apart from the rush hour.

You have a place in Montana — there must be plenty of wide open spaces there still?
You know, I actually live in southern California, though we have a ranch in Montana, where my wife and I try and spend two or three months in the summer. I have quite a love of fly fishing for trout — which, by the way, was developed in this country of yours, on the rivers Test and Itchen. One of the reasons we spend part of the summer in Montana is because of the fine trout fishing there. Of course, the beautiful scenery, the mountains — it's nice to breathe some clean air away from Los Angeles.

Like playing the guitar, fly fishing must be a very demanding skill.
It is. It requires a good technique. I used to compete in tournament casting. My dad and I competed in the western United States Championship in casting. It requires a fairly decent technique in order to be effective. Wrists, timing, a good eye, and proper equipment — and then, as far as success in fishing goes, it's knowing the water and knowing where the trout lie. I doubt that your readers would be very interested. Is it a fishing magazine now?

Perhaps I'll send this interview to the Angling Times. But I wondered if the two techniques, guitar and fly fishing, were of mutual assistance in any way?
Well, I think probably with any sport there is a relationship at least with the discipline that one needs to get good at it.

The other thing I wanted to mention is your religious involvement. There seems to be a movement back towards a deeper spiritual attitude to music among some guitarists, of whom Thomas Heck is one notable example. Have you noticed any trend there? And can you define your own attitudes and beliefs as they relate to guitar music?
You know, I've always been greatly influenced by the music of Bach. He said, and I'm quoting, that the aim and final reason of all music is none else but the glory of God. And as you know, he wrote at the end of many of his compositions the initials S.D.G. — Solo Dei Gloria, for God alone the glory.

I became a Christian about eight years ago, and it had a great effect on my guitar playing. In my twenties I played over 90 concerts a year, actually with the idea of retiring at an early age — which I pretty much did. I took several years' sabbatical, you might say; I had everything that I thought would make me happy; I had my ranch with the trout streams on it; my wife raised horses, and I didn't need to make any more money playing the guitar. So for a few years I stopped playing. Then, when I became a Christian, I realized that there was a better purpose for playing the guitar, for me, than just to use the instrument to make money to buy what you want. Consequently, when I became a Christian, I read in the Bible where it said, whatever you do, do all for the glory of God.

I only knew two things: one was fly fishing for trout, and the other was playing the guitar. It seemed that the second of these was the better option to pursue. So I started playing and recording again, but this time with really a whole different motive. It's given me a quite a bit more fulfillment in my life, and is really the major reason why I'm playing the guitar now. I feel I would like to use whatever ability or talent the Lord has given me to try and give Him glory and give some pleasure, hopefully, to the audience.

One of your records is called Sacred Music for the Guitar, or 'Simple Gifts'. Is sacred music a very rich area for the guitar?
I found that some of the most beautiful pieces ever written were written expressly for the glory of God. I don't think that because you're playing sacred music it has to be inferior to secular music. However, I also don't believe that it's necessary to play only sacred music in order to fulfil your purpose. So I'm doing a variety of music. For instance, the program I'm doing at the Queen Elizabeth Hall will be all secular music, apart from perhaps an encore I might play from that

Simple Gifts album. Then there's another album I did with the soprano Kathleen Battle. She has a beautiful voice, very high and clear and pure-sounding; it's a nice blend with the guitar, I think.

You have no shortage of great guitarists here in England. Julian Bream and John Williams — my goodness! I saw John Williams when he was in Los Angeles; I was in a guitar series with him and Julian Bream and Segovia. I was on tour when Julian Bream was in California, so I wasn't able to see him, but I was able to have lunch with John Williams, and a nice chat. Such a great player!

Of course you met Segovia again during his recent masterclass at USC....
There was a panel, with some of Segovia's older students, like Oscar Ghiglia and Michael Lorimer. As a matter of fact, they asked us some questions which were related basically to what we felt when we were studying with Segovia. The Maestro was sitting in the first row, so he was hearing all of our comments. He seemed to be pleased and also amused by them.

I was able to have dinner with Segovia, and got a chance to spend some time with him. He's very well, I'm happy to say, and just as witty as ever. He was very sharp in the masterclass in California; his principal criticism was the interpretation of the music, and

he would go over and over phrases with students to improve their interpretation. When I asked him what he felt about the class, he gave an interesting comment. He said that all the students, and I believe there were twelve performing students, had more than enough technique, but only one had music in her heart. I found that an interesting comment, that out of that whole class of twelve only one had that innate musicianship which he was looking for.

These days, with teaching so much improved, we should take technique for granted.
I agree. The standard of guitar playing has come up so much.

So what do we need to make us all better musicians? Can we do it ourselves?
You know, I had a very wonderful beginning in regard to that. When I went to the University of Southern California, there was no guitar department per se, so in order for me to finish my degree I had to study interpretation. Heifetz was there, and Piatigorsky was there. So my IBM card read 'cello major'. But I didn't play a note on the cello!

So I was forced into studying interpretation of the music with these fine musicians, which was actually, as I found out later, a real advantage. Because they would look at the music unbiased from the standpoint of the problems that a guitarist might face. They would just strictly look at the music. So it was a real blessing for me to be able to work with such great musicians early on. Of course, I also studied privately with Segovia every time he came to Los Angeles, along with Castelnuovo-Tedesco — privately — and the interpretation of his music. And with Joaquín Rodrigo when I performed his two guitar concertos throughout Japan. Studying with him was also a great experience.

So one of the answers would be for a guitarist to seek out good musicians, irrespective of whether they play the guitar or not?
I would certainly recommend that.

On the other hand, it's rare for a violinist to go and study with a pianist. I suppose there are more good teachers for those instruments.
That might be true. There's certainly a wider range of excellent musicians to choose from. I worked with a violinist, a cellist, a pianist and a harpsichordist. In every case, they enjoyed working with the guitar. It was kind of a break for them, from always being near

their own instrument, and perhaps they enjoyed the change from routine.

You and others who were at the USC masterclass have confirmed that Segovia's wits are as sharp as ever. Some people — quite unreasonably — tend to associate him with a beautiful tone but not much else. But Eliot Fisk said that the qualities about Segovia that impressed him, even at the age of 90, were his 'passion, expressivity and daring'. Is that your experience of him too?

I would totally agree with everything he said. Segovia has that magical combination of technique and the sound which goes with technique, innate musicianship, that artistic instinct which he has in combination with his charisma on stage. Put all that together, and it makes for a great artist, to whom we are all certainly indebted. I admire him so much.

It's amazing to me, every time I see Segovia walk on stage, that he can play so well. He's just an amazing person all the way round. I really don't think that anyone will ever do for the guitar what Segovia has done for it. I'm very grateful to have had the opportunity to work with him, certainly in his prime.

Do you play much contemporary music?

Not too much. I guess I would have to say that I am a little old-fashioned, in that I favor more lyric and beautiful music as opposed to strictly atonal music. If the music moves my heart, I guess that's what's important to me — something that is beautiful. Then I feel that I have a chance of interpreting it correctly. I have to love a piece of music.

I know that Bach is preeminent among the composers whose music you play. Who are some of the others who have a special significance for you?

Oh gee, there are so many that I enjoy. The program on Monday night will rely heavily on Spanish music, principally because I'm doing an all-Spanish album. But I love the music of John Dowland, and certainly individual pieces by certain composers will take my fancy.

When you play concertos, you amplify, presumably?

As I mentioned to you, I played for over 11,000 people in the Hollywood Bowl last Thursday night, and of course in an outdoors amphitheater, especially with an orchestra, it's mandatory to amplify the guitar. But if you have a good microphone and a good sound man who knows what a good quality of sound is, and what a proper balance between orchestra and guitar is,

then I think it's possible to create a nice experience for the listener.

As a matter of fact, the reviewers were saying about the concert that the Hollywood Bowl was transformed into a kind of cozy living room. They all mentioned the fact that the sound was excellent. That, of course, is due to my sound man in Los Angeles. With orchestra, I think it's mandatory: a discreet amount of amplification, hopefully something that sounds quite natural and preserves the beautiful sound of the instrument.

In halls of 1,000 to 1,500 seats with good acoustics, I will generally not use a microphone when playing solo, but in halls with 3,000 seats it's necessary. I talked to John Williams about the type of microphone he used, and ended up by purchasing one myself. I carry that with me wherever I go, then at least I'm feeding the house system with a decent sound, a good signal.

Most guitarists have to be content with using the house system with all its imperfections. That doesn't do the guitar any good in the long run, does it?

If you're not able to take your own personal sound man with you, the next best option is to have friends who can advise. I have friends in each major city, and I pretty much trust their ear. So I'll invite them to the rehearsal, and they will work with the house sound technician, getting a nice balance and a good quality sound. And of course I'll take my own microphone, so that's half the battle.

So the least a travelling guitarist can do is to invest in a good microphone?

At least that — and carry it with them. At least feed the system a nice sound. It would be awkward, at least for me, to carry around my own amplifier and speakers and mixing console and all that.

Segovia can still attract several thousand people to a concert hall at the age of 93. Have you any ambition to play as long as that?

I'll play as long as the good Lord thinks I'm able. I can't envisage myself living that long, frankly.

CC

JOAQUÍN RODRIGO

This interview took place in 1992, shortly before the 91st birthday of the most celebrated Spanish composer since Manuel de Falla. Joaquín Rodrigo was in London with his daughter Cecilia. There had been a reception at the Spanish Institute to mark the publication of his wife's book, *Hand in hand with Joaquín Rodrigo* (by Victoria Kamhi de Rodrigo, Latin American Literary Review Press, Pittsburgh, 1992). The next morning I went to his hotel with my colleague Thérèse Wassily Saba, armed with the usual paraphernalia of tape recorder, camera, flashgun. The maestro was visibly tired, and barely responded to questions. There was no need to worry, however, because Cecilia, a devoted daughter if ever there was one, knew all the answers. For instance, to my question about which of his very many guitar pieces meant the most to him, his sleepy response of 'No se' ('I don't know') was speedily translated by his daughter into a list of three works beginning with the *Aranjuez* Concerto and including *Invocación y Danza* and, if my memory is correct, *Tres piezas Españolas*. It was amusing, but it was also touching.

Joaquín Rodrigo was born on 22 November 1901 (St Cecilia's Day) —not, as several reference books would have it, 1902. In 1991 the Sociedad General de Autores de España in association with the Spanish Ministry of Culture and the Quincentennial Society of Spain paid homage to Spain's most distinguished living composer in the form of an international festival of his music, the first time in Spanish history that a living composer has been honored in this way. The festival took place in 15 musical capitals of the world, culminating in a closing concert on 12 September 1992, given as part of the World Fair Exhibition in Seville.

To be able to compose at all is a tremendous achievement for someone who has been blind from the age of three years. The cause was diphtheria, a disease that killed many children before an efficient preventative was found later in the century. But it led the young Joaquín Rodrigo towards music, and at the age of eight he began to study sol-fa, piano and violin; harmony and composition began later, at 16. Few non-afflicted members of an audience ever reflect on the exceptional will power that such an undertaking entails.

In 1927 Rodrigo went to Paris to study with Paul Dukas. He became known as a pianist as well as a

Courtesy Classical Guitar Magazine

composer, and was the friend of Falla, Honegger, Milhaud, Ravel and many others. He married the pianist Victoria Kamhi in 1933.

Guitarists know Rodrigo chiefly for five concertos and a considerable number of other works for guitar, although not many of those have found their way into the general repertoire. Of these, Rodrigo said, he has a special feeling for the *Tres Piezas Españolas*, *Tríptico* and *Invocación y Danza*, the last of which won a prize in Paris and turns up regularly in recitals and competitions. Among the five concertos, the *Aranjuez* (1939) of course is the most popular, but the *Concierto Andaluz* (1977) is getting more and more performances — partly because the number of guitar quartets is increasing by leaps and bounds, and partly because people like the work.

'I was in Vienna last week,' said Cecilia Rodrigo, Joaquín's daughter. 'The Romeros Quartet played to about 2,000 people, the hall was full, and some people were standing, and after the *Concierto Andaluz* they were clapping for more than a quarter of an hour.' The concerto was an undoubted success, and so, added Cecilia Rodrigo, was the *Concerto Madrigal* (1969) for two guitars and orchestra. 'They are catching on, little by little,' she said. Strangely enough, although the *Concierto Andaluz* is popular in the United States and in Europe (particularly in the eastern countries and in Germany, though perhaps not so much in Britain), it has never been performed in Spain.

It is only comparatively recently that Cecilia Rodrigo, with commendable initiative and enormous energy, has been able to devote time to the promotion of her father's music. To that end she has formed her own publishing company — Ediciones Joaquín Rodrigo — and has begun the lengthy and often tedious process of retrieving the various copyrights from other publishers, some of whom have not been able to maintain her father's work in print. This venture has brought her into contact with more guitarists, and she is impressed by the network through which information is disseminated. 'Everyone knows one another, and everyone knows the music,' as she put it. It is this unstructured but complex organization that has enabled the first but unpublished version of *Invocación y Danza* to be performed by numerous guitarists despite the differences from the published version. Rodrigo himself prefers the original version; and his daughter would like it to be publicly known. How many guitarists can actually play the first version (it is widely held to have some impossible things in it) is another matter.

Rodrigo still composes, but he does not dictate any more: the work of dictation is extremely hard, needing a lot of concentration. He composes at the piano, recording the notes in braille, always standing up in front of his machine to do it. He returns to the piano for revision. It will mean a problem for future scholars, because only he can read his own manuscripts: not only are they in braille, but they are in a very personal form of braille, and not even another unsighted musician would be able to understand them. Deciphering Rodrigo's late manuscripts will be akin to deciphering the Dead Sea Scrolls or Linear B.

'Audiences don't always realize what it means to compose when you are blind,' said Cecilia Rodrigo. 'There were times when he had to compose during the night, because in the daytime he worked and did other things. It was after ten at night, after dinner, that the copyist came, and my father would dictate until two or three o'clock in the morning. That went on year after year, day after day.'

Cecilia Rodrigo was trained as a dancer in the Royal Ballet in England. She opened her own ballet school in Brussels, but gave that up in order to become a publisher in 1987. It took her two years to establish what had to be done, and the publishing company was eventually was set up in 1989.

'I concentrated my efforts on recovering most of the catalogue which was in other publishers' hands. We recovered quite a lot in fact. We have most of the important symphonic works, we have the violin concerto, and quite a few works for guitar. A wide and large range.'

An important factor is the support provided by the Spanish Society of Authors, which makes it easier for the Rodrigos to attend and to exhibit at large events like the Frankfurt Music Fair, where Ediciones Joaquín Rodrigo had their own stand. Cecilia sees this as a shrewd investment; it means that Spanish music is overcoming a previous tendency towards isolation and is becoming much better known around the world. 'For me it's very easy, because most of this music is well known. But very often people couldn't find my father's music. They would ask for titles, and they were just impossible to find. I don't know what they were doing, these publishers.' It is by no means an uncommon story.

Part of the operation involves Ediciones Joaquín Rodrigo sending music to countries that would otherwise have difficulty in obtaining it — Cuba, for example, where a donation of music has been made to that country's Society of Composers. In the International Guitar Festival of Havana in May there was a concert devoted to Rodrigo's music that included the *Concierto Andaluz* for four guitars. 'We donated the scores, as we are doing in other countries such as Russia. It's a way of making the music known and promoting it. Before, I couldn't do this, because I wasn't a publisher and I did not have access to the scores. I can tell you that in only three years this way of working has produced an effect.'

She finds it hard to understand why publishers don't reissue the works. 'A publisher should always have the music available. Always! Even if it is not successful, if you have a contract, you must honor it.

'Thanks to the help of many people, I think I have been very successful. It is something that a composer cannot always do, because he is composing, he is doing his job. I think I was very lucky to be able to realize soon enough that I could do something. I mean, I think it was a little bit late — but not *too* late.'

Cecilia Rodrigo has recovered the whole of the Rodrigo section in the Max Eschig catalogue, some 22 works, many of them important. 'The *Concierto Andaluz* was formerly published by Salabert. We got the *Cello Concerto* back as well. I think we have done very well, and I am very happy. But everyone is helping me. At the moment we are printing the *Violin Concerto*.'

Joaquín Rodrigo is one of those composers who understand the importance of a good title. Not for him the Opus 17 or the Study Number Seven or the Prelude in B flat minor; his titles convey the scents and sights of Spain, and they are memorable: *Aranjuez, Andaluz, Madrigal, Fantasia para un Gentilhombre, Invocación y Danza, Sonata Giocoso, Bajando de la Mesta*. Away from the guitar, it's the same story: pianists have *El Album de Cecilia, A L'Ombre de Torre Bermeja, Danza de la Amapola, Gran Marcha de los Subsecretarios, Preludio al Gallo Mañanero, Zarabanda Lejana*; and his orchestral works are no less colorful: *A La Busca del Más Allá, A Sagunto, Dos Piezas Caballerescas* (a version exists for four guitars, incidentally), *Homenaje a la Tempranica*, and many others. These works are not widely known, partly because they are often difficult to obtain, and partly because orchestras (not to mention guitarists and other instrumentalists) generally play safe and stick to what they know. Among guitarists, *Invocación y Danza* has caught on; it is a rewarding piece, full of poetry and subtle allusions to Falla, but one would welcome the opportunity to hear some of his other guitar works for a change. There are 24 altogether listed in the Catálogo General, not counting the concertos; guitarists generally play no more than five or six at the most. Why? Have they tried them all and found the other 17 deficient in some way? And if they haven't tried them, how do they know they are not missing a masterpiece? Why must guitarists be so unadventurous?

Joaquín Rodrigo has written a ballet called *Havana Real*. It has been performed in Germany and Spain and in Buenos Aires. It is not in the catalogue, but an orchestral suite is to be made out of it. In the ballet is a Romance for solo guitar, *Romance de Durandarte* (originally written for piano in 1955). 'Always the guitar everywhere!' said Cecilia Rodrigo with a laugh.

She does not, however, think that there will be any more guitar works, though 'He always says that he will never again write for the guitar, but he's been saying that for 20 or 30 years.' Why has he changed his mind so often? 'I think it is because he has so many guitarist friends. They approach him and ask him to write something. So he goes on writing.'

One of his most recent guitar pieces is *Un Tiempo Fue Italica Famosa*, five minutes long and written in 1981. It is published by Schott, with fingerings by Angel Romero.

Like Segovia before him, Rodrigo seems to travel rather more than one might expect of a nonagenarian. 'He feels a little bit lazy each time I tell him that we have to go somewhere,' said his daughter. 'But he's so nice and so easy to convince, and he usually says "Well, let's go!". But he doesn't complain much about going to London. It's become a habit: he's been so often that he doesn't mind.' Rodrigo's wife, Victoria Kamhi, had stayed home in Madrid on this occasion. Cecilia, an only child, was missing her, but her mother has some difficulty in walking now and, understandably, it places too much of a strain on Cecilia to accompany both parents on a trip abroad.

She thinks her father is often unaware of just how popular his music is. 'He has always been very humble, very modest, and now, with age, he can't realize any more how things are going. I tell him that such-and-such a work was played and there were so many thousand people in the audience, and he says "Really?" I say how many records have been sold, and he says: "It's impossible! I can't believe that."'

Joaquín Rodrigo is a worker. His early struggles would have defeated a weaker and less strong-willed man. Fame was not something that was actively sought, but something that came as a kind of by-product of his composition. Cecilia herself was not aware of the increasing fame as she grew up. 'I never

Photo by Colin Cooper

69

took much notice of his music, as a matter of fact,' she admits. 'It was so normal. I began to realize much later on. Now people are very kind to him. We often receive letters from English people, who don't know him but want to say how much they like his music.' And each instrumental work brings letters from instrumentalists, expressing their appreciation. The two Cello Concertos seem to have attracted a correspondence in this way.

There was a guitarist in Holland, said Cecilia Rodrigo, who wanted to transcribe the Cello Concerto *In Modo Galante* (1949) for the guitar, but Rodrigo said 'No. There is enough guitar already.' The *Concierto Andaluz* has been transcribed (from four guitars to eight guitars), but there had been no objection to that. It had been done for a guitar orchestra in Munich, Germany, who are recording it.

Talking about transcriptions, Cecilia Rodrigo said that she had been angry at some of the criticisms that had been made against the *Fantasia para un Gentilhombre*. 'They said that the music was by Gaspar Sanz and that Rodrigo had only made a transcription. It is not true; the Fantasia is such a personal and beautiful work.' Here Cecilia Rodrigo opened the book (*Hand in Hand with Rodrigo*) in order to quote something that Segovia ('a very clever man') had written to Rodrigo at the time of the first performance: ' I hadn't wanted to say anything, but being familiar with Gaspar Sanz's work, I did feel that the founding for the basis of the work you were starting was very weak. Fortunately, like a spider, you produced the thread you needed to weave your own work.'

Some weeks previously Rodrigo and his daughter had dined with Sir Michael Tippett. She had the impression that Tippett's music was played far more in Britain than her father's music was played in Spain. Spain, she felt, was backward in appreciating the genius of its own artists.

Could that in some way be a legacy from the turbulence of Spain's recent history? Cecilia did not want to talk about that; her father was non-political, and had been consistent in his non-political stance. 'People were wondering why, when so many other composers were leaving the country, he came back after the war. He was different, he writes differently from everybody else, he does things in his own particular way.' He was criticized for it, of course, and it was sometimes assumed that because he returned to live in Spain

when many other prominent artists stayed away that he was a supporter of Franco. Nothing could be further from the truth, declared Cecilia Rodrigo. 'A letter from my father addressed to my mother states very clearly that he came back only because he wanted to return to his own country. He had been away for twelve years, studying and working with difficulty, and he wanted to come back. And that was all.' Spain, felt Cecilia, was a country where you were knocked if you became successful, and knocked as strongly as possible. Nevertheless, Joaquín Rodrigo had achieved success in Spain, not only for his music but for his qualities as a human being.

When the interview was over, Joaquín Rodrigo sat at the grand piano that stood in the hotel lounge and played the slow movement of the *Aranjuez*, missing out a few notes but going back, sometimes more than once, to correct them. When that was over, he launched into a Bach fugue, much more sure of himself and rapping out the voices firmly and clearly and without mistakes: an impressive performance by any standards. Rodrigo at 90 is not only a figurehead, an icon, but a living artist, still capable of producing good work. It seems certain that there will be no further guitar pieces. Before we say, automatically, 'What a pity!', we should reflect on what he has already contributed to the guitar. Few composers, dead or alive, have done as much.

CC

ANGEL ROMERO

In late August 1982 Angel Romero was in London in order to record a concerto. He telephoned me, and we met for dinner, after which we sat in the foyer of his hotel near Swiss Cottage and talked. What followed was not a formal interview, guided by prepared questions: but a spontaneous conversation which, rather than rearrange in logical order, I have preserved more or less as it unfolded, trying to preserve some of its informality. Angel Romero is a man of abundant good humor — he laughs a lot — but you can't write that down.

I don't remember you playing in London before, except for recording sessions.
Angel Romero: Some time ago, maybe when you were out of town, we snuck into London and played a quartet concert in the Queen Elizabeth Hall — about twelve years ago. Maybe I dreamed it!

There's hardly a time when one of you isn't here.
I know. I love London. Although a Spaniard I feel extremely comfortable here; sometime I want to get a flat and live here.

Courtesy Classical Guitar Magazine

When did you leave Spain?
In 1958. I'd just had my birthday. The day I began my sessions this time, recording the Giuliani Op.30, I had my 17th — no, I wish (on one leg) — I turned 36 on the 17th August. I'm two and a half years younger than Pepe.

Did you begin the way Pepe began, playing flamenco?
No I did not. I began singing flamenco, which didn't do me a bit of good on the guitar. We started basically from my father — when I was about six or seven years old I played a bit of flamenco, nevertheless not as

seriously as Pepe. I was more interested at the time in the classical pieces, so was Pepe. Of course Celin too — he taught us both when my father was out concertizing. He's the oldest — he's 42.

He's the one who doesn't seem to make solo records. He's made a couple of duo albums with Pepe, but he's been our elder brother, he feels very protective towards both of us and he has held his ground, waiting for both of us to make our moves; now he's going to do some solo recordings.

There are a lot of Romeros on record...
Too many! Maybe we should change our names.

Your musical tastes and horizons — earlier on you were saying you don't like 'funny noise music'. Where do the 'funny noises' begin?
Well you know, I take music like food. In essence it's food for my soul — without trying to be too romantic with my words. But, being absolutely honest, it's like food — if something doesn't taste good and doesn't titillate my taste-buds then I don't follow it. I figure I can eat only so much food in my lifetime, so I should enjoy it.

Don't you find your taste changing?
I do. I like carrots — I used to hate carrots. The other day I was absolutely shocked by Schoenberg; I never was fond of him. I heard a composition of his for orchestra and choir and it was thrilling, it gave me chills. Taste does change but I don't believe in rushing it; it's something that happens naturally, something that matures. Speaking about that — variety — what I have in front of me *(earlier in the evening I had given him a copy of my list of works — JD)* — do not take this out: I am sitting here with Mr Duarte in the lobby of my hotel and I just had my mouth drop to the floor, because I have known for some years you are a prolific writer, but my God! This brochure — it's unbelievable, like a wonderful menu. Out of this I'm going to get a lot of coverage because I certainly want to play it.

I'm a bit older than you are (AR: Two years? JD: It depends when your birthday falls) *but I hope I haven't stopped yet — haven't closed my mind and decided that music is here and non-music is the other side of that line.*
Well you are a creator. I don't limit things, talent limits me to being able so far to interpret within my 'degree of interpretation'. But I have so many ideas about life itself, I express them through music — but I wish I could write something. I never write, it's almost as though I'm afraid.

Do you improvise?
Yes, I do, but sometimes in a very frightening way; I improvise in the middle of a Bach fugue.

When you forget?
That's right. On the concert stage — and then it's very frightening, that's when the cold sweat comes out. But improvising for its own sake, that's a very difficult art and I have done this. When I have improvised on stage I have said nothing, I have sat down and started to improvise. Then, if the audience likes it I say: 'Ladies and gentlemen. I have just improvised on such and such a theme'. If they don't like it, if the applause is low, I make up a false name of a composer and say: 'Forgive me for having forgotten to tell you who wrote it before I played it'. If you promise to be good I'll never put your name on it — 'this was a sonata written by my dear friend John Duarte'. Right after we were talking about where does music stop and noise begins.

The Romeros have been closely identified with Spanish and romantic music. When one moves 'backward' and plays Bach romantically it can be all wrong.
You've never heard my Bach? It's good. It's very stolid (*said with a smile — JD*) — no it's not; I play Bach as I feel it — maybe you like it, maybe you don't. I don't believe in romanticizing music for the sake of being romantic.

No, I'm sure it's something in your own nature.
Exactly. You know who was extremely romantic in his playing of Bach? It was Casals.

If you play baroque music in proper baroque style it is in a sense very romantic — not in the later sense but very expressive; expressiveness is what it was all about.
Yes, right.

Bach wasn't just a kind of musical mathematician.

No, just listen to some of the sarabandes, they are unbelievable.

How about moving forward ?
I *am* looking forward very much to new music — I mean music that could have been around for quite a bit, but new to me.

Come to think of it, you don't seem to play much of Ponce's music.
No, but I recently played the Sonata with harpsichord with Igor (Kipnis). I've been quite busy with so much repertoire but I haven't yet played everything of my choice. I'm still in the middle. It's like being in an ocean, still getting to the other side: I'm still paddling. I haven't played any Villa-Lobos either.

I can't remember you or Pepe playing any music from south of Florida.
No. I used to play some Lauro, but there are so many fabulous things that it's hard to keep a foot on everything. But it isn't that I've discarded the idea. I absolutely *will* cover it.

What guides your choice?
When I was very little I loved Mozart, Sor and a lot of composers, but I took only a few and I'm still learning how to play them. I'll be learning until I die — I mean that sincerely. So, instead of being a jack-of-all-trades and good for nothing I want to analyze everything I'm doing. I've taken a lifetime — mine, so far — trying to play works like the Sor Variations (*Op.9 — JD*) and pieces that are so-called 'standards' and workhorses but have been very much mutilated. I'm not talking about technique, I'm talking about the lack of understanding of the flow of the melody, the sequence of phrasing, the harmonic ambience of the piece. If you think of a piece in that way, which I really do, it takes an endless amount of time — even though I can learn a piece and perform it after one week.

What goes through your mind when you play?
I'm trying to analyze myself while I'm playing, I'm creating a mood — a thought — but it's difficult because you're doing it with someone else's tools. When I'm playing I get almost a sense of embarrassment, like walking on ice. I'm of a positive nature but at the same time I don't want to do wrong. I don't mean to blow a scale. Because if I do, that's *nothing* — the next one will come out — the real sacrilege is the one of not having taken the time to analyze the piece, the lack of seeing what the piece is about, the negligence. That's what I would give the 'ticket' to —

like a policeman. There's a lot of people who will cover a lot of repertoire and they play anything from Bach to Lauro; a lot of people and even critics will say 'My God! This man has advanced into so many areas of music!'. But no, he hasn't. I don't like to bite more than I can chew.

Some guitarists have the delusion there is a 'standard' repertory they are obliged to play in order to prove themselves. There are no 'musts' — you should play only what you really want to play.
I *want* to play Villa-Lobos and I haven't really played Bach, though I want to. When I was very little I used to wait until my father and mother would leave the house so I could put on a record of the Fugue in C major on the organ. I used to put my ear right to the speaker and it would saturate me, make me vibrate. I believe technique on the guitar is a vehicle — rather, it's the track, musicality is the train. A good technique on the guitar is the track; I have laid all the track and I'm waiting for the train. I have a good track, a solid one, and I don't have technical problems; now I want to mature and have an equally solid train. You could be tempted, being in the public eye and concertizing, to fall into the thing of 'I know it all', but I *don't* know it all.

So what you're really thinking of is the music.
Yes, just the music. My ear, my soul knows when I'm not doing justice to it musically and then I don't enjoy it. If you can't do that — think only of the music — you don't have any right to play it.

Your statement about not worrying if you blow a scale is important. There are two kinds of 'nerves': one is just the excitement, the flow of adrenaline like you had when your father first took you to a theme park, the hype, and that's good — a sign that you are toned up to the performance; the other is anxiety — when you blow the scale you know it is because you were always liable to do it, that you weren't really on top of the piece technically. It doesn't worry you *because, as you said, you know it will come out next time, it was just a slip.*
If someone takes notice that I have blown a scale it's because I wasn't putting forth enough music to demand their attention — and for them not to notice it. Either they are not musical and don't listen, only to hear whether I make all the notes or not (that's juvenile) or it's someone who loves music and I've been worried about something else and I have not captivated their mind.

I wrote an article in 'Guitar Player' magazine on coordination that seems to tie in with what we've been talking towards. It isn't a question of coordinating one hand with the other...
No, you'd go crazy trying to do that!

It's a matter of coordinating each hand separately, with the 'time spot', the instant when the metronome in your head ticks and says there should be a note; when you do this, one hand coordinates automatically with the other as a sort of by-product. Pepe (Romero) makes the same point — I referred to his view in my article — but he doesn't call it the 'time spot', he refers to the 'desire for the note'.
Exactly. Often when I play, if you put a microphone to it, I'm singing. If I sing it then it comes out beautifully; if I play it and I don't sing it, it doesn't come out as well. Today in the recording of the Giuliani I was humming it to myself.

Time and the eventual issue of the recording will tell whether Angel Romero will emerge as a guitaristic Glenn Gould, joining a 'club' to which Oscar Ghiglia already belongs. Time will tell, too, when and in what way his music-making will develop. Whatever the outcome it will have been reached by an amalgam of the subjective and the objective, for, beneath the boisterously humorous exterior lies a man who takes what he sees as his responsibilities very seriously. We too are waiting for his train to carry him along his well-prepared tracks.

JD

73

PEPE ROMERO

See him going for a walk in the park, and you will surely never suspect that there goes someone quite out of the ordinary. But conversation enlightens you rapidly. Some critics say he is one of those rare all-time virtuosi, projecting his genius onto the six strings of an instrument that is heavily involved in the fight for survival among all the other classical instruments; others are associating him with names like Franz Liszt or Alexis Weissenberg (b. Sofia 1929), both pianists. I believe Pepe Romero to be one of the last true romantics.

Romantic? Yes, in the sense of being dedicated to the arts, bound to music, living for the guitar and the beauty of its music, not caring about fashionable evolutions, compromise or trends. But Pepe Romero, as he says, tends towards being happy, and although that is easy to read it is to be seen in different aspects: playing the guitar, having plans and ideas, always being creative and not static, loving people and giving them what they might regard as an enrichment.

I don't think anyone can really say what the guitar means to Pepe Romero, but two episodes speak for themselves. Years ago he engaged in some jogging sessions, but while his thoughts were probably circling around a concert he had to give on the following day, he broke his ankle. Mounted with a heavy plaster of Paris dressing, unable to walk except on crutches, he was driven the next day to the concert hall, where he was heaved on to his chair by the conductor himself. Another chair supported the aching gypsum-covered leg — and Pepe was playing the *Aranjuez*.

In 1986, a large truck caused an accident on an American highway. Pepe's car was pushed off the road, and looped the loop several times. He tells the story:

'Being then in a desolate situation, with my head downwards, I was asked by the truck driver if I were dead. I was not, so I told him; but I felt that man was closer to shock than I myself, asking me if there were *anyone else* dead! No one was, but I felt my left wrist aching, and I thought the best way to find out if it was broken or not would be to play the guitar. The hard guitar shell had hit me right in the back, so I was aware where the guitar was. Somehow I managed to get out of that crumpled car. I found that the guitar had not suffered at all from the crash, and so I played it. Afterwards I was told that people were standing

Photo by Philips Classics Productions/Christian Steiner

around me with strange looks on their faces.'

It was July 1986 when we met again, at Salzburg, where the International Summer Academy Mozarteum had invited young and gifted musicians from all over the world. Pepe was leading a masterclass there. He did not have a guitar with him. 'No, I do not play to let the students know what probably could be done better,' he said. 'It's up to them to discover the things that have to be changed. I am there to watch them play, and after that we speak about this or that. So we come closer to the essential points, I think.'

He is calm when talking, and less vivacious than you might expect. 'Students do not need sermons,' he explains. 'A few words hitting the mark are more effective than lots of sentences.' And he respects the individual: 'I always try to put myself into their place, so sometimes there really are two or even more different teaching methods relating to one and the same thing. What's good for one does not necessarily have to be good for the next one as well.'

They had come from different parts of the world to join that masterclass: England, Italy, the USA, even Brazil. Asked why she had crossed half the continent to attend Pepe's masterclass, a young student said: 'I've never watched Pepe teaching, but I have heard so much about it. Maybe I was looking for that special atmosphere where teaching can change so many things.'

Another student: 'Pepe Romero is the guitar authority to me. But I know that he himself is far from being an authoritarian, and I would have flown to China if necessary.'

'Teaching,' Pepe says, 'is something important and essential. If there is something you are able to offer to others, you should do so.' Watching the students' reactions and recognizing the effects of his teaching, one senses a special atmosphere being built up, a natural 'student—music-teacher' relationship that enables everyone to verbalize his or her problems. 'No, there are no plans, rules or things like that,' Pepe admits. 'Maybe you will miss a special kind of preparation. There isn't any. But there is an order in it, of course. So, the first thing is to hold the guitar in the most comfortable way. Many a guitarist, even a good one, does not know that things could be more comfortable if he held the guitar in a correct way. And "correct" means fitting to the individual. The second step: the students are to play themselves, pieces they feel at home with. We all listen to them, and then I look at the mistake or mistakes that really have a chance to be eliminated during this three-weeks course. There is no use sticking to a problem when you know that it is really impossible to eliminate the mistake while we are together. The student must not go home and rack his brains about something the teacher might have had in mind and that he can't recall concretely. So we look at what can be done during these three weeks. Having heard him play for the first time, we will see what comes out the following day after several hours of practicing alone, and then there are concrete plans how to proceed. So, technical things come first, followed by questions relating to the music itself. During the course, and at the end of it, each student is given the chance to perform, and there's a wide variety ranging from guitar solo to guitar with oboe, or even guitar and orchestra. We prepare for these events very carefully. I will attend each concert, and afterwards we discuss things relating to the performance.'

Then we changed the topic. Asked what the guitar meant to him, Pepe answered: 'It could be easily said: my life, my love.' The guitar is for Pepe Romero a subject of total integration and identification. Whatever he plays, it is interpreted with the authority of a man who knows exactly what he is doing, with a tremendous knowledge of the relevant backgrounds.

'It all depends on the way in which it is done, or in which it should be done, at least. It depends on one's own ideas and the will to bring those ideas to a realization.' And Pepe plays the Bach Partita as if there were just one legitimate 'idea', that of the composer himself. 'People can do anything on or with the guitar; they may transcribe or arrange whatever they think could or should be done. There is no question about what is allowed or what is not,' he adds, with past discussions in mind. 'The contradictory aspects of last year's emotions and discussion often demonstrate an inability to accept things which others have seriously thought about. I do not think that there are strict rules in general when we are talking about the pros and cons of transcriptions and arrangements. Music is living, it is far from being a static something. Why not wait and see what the future brings?'

I asked if *Pictures from an exhibition* would be a challenge for him.
(The Japanese guitarist Kazuhito Yamashita had recently caused a sensation by playing an arrangement for solo guitar of Mussorgsky's piano work. — Ed.)

'I don't think so, at least not at the moment. There are other things of more interest to me. I am seriously thinking about recording Giuliani's *Rossiniane*; they are beautiful compositions and very demanding for the player. There is so much good music that has not been played before.'

We talked about the guitar today and its related activities. In every country one can see tendencies that make one ponder on the future of the instrument. To put it another way, is there a future for classical guitar music?

'We know that there are fewer people deeply interested in or involved with classical guitar music than there were, say, three to five years ago. But on the other hand, we certainly have more splendid young guitarists than probably ever before. In my opinion, so long as there are enthusiastic people like Brian Jeffery and Thomas Heck, who are doing important research into composers' lives and music history in general, we need not be too nervous about the future of the classical guitar. I think we happen to he living in a really exciting time in which many pieces, even masterpieces, by many a brilliant composer of the past are being discovered, and many contemporary composers are engaged with the concert guitar. So maybe one should ask the same question again in ten years. No one really knows what's going to happen.'

Finally, we talked about the different styles of guitar music, about those seemingly endless discussions concerning the question 'What is classical?', and if folk music should or should not play a part.

'If there is a tendency in Germany or elsewhere to make a strict difference between the so-called "classical" and the folk elements, it is another thing in America or Spain. I myself do not like those analytical characteristics, for music is so far-reaching and extensive, especially guitar music — simply because the guitar has been influenced by so many important movements in its history, and the instrument developed side by side with the technique. This was as true in the 16th century as it is today.

'Those who try to see the guitar simply and solely on just one branch — the pure, classical branch — have not understood the essence of our instrument; they are used to sticking obstinately to only one aspect and, for whatever reason, will not tolerate any deflection. But one should not overestimate things like that. Art means, not least, freedom of thought. It is not a means or a medium for accomplishing one's own will.'

HH

Photo by Philips Classics Productions/Christian Steiner

DAVID RUSSELL

It was the late 1970s. Coming down from my study for a mid-morning cup of coffee, I switched on BBC Radio 3. A guitarist was playing, Normally I would have turned up the volume and gone into the kitchen. This time I stayed until the end, not wanting to miss a note, eager to hear who the player was. It was neither Segovia nor Bream, whose respective styles I knew well enough. It was not John Williams, whose playing I had also come to recognize. I ran through the list of possibles. Diaz. Bonell. Parkening. Lagoya. Behrend. Rey de la Torre. No one I knew of fitted the bill. There was something unique about this player's graceful but sinewy melodic line, so finely crafted, leading you on to expect more — and then giving it to you. I have never been in such a state of suspense when listening to a piece of guitar music. As in a story by Raymond Chandler, I wanted to know what happened next.

The name meant nothing to me. David Russell. To an Englishman, it sounded very ordinary. But I remembered it, and when he came to play at a community centre not far from my house in north London, I naturally went to hear him. There were just twelve people in the audience. David's partner on that occasion was an excellent double-bass player, Dennis Milne, whose promising career was not long afterwards brutally terminated in a tragic car crash.

David's solos fulfilled expectation. Youthful vigor, a singer's way with a melody, a perfect balance across the six strings, a seductive sound, and above all this rhythmical strength, convinced me that here was a very special talent.

His apartment in Golders Green was only a mile or two from my house, and I became a frequent visitor. I would often go by bicycle, avoiding the frantic traffic in Lyttelton Way as far as I could, arriving slightly out of breath (there were three flights of stairs to be negotiated before you reached David's rooftop flat). 'Listen to this,' David would say as he began to play his latest discovery. He would not be sitting down in a formal posture, but standing and resting a foot on a chair, or perhaps squatting or sitting cross-legged on the floor. David's athletic body can adapt itself with ease to virtually any playing position the circumstances require.

Thus I heard, among other things, the Carnival of Venice Variations by Tárrega. Not great music, but certainly great entertainment. 'Will you play it in public?' I asked, recovering from my astonished wonderment. 'I don't know,' he replied. But he did, and it was a success.

After our first interview, we went up to the roof for some photography. One of the shots turned out exceptionally well. Long blond hair blown by the wind, an engaging grin, guitar held casually, he looked the very picture of a young and vibrant artist, open and friendly, offering his talent to the world with the hope of youth but also with the confidence that comes with a sense of one's own ability. That picture was reproduced over and over again in guitar magazines, newspapers and record sleeves.

Time passed. David became internationally celebrated, and other photographers took over. But I was quite pleased with that early photograph. And when I count up the hours I have spent listening to David's magnetic playing, I realize how fortunate I am to know so remarkable an artist.

My first question concerned his ability to give his audiences something to hold on to at every level. Even if they knew nothing about the guitar, there was always something to attract them; yet at the highest level the sternest critic could be satisfied. No one felt left behind, or too far ahead.

David Russell: I think there is a basic kind of musicality. In some ways a simple tune is musically the most powerful or the most intimate, the part that can get past all the intellectual criticism, the equipment that is there to analyze and to tear apart. When you get past that, you come to the depth, a deep subconscious feeling.

There are two ways past it. One is through complete simplicity, where there's nothing to criticize anyway and all a player has to do is produce a beautiful line with good tone, simple notes that in theory a beginner could play. That is one route to a beautiful musical experience, which may be technically difficult or it may be technically easy.

The other way is through the overwhelming of the analytical and critical faculties by means of sheer excellence in technique and style. I find that experience in some of Bach's complex fugal works, where at first the mind is analyzing what's going on. Eventually it blows the mind, because you can't hang on to all the strings and keep track of what's going on. And then I start to get a musical experience.

Sometimes my analytical apparatus is overwhelmed because the player I'm listening to is playing so well. Or the piece is so simple and straight that my analytical abilities have nothing to do. For example, the performer can leave a space of silence, and you can feel the whole hall listening to that silence, no coughs, no nothing, for maybe just a second or two. That is something slightly more magical than normal everyday life.

Those are the sort of things that my analytical abilities have nothing to do with. Yet there can be a magical feeling. And sometimes, in my own concerts, when I reach the end of a movement, there's that little space of time before the next begins — and that can seem almost the whole reason for that movement. Or within a piece you sometimes have a huge pile of notes and you think, 'This is really exciting', but it's at the end of it, moving into another passage, that you have the most beautiful bit. The three minutes of excitement before existed only for that moment of transition.

They're all ways of getting past the analytical. That's why people write new languages or extend the language. Because if you work too much within the language, then everyone begins to understand too much what's going on.

It seems that too much understanding can drive out the magic. How does that apply to modern music?
I find that a lot of modern music tends to be an intellectual endeavor, especially at first. After a while I'm able to achieve a certain, for want of a better word, spiritual feeling through certain kinds of music. One of the problems is that nowadays there's a lack of tradition, or the tradition's not used so much. So composers and groups of composers are trying to invent their own language rather than extend the existing language. Originality and 'differentness' have become such important things for this century. Because historically some people were the first to do something, they are now considered to be the best or the most important, rather than those who developed it or who used it best.

Many composers are trying to do original things now. Sometimes it's very good; sometimes it just means there's another language to learn before you can get any real musical feeling out of it. If you relate it to poetry, someone may speak rudimentary English well, but they're not going to get a really deep feeling out of poetry until it's virtually their own language. And they're not going to be able to give a good recital of

Courtesy Classical Guitar Magazine

poetry until they really do understand it.

I think the same thing happens with a lot of music. If the language is difficult, new or whatever, then it's difficult to give a good performance. We've got to bash away at it and work really hard, trying to understand it in order to give a good performance. So I don't want to rush through all the modern repertoire until I start enjoying it — and I don't want to play anything that I don't enjoy. I would like to have the feeling that every time I'm playing something, it's my favorite piece — at that moment.

Having said all that, I play modern music most weeks. Sometimes I enjoy it, sometimes I don't. Sometimes it's not the sort of thing I want to do. I find it easier to cope with when I'm feeling settled and comfortable. When I'm not particularly settled, I prefer soothing or abstract pieces in a language I understand very well, like the baroque and the later classical.

But as guitarists we have to be pretty omnivorous and play a bit of everything, so I don't want to restrict myself. I don't go to modern music concerts for personal enjoyment — more for instruction. It's something I want to know more about.

I was reading your interview with John Williams, who said that it was funny that all his playing of modern music had gone unnoticed. It's the same with me — I play it every week. But I play a whole lot of other stuff as well, and that tends to be the most memorable part of the concert.

I have to play at many concerts. I have to give musical pleasure to many different kinds of audience, so it's necessary to find out what people enjoy as well as what I think I should be playing. I don't teach anywhere, I make my living out of doing concerts. I need people to come to my concerts. I don't want to play Villa-Lobos and Torroba all the time, yet I know hundreds of people in many places would enjoy that program. On the other hand, I don't want to play hundreds of pieces that are not going to attract anybody. Because nobody would come to my concerts, in which case I'd have to take on some teaching position somewhere. I'd also probably have to see a psychiatrist! For that reason I prefer to play accessible music. Maybe one or two pieces that are not so modern, which anyone can enjoy, and a few pieces of modern music as long as they're well placed in the program and well chosen. An accessible program of not very well-known music. I spend a lot of time searching around.

There used to be a saying that the problem with the guitar is its repertoire. I don't think that's the problem with the guitar; I think it's a problem with guitarists. It's their repertoire, the repertoire that has been played, not the existing repertoire. There's a lot more to be played. And there is still a lot in the modern field that is accessible and has yet to be played.

If I want a really musical experience, I don't usually go to a guitar concert for it. I go to a guitar concert for instruction, out of curiosity, perhaps because I know the guitarist, or I want to hear the repertoire. Sometimes I get a musical experience, but I know what's going on, I know what a person is doing, and the magic disappears a little bit. There are times, certainly, when some of the best players — and even some of the not-so-good players — have given me a good musical moment. But if I go to hear another instrument, the technical elements don't involve me, so basically I'm open to more enjoyment.

I think that's one of the things that kills your enjoyment. We increase our critical abilities, so we become less innocent. But the less innocent we are, the less likely we are to enjoy something.

Perhaps I'm talking in black and white. We need a certain amount of knowledge to be able to enjoy something. But if you go to something that you know a lot about and you go with a critical eye, you will get an intellectual experience. On the other hand, if you go with a non-critical open-hearted feeling, you're likely to get much more of a heartfelt, spiritual experience.

When I go to a concert, I can hear the things that are going wrong. But perhaps the person sitting beside me doesn't notice these things and is consequently able to see a lot of other things that I'm missing. But I can't help it. And when I'm playing myself, I wish I didn't notice those little things that no-one hears from ten feet away. So it's not that you get less from it; it's just that it's more *difficult* to enjoy.

One of the reasons why the standard of playing is going up is because people are becoming more critical. They are not getting musical enjoyment out of a duff concert. The players have to be better, they have to play more musically. You can't get away with just a beautiful sound nowadays, nor with just plunking all the notes. It has to be on a higher level altogether. Which is good.

On the other hand, I sometimes hanker for those moments when I was 15 and used to play some of my records and they made my back shiver. Now I can understand what's going on, and it's very seldom that happens.

Now you are in the business of making other backs shiver — of creating magic for other people to enjoy. That can't be easy in front of a sometimes restless audience.
I think you have to draw people in. The audience have to participate, in a way. It shouldn't be a conscious thing, although that may be necessary at first. I think your mind should be free to wander — though with the music, not off on its own. As long as you're playing really well, your audience is with you. When you're not playing particularly well, you notice that people cough more; you lose your audience if your playing begins to get ragged. It's a fact of life.

The guitar's an unfortunate instrument in that mistakes and buzzes are actually louder than the good notes. You move a finger from B to C and there's a big squeak, louder than the notes. Then you buzz on the F, and it's louder than the last three notes put together. It makes it very difficult for all players. It also makes it very easy for the listeners to notice the bad things — and more difficult for them to immerse themselves in the good things. But perhaps the very fragility of it is one of the charms of the instrument. It's also one of the challenges.

79

There's one thing I wish didn't happen. Sometimes you can build up to a moment of complete silence, after a beautiful short passage, perhaps a group of only three or four notes but the centerpiece of a big passage. On the guitar they are very often the more quiet and intimate notes rather than the large and extravagant. And someone out of the 500 people chooses that moment to cough. It makes me feel I want to go over that bit again. It would be nice not to do concerts in February or March.

When you played L'Aube du Dernier Jour, *by Francis Kleynjans, at the Wigmore Hall recently, you got another kind of audience reaction — a laugh when the 6th string imitates the opening of the cell door after the footsteps. What attracted you to this particular piece?*
Well, I do a lot of concerts that are not just for guitarists. And I like to have some modern pieces. When I heard it, I enjoyed it, and that's the main reason. It uses the guitar in quite an original way, even if some of it verges on Hammer horror movies. Someone is describing how it feels, waiting for execution. You have that marvellous clock at the beginning. And the chimes — a marvellous sound. Then the jailer comes up and opens the door — and so on.

It was the first time I'd played it in public. I don't really want a laugh there, obviously. I would prefer the piece to be taken seriously. But people sometimes laugh when they feel uncomfortable. Just a touch of fear can induce humor. It goes up the wrong emotional channel, if you like.

We're talking about the ways people protect themselves. They can do it with criticism or with an analytical ability. And I think cynicism is in some ways a protection against other emotions, perhaps the more dangerous or disturbing ones. Cynicism says 'I know better than this'. I suppose many guitarists have done that opening-door trick. The strange thing is, the chimes just before the door opens don't make anyone laugh.

How do you get that effect?
You pull the 6th over the 5th and hold it down at the 7th fret. Instead of plucking the 6th string, you pluck the 5th, very gently, near the bridge. It rings on. If you pluck the 6th string, you get the snare drum effect. It's because it's not a clean note that you get so many partials, as in a bell, which create the effect. Sometimes even the fundamental gets lost in the dozens of strong harmonics.

We were talking about moments of silence. That was one of them. I'd just done the tick-tock effect after the chord, bringing it up very loud and taking it away again. Now people were still listening for it. When it died away to nothing, I played the 'bell' effect, very quietly — because people's ears had tuned right down and there was complete silence. I was lucky that there was no Bakerloo train going past underneath. (*A well-known hazard at the Wigmore Hall — Ed.*).

A great piece of story-telling — but is it also a great piece of music? Will people be playing it in a hundred years' time?
I don't know what's going to happen to music. But it's a piece that fits into the repertoire. It suits the guitar so well; it fits on the guitar, it's guitaristic. Parts of it are difficult, but certain things that sound extravagant, with piles of notes flying out all over the place, actually fit into the fingers very well. It's not like the Santórsola piece I played last year, for example, which didn't fit into the fingers; he wanted certain kinds of sound which were really quite difficult to achieve on the guitar.

After the Kleynjans, I played, for an encore, some Bach that I think is a great piece of music. And it's a very simple tune. That would rank as a great piece. And a lot of Mozart is very simple, yet you would have to call it great.

In tercentenary year it's inevitable that we should be getting a lot of Bach and, to a lesser extent, Scarlatti on the guitar, but not much Handel. You have arranged a Handel suite with distinction, but on the whole his music is not guitar territory.
With every centenary, Bach is there in front of him, so he gets a little bit overshadowed sometimes. But I love Handel's music.

More theatrical and outgoing than Bach's, so possibly not as suitable for the guitar?
More extrovert, yes. His harpsichord music, which is perhaps the first or even the only thing a guitarist would look at, is very 'notey' sometimes. He uses the instrument a lot. Bach's music is often more abstract, but Handel's is more directly on to the instrument, which makes it more difficult to transcribe.

I didn't have to make too many changes in the suite I transcribed, but it's difficult to play. I had to thin out the Overture quite a lot. Bach has moving lines, but Handel has those big chunky chords, with three octaves repeating one note. And often he's got lines that are going in thirds and in octaves, so it can actually work very easily on the guitar.

When I first started doing transcriptions of Handel I was viewing them with the same sort of view I take with Bach, where the bass line is very important; the way the counterpoint works, the way you think of things in a linear way. In Handel it's not so necessary — though of course sometimes it is. At times he's very concise. I think he forgoes some of that kind of almost mathematical precision in composition, and I think it takes a while to understand what he's doing. But I love the music, and it's really enjoyable to play some stuff that guitarists haven't heard.

You have an international reputation as a soloist, yet you play a lot of ensemble music — your duo with Dennis Milne, with Raphaëlla Smits, with Robert Brightmore, to mention only a few. And now you're working with a singer.
If most of your work is doing solo concerts, as mine is, people don't notice the other things you do. It's other people who put the labels on, other people who make your reputation. John Williams said, indirectly, that all the time he was doing one thing, he was also doing other things. The labels are put on by the people who

listen — and they tend to listen to what they like most.

What I said earlier about some modern music doesn't reflect all my views, because I do play a lot of it. Yet certain people would label me as a non-modern music player. I would say that modern music makes up about 20 per cent of my repertoire. It's a fair amount.

What do you think of the current fashion for speed?
I don't particularly like the way some guitar enthusiasts place speed quite high up on their list of necessities, the idea that if you can play fast, then you're a virtuoso. I think it's unfortunate that, because it's difficult to play fast on the guitar, it becomes an important thing. It's necessary to play fast sometimes, because much of the repertoire is soloistic, virtuoso stuff. But I can sit down at the piano and with two fingers play faster than I can on the guitar. And so can anyone.

There's a difference between something being a necessity sometimes and actually making a feature of it. There's a difference between art and athletics.

It's not my place to criticize other players. They're my colleagues, not my adversaries. And I don't think it's right for a player to be a reviewer. In private I'll certainly have my views on different ways of playing.

Sometime I'd like to give reviewers my point of view on what they do. And perhaps on the way they affect us players. Most of us get very affected by, for example, the way an audience reacts. So I get upset when, playing a concert, I see a whole audience clapping except for one guy sitting there, determinedly not clapping because he's come there in a professional capacity. I'm sure you know the kind of thing I mean. Sometimes you try to do a certain thing, and the reviewer or critic misinterprets it. Obviously it's bound to happen. I'm not saying there's no place for it, but, as we mentioned before, if you look at something with a critical eye, you're to some extent insulating yourself from the appreciation of some of the other qualities that lie behind the intellectual.

If a reviewer goes along with certain tastes, it can be difficult for that person to appreciate some of the other things. There's also the unfortunate situation where you don't particularly care for the person who's doing something, so it's easy to have negative feelings about many of the good things they're doing. On the other hand, I may go to someone's concert, someone whose style of playing is completely different from mine, and

I may really like it.

It's sad if the reviewer happens to be a modern music buff and the guitarist doesn't play any modern music. What's the reviewer doing at that concert? I've read unjust reviews which may be just from the point of view of the reviewer but which have missed the whole point. And the unjustness goes both ways, in that concerts that in no way deserve a good review sometimes get one.

A review in some ways should be an explanation of what happened. Perhaps the critics can write some of their opinions into it — but they are only opinions, and opinions that very often are by very opinionated non-professional musicians. In the magazines, the part where it says 'Reviews' should say 'Opinion'; and the reviews should be an explanation of what happened.

By professional musicians?
By non-professional musicians who are professional writers. And unprejudiced, you hope, by the professionalism in the same circle. Certainly they have to be knowledgeable.

I do get affected when I get adverse criticism. Some people are able to cope with it better than others. I'm less affected by fair adverse criticism than by unfair adverse criticism, which I have no way of understanding. It only makes me slightly angry.

Perhaps I shouldn't talk about my own experiences. But a reviewer who is a non-professional musician often has a scale of expectations and so criticizes this player at one scale and that player at another. A reader in some little town in the north of Scotland gets the impression that the two players are on a par, whereas player A is on a higher level than player B. But the reviewer has lowered his expectations for player B, and consequently enjoyed the concert much more than A's, which he went to with higher expectations.

I don't want to mention any names, but some of the best players have suffered in this way. I realize it's a great problem for the critics, to know how to balance this up.

Ought we to have a scale of absolute values?
That's the difference between a review and a criticism. If we have absolute values, then we all become critics, pigeonholing players according to their level. On the other hand, you can't review a concert without actually giving your view of it. I would prefer to have

someone saying in a review, 'I didn't particularly enjoy this piece', rather than saying 'The player did this wrong and that wrong, and didn't play this in style, and made some stupid ornaments there'.

I have been very lucky in that generally critics or reviewers have been very good to me. But, you know, I've had a few good reviews of concerts that I didn't feel deserved a good review. Those you just forget about. It's a nice bonus.

CC

ANDRÉS SEGOVIA

Although I had heard Segovia in concert on two or three occasions, it was not until 1982 that I was able to interview him on behalf of the newly launched Classical Guitar magazine. He was in London to give a recital at the Barbican Centre, which possessed a somewhat more satisfactory concert hall for a guitarist than the cavernous Royal Festival Hall where, if you sat more than halfway back, you missed a significantly large proportion of the guitar's color. This simple observation, I could not help noticing, was often flatly denied by guitar grandees who themselves never sat in the poorer seats.

Segovia himself was a determined advocate of playing in large halls, for the simple reason that it brought the guitar to more people. It was, however, only the well-off people at the front who, like the first-class passengers in a large liner, enjoyed the experience to the full. The Barbican Hall's acoustically preferable shape enabled very many people to hear Segovia properly for the first time. It was their bad luck that, by that time, his great age — he was 89 in 1982 — was beginning to be all too noticeable. His left hand, never the stronger, quickly became tired, to the detriment of clarity and articulation. In contrast, the right hand, as it tired, seemed to produce tone of an ever-increasing quality, so that by the end of the concert one would have been satisfied if he had played a series of open-string arpeggios in that inimitable style of his. But of course there was always more than that. Segovia remained a great artist to the very end, even if he was no longer the great guitarist that he had been; and ultimately it is artistry that the human sensibility demands.

I telephoned him at the Westbury Hotel in Mayfair, where he habitually stayed when in London. 'Come tomorrow at half past six,' he directed, and hung up without waiting for confirmation. I looked in my diary and found that tomorrow he was to play his recital at the Barbican Hall, one hour later at 7.30. Surely he did not mean to restrict the interview to a mere few minutes? Would he want to speak to journalists at all so soon before a concert? A simple mistake seemed the cause; his wife was not there to look after such arrangements, and he had been known to ring friends in London to inquire 'Where am I playing tonight?'

Accordingly, I rang back immediately. He sounded irritated at being disturbed a second time, and I reminded him that, since he was giving a concert at 7.30, he would scarcely have time to speak to me an hour beforehand. There was a long silence. Then, accompanied by a rich chuckle, came the words: 'I am very sorry. Come the day after.'

David Russell came with me. He had visited Segovia the year before and had played for him. He had been complimented. This time he left his guitar behind, not wanting to hinder me in my work. I was sorry; it would have made my photography more relaxed if David had been playing while I was taking pictures of the older maestro.

Segovia, we were told, had gone for a walk. We sat down to wait. Then, through the door came the burly figure of the great man, wearing his black beret and holding his silver-topped cane. He walked, surprisingly briskly, to the reception desk for his key, and we introduced ourselves.

He asked us to wait for ten minutes, and walked towards the lift. It was his platform walk, slow and stately, far removed from the brisk and energetic stride he had used as he came through the door. Segovia had dropped, simply and innocently, into his performing mode.

In his room I gave him a copy of our first issue, with Julian Bream on the cover. It prompted a mischievous story of how, the year before, he had seen a picture of 'an old, bald-headed guitarist' on the TV screen and had not recognized him. His young son had confirmed that it was Julian Bream, and Segovia exclaimed: 'But he is so old! And I am so young!'

It was the first of many anecdotes, signalled in advance by gesturing to me to switch off the tape recorder. While the machine was running, I was given the standard interview that had appeared in numerous publications. Another off-the-record remark concerned his disappointment with John Williams and his association with the pop group Sky. He did not see it as an essential part of the younger guitarist's search for a new identity, but felt that John Williams should have been content with carrying on the good work that he, Segovia, had initiated. Then there was a furious denunciation of the publishers of his autobiography; they had, he claimed, deprived him of the Spanish rights, which he had particularly requested should remain his. 'To cheat me, an old man, like this!', he stormed, and Andalusian fire raged in his eyes. 'Terrible! Terrible!'

He leafed through our first issue. 'Duarte,' he muttered. 'Again Duarte. And more Duarte.' His meaning was not clear. Was it a criticism? An expression of approval for the industry of his old friend? John Duarte did put in a tremendous amount of work in the first two issues before departing to help revitalize another guitar magazine (Guitar International, now defunct), after which his contributions to Classical Guitar became less frequent.

I was left with the impression of a man of formidable musical power but possessed, notwithstanding, of a lively sense of fun and a love of company. Segovia liked to talk. He was also surprisingly docile when it came to photography, obeying every instruction to turn his head this way or that way or to 'Look into the lens, Maestro'. I have photographed a great many guitarists, and the only other to have behaved with such impeccable understanding turned out to have done some professional modelling before his guitar career took off.

There were to be later meetings with Andrés Segovia, but the first one remains the most vivid.

CC

Courtesy Classical Guitar Magazine

The Barbican audience had been highly appreciative, giving him a standing ovation at the end. But there had been some trouble with the footstool, which had collapsed. It was terrible to be distracted by that kind of thing, said the maestro, because the fingers were accustomed to the discipline, and as soon as the discipline was relaxed the fingers could not perform their task. But he had enjoyed playing at the Barbican.

'The acoustic may be a little better than the Festival Hall's, where people come once but not any more if they don't hear the guitar very well. There, I was always looking to see if people were applauding. If they weren't, it was because they couldn't hear. It was a phenomenon in all the concerts there.

'Last night there were two or three coughs, on my left.

You know, I was once playing the Suite by Bach — the Sarabande, a long movement, expressive, then...' (a realistic cough to illustrate his point) '...then I stop. I look at the place where I hear the cough, and...' (here followed a handkerchief-to-mouth mime, designed to effect an instant cure for bronchitis). 'Everybody laughed — but no more coughs. A handkerchief to the mouth disturbs neither the neighbor nor the artist.'

At the beginning of his career Andrés Segovia had set himself four aims: 'To redeem the guitar from flamenco and other folkloric amusements, to persuade composers to create new works, to show the real beauty of the classical guitar and to influence schools of music and conservatories to teach guitar at the same dignified level as the piano, violin and cello'. Did he feel that he had achieved those four aims?

'I think I have succeeded in my purpose. Because first I redeemed the guitar from the captivity of the flamenco — apart from Tárrega, because Tárrega did not give concerts frequently, not in concert halls or theatres. He was, rather, surrounded by several friends, and he played for them. He received a very modest remuneration. It was a difficult life.

'I did not know Tárrega. I was a little boy when he died. He intended to come to Granada, where I was living, because a friend of my family wrote to him. He answered and said he would come. But in the meantime he died.

'The second goal was to create a repertoire which was not a repertoire by guitarist composers — with the exception of Sor and Giuliani. Tárrega was not a big composer; and the other composers were not very musical. I began to ask the real composers — symphonic composers — to help in creating the repertoire for the guitar. The first to answer was Torroba, who died recently. He was then a young composer of great

84

talent. The first composition he did for the guitar was the dance, in the Suite *Castellana*.'

After that, many composers who heard Torroba's work played on Segovia's guitar were stimulated to produce their own guitar pieces. Torroba himself went on to produce 200 or so. Castelnuovo-Tedesco wrote more than 120 pieces, Turina only about a dozen but of good quality, Villa-Lobos many — including a concerto — and of course Ponce and Tansman.

'This was achieved. Between, I had the transcriptions that I made from vihuela and from harpsichord and from piano, and the pieces that had been composed by real composers foreign to the guitar. The repertoire had 300 or more pieces. This broke the vicious circle the guitar was in. Because there were no composers, there were no artists. And there were no artists because there were no composers.'

Segovia was also concerned about projecting the sound of his guitar, since both Tárrega and his brilliant pupil Llobet both thought that the guitar could not be heard beyond a very short distance. He played his first concert in Granada at the age of 16, then went to Seville, where he performed many times despite the limitations of his repertoire at that time. From Seville he went to Madrid, and thence to Barcelona. It was here, at his second concert, that he decided to make the experiment in sound that opened up the way for concert guitarists ever since.

The first Barcelona recital had been given at the *Sala Granados*, where incidentally he first met the young woman who was to become his first wife. It was, he says in his autobiography, of a great significance to guitarists throughout the world. The *Palau de la Musica Catalana* held over a thousand people — an unheard-of audience for a guitarist — and when Segovia announced that his farewell Barcelona concert would be held there, he was greeted with howls of derision from what he calls the 'simple minds' of those who had taken Tárrega's opinion at its face value.

'Llobet thought that I had lost my mind. But I made the experiment in this way. I told the manager of the hall, "Go throughout the hall and tell me if you hear this —"' Segovia clicked his fingers several times, not very loudly. 'He said yes. I said, "All right, now go over there while I do the same thing". And I noticed that the quality of the sound was exactly the same throughout the hall. The *Palau* was almost full for the concert. The public was happy. And I was more happy.'

The story of how, in Madrid, he had gone into the workshop of Manuel Ramírez has been told often. Ramírez, after hearing him play, put a good guitar into his hands with the words 'Pay me without money'. The debt must have been repaid many times. In every concert Andrés Segovia gave, he played the Ramírez guitar, and people knew it was by Ramírez.

Later came Hauser and Fleta. In recent years Segovia seems to have alternated between Ramírez and Fleta to some extent. Was there some particular reason for that?

Fleta, explained Segovia, built his guitars in one of the most humid cities in Spain — Barcelona. The wood absorbed moisture, so that when you took the guitar to places that were drier — he mentioned Scandinavia, North Germany, Canada and the United States, possibly having in mind the intensity of the central heating in some of those places — severe damage could be caused to the guitar as the wood dried out. Ramírez, aided by the drier climate of Madrid, had to a considerable extent contrived to extract the moisture from the wood before manufacture. Segovia loves the Fleta sound — especially for intimacy, he says — but an experience in the United States two years previously, when his Fleta had become unglued, made him turn again to Ramírez.

'The Ramírez guitar was stronger, more resistant to the heat, to the change of temperature. Two years ago I took a Fleta to the States. Before the concert, in Washington, I had to telephone my wife in Spain and ask her to send me a Ramírez guitar by our airline, Iberia. I received it only a few hours before I was to give the concert.

'Now there is another inconvenience — the strings. Dupont made the first nylon strings for me in 1947. They were superb. I had them for eight months before changing them. But about three years ago I telephoned Dupont to say that their strings were very bad. They told me that when I came back to New York they were going to send me the head of the plastics section.'

Had he said the head of the head of the plastics section, we would not have been surprised. However, Segovia received him in New York: 'Then I called Augustine, because Augustine had made the strings. And the head of the plastics department told me that the quality of the nylon they had sent to Augustine was not so good on account of the crisis in petroleum. He told me that as soon as they got out of this crisis they would send me a better quality of nylon. The petroleum crisis — can you imagine!

'I practice two hours with the same strings, and already they do not sound very good. It is a case of "Very well, I am going to change the second and the first".'

In spite of that he still used Augustine strings.

'Many others have taken up the possibilities of making nylon strings But it is the same situation. I have no obligation with Augustine. I never accept any obligation, either with strings or with the guitar. No, no, never. But I have to admit the truth: that the best strings are Augustine.'

We talked then about his autobiography, the first volume of which appeared in 1976. When were we going to see volume two? It appeared that he had been having trouble with his New York publishers. He now had a new publisher (William Morrow) and everything seemed set for the second volume — and more.

'Now I am going to begin the publication of my second, third and fourth volumes.' Originally his publishers had wanted to confine his autobiography to a simple index of concerts and musical success. But, as he said with a chuckle, 'My life has been not only long but broad'.

'I enjoy writing very much. But I erase more than I write. My writing is in Spanish. I always look for the word that is just the right one, you know, the one that carries the meaning that I want. I know my language very well, and I like to write well in it. Perhaps I ought to have been a writer.'

We wanted to know why so many of his old records were so hard to get, and whether any arrangements were being made to reissue them — perhaps in tribute to his 90th birthday in February 1983. He did not know the answer to that. He agreed that his older records sound 'very nice' — adding that he never played them himself — but was far more interested in the possibilities of making new recordings. It was not easy to find the time.

'Last July I was in Japan. I had to give three different programs in Tokyo. That represents about 50 pieces that had to be memorized, practised and performed. I did not have the time to prepare one record, apart from the one that has the little pieces by Schumann, which are very nice on the guitar.

'Soon I am going to do the *Fantasia* for piano and guitar by Castelnuovo-Tedesco, written for my former wife, who died. I am going to do it with a friend of mine who is a very good pianist. That will be one side. On the other side — solos.'

He talked about his old friends Falla and Ponce. 'The sonata by Ponce — the first sonata — is very beautiful. The theme of the *Sonata Clásica* was deliciously put by Ponce. And then the *Sonata Romantica*: I remember the great French composer Paul Dukas, who played the piano. He deciphered the Sonata for piano and told Ponce: "This is good Schubert — but without the divine length". The Andante is deep poetry. And also the Moment Musical, the Intermezzo. Very nice. Sometimes I play it with the other intermezzo. Because the *Sonata*

86

Photo by Colin Cooper

Mexicana was the first thing he wrote for me, in Mexico. The first thing Ponce wrote for the guitar was the little serenade, in the *Sonata Mexicana*. But this is, how shall I say, a little shy, a little timid, you know, because it is the first thing he did. When he wrote the sonata with three movements I told him, please put that intermezzo in. But later on he wrote the other one. When Falla and I were together, he wanted to hear this little intermezzo. It is beautiful.

'Ponce has been magnificent for the guitar. He was a real composer. Everything he did — the preludes he did for me, for instance — was first class. He did not have the least intention of appealing to the public. His aim was to use the poetry of the guitar. He composed one sonata that I have lost, because I lost my entire house in Barcelona at the beginning of the Civil War. I lost many things by Ponce because, you know, he used to send me the original without making a copy. I told him about this many times.

'I lost seven or eight pieces in this way. A sonatina I asked him to write in homage to Tárrega disappeared — and the worst of it is that the first movement was a very big emotional thing. Great emotion. But still I think that the greatest thing he composed for the guitar was the *Theme, Variations and Fugue on La Folia.*

Segovia played a little joke on Ponce in the matter of the variations. Ponce had sent him the variations, telling him to reject the ones he didn't like. Segovia wrote to the composer to say that he couldn't do much with the variations, apart from four or five at the most. Ponce concealed the disappointment he must have felt, but was delighted when Segovia turned up with the printed music, which Schotts had meanwhile published, of all 20 variations together with the fugue.

Segovia had spoken to Falla about Ponce, arousing his curiosity. Falla was to conduct at the Venice Festival, where Segovia was also due to perform. From Geneva Segovia telephoned Falla, who was in Barcelona at the time, offering to pick him up at the frontier and drive him to Venice, departing 15 or 20 days beforehand so that they could enjoy themselves in every place they liked between Barcelona and Venice. On the journey they talked about Ponce.

'I was speaking about him in a very tender way, because I knew Ponce very well. He was a spirit, you know, who never took a single step for himself. And Falla, after hearing my description, had a great sympathy with Ponce, but still didn't know anything by him.

'In Venice I was practising the *Theme, Variations and Fugue* — not all the variations, because the work was too long for the concert I was to give.

While I was practicing, Falla said "What is that?" Further on he said again, "What is that? It's very good, that". Finally, when I played the fugue, he said, "What is this? This is very good". And I said, "Do you know, it is by Ponce". And he said, "I am very glad to unite the estimation of the music to the sympathy of the person".'

CC

DAVID STAROBIN

Few guitarists have done as much for contemporary music as David Starobin. In addition to his activities as a performer, he is the president of Bridge Records, which he runs in partnership with his wife Becky. The contribution made by Bridge Records to the contemporary repertoire is enriching beyond calculation. One of his projects has been the commercial release of historical recordings from the Library of Congress.

He is also an ardent exponent of music from the Romantic period. In particular, his championship of Regondi's 10 Etudes, thought to be lost until Matanya Ophee rediscovered them in Russia, did much to rehabilitate that Chopinesque figure of the 19th century.

It might seem odd, this juxtaposition of the old with the new — Regondi alongside Elliott Carter and Poul Ruders — but when you have heard David play you realize that it is all of a piece with his incandescent musicianship, his drive to uncover the good music, whether old or new, that is often obscured by dogma and suspicion. Elliott Carter difficult to understand? Regondi trivial? David Starobin will have none of this 'received wisdom'. In unfolding the music for you, he overcomes all objections; you find yourself listening as you have never listened before. And as you listen, the music invades your unconsciousness, opening doors that have remained locked for too long.

Yet, despite his persuasive — and successful — work to establish the music of the composers he admires, David remains a musician first and a pioneer second. To put it another way, the pioneering is accomplished through his music-making, and it is that which has secured this unique guitarist his very many admirers.

Does your forthcoming Wigmore Hall program of 19th-century music represent a turning away from the contemporary music you have pioneered so successfully in the past?

David Starobin: Well, looking now in my datebook... in a way it does. I've got a ten-day hiatus between Amsterdam (where I'm playing American guitar music of the 1980s) and the 19th-century Wigmore program. I'll be turning away from my Humphrey and intensively playing the Panormo for the better part of those ten days.

Seriously, though, I've been playing the 19th-century guitar repertoire since the age of seven. My first instructor, the late Puerto Rican guitarist Manuel Gayol, was a fanatic about the stuff. We played reams of Sor, Giuliani, Legnani, Molino, Carcassi, Carulli and Mertz. I still keep the notebooks in which he would copy out (from memory) this then unavailable repertoire.

For me, the cornerstone of my chamber music activity has been the chamber and vocal works by Boccherini, Paganini, Giuliani, Weber, Hummel, Schubert and Spohr. While I was still in school, I was extremely fortunate to perform and record works by Boccherini and Paganini with the beloved Italian violinist Pina Carmirelli. Pina's pioneering Boccherini research has saved much of this beautiful music from obscurity.

Do you play chamber music using period instruments?
Yes. I perform in a duo with violinist Benjamin Hudson. Ben is known in England as leader of the Hanover Band. We play a lot of Paganini and Giuliani. With these instruments, it's possible to put the 'V' back into virtuosity.

Could you be a bit more specific?
Well, first of all, there is the matter of string length. I'm presently playing a Panormo copy (built by Gary Southwell) which has a 63cm scale. This allows me (and I've got fairly large hands) to make all of the reaches that Sor asks for, without crippling myself. Given average hand size, playing on a smaller scale allows the player a shot at tempos which might be unattainable on a 66cm scale.

With the lower action and string tension of these instruments, left-hand articulation becomes a relative breeze, and the resultant sound quality is different too. On a large modern instrument, the gap between normal plucked sound and left-hand articulation is quite wide. On my Panormo, the left-hand articulation is closer in amplitude and color to a normal plucked attack. This makes for an integrated sound world that I find quite thrilling.
Even more important, though, is the balance between the treble and bass choirs. The comparatively duller treble of a Lacôte or Panormo actually *emphasizes* the contrapuntal nature of a composer like Sor. Bass lines come to the fore, and middle voices cut through independently and with warmth.

I try not to ignore the areas in which modern instruments surpass these little guitars. I presently play all of this repertoire on both old and modern instruments. The possibilities of each instrument seem to contribute a lot to my learning process.

19th-century solo repertoire sometimes comes in for criticism, mainly, it seems to me, because it is hard to measure against the acknowledged masterpieces written for the piano. What do you really think of our 19th-century solo guitar repertoire?
With the republication of Sor's complete guitar works, it became apparent to me that the best guitar music of this period had been virtually gathering dust. In works such as his Opp. 30, 56, 59 and 63, Sor shows us that though he is not a music revolutionary, he is nonetheless a musically progressive romantic poet, capable in his best pages of the soulfulness of a Schubert and the impeccable instrumental virtuosity of a Chopin.

We are only beginning to learn how to perform these long-dormant treasures, and it is safe to predict that Sor's reputation will only grow as his best works are more frequently played. Guitarists everywhere are indebted to Brian Jeffery for his research and publishing activities. With Thomas Heck's pioneering Giuliani research, Jeffery's recently completed Giuliani edition makes it possible, for the first time, to evaluate the other key figure in the 19th-century guitar's history.

For too long, bad scholarship and ignorance have been the guiding factors in our view of the instrument's repertoire. Can you imagine the piano's two greatest 19th-century composers being subjected to incomplete, poorly edited editions until 1989? A good many of these Giuliani and Sor works (including some of the best) could not be found in any edition.

Where do you see your tastes and inclinations leading you in the years to come?
To answer that broadly, I'd have to say 'give me more of the same' — that is, lots of variety. To be more specific, I should explain that my musical activities are somewhat segmented. In addition to the guitar playing, I maintain a handful of university positions, and I'm one of the conductors of Speculum Musicae, a terrific new music ensemble in New York. I try to spend spare time with my wife and two children.

I'm looking forward to the coming season with great anticipation. Many new works are being written by composers whom I greatly admire. In November I'll play two new works: a Trio by William Bland, and a chamber concerto by George Crumb. I've been asking Mr Crumb for a piece for 20 years, and the confluence of his interest and a commission from Augustine Strings will finally make that dream a reality.* Later on, I'll be playing a MIDI guitar in a new guitar duo by Tod Machover. The other guitarist is Pat Metheny, and I expect we'll have a blast playing that one. The Danish composer Poul Ruders and the American composer John A. Lennon are both writing me concertos, and Milton Babbitt is writing a flute and guitar duo.
I'm also playing a lot of duo concerts with my long-time baritone partner Patrick Mason. Pat and I are celebrating our 20th anniversary as a duo by touring in the US, the UK, Holland, Luxembourg and Japan. For the far future, Paul O'Dette and I have been threatening to record Sor duos on little guitars. I recently took off my nails for a bit of preparatory experimentation.

What about your record production activities?
My next two or three months are also eclectic. I'll be finishing production on a Mahler/Berlioz disc, a disc of Elliott Carter's vocal music, a disc of Tibetan Buddhist rituals. A disc of Balinese Kecak, and the four Ives Violin Sonatas. Help!

How do you keep from drowning in it all?
My wife Becky. It's really that simple. Our lives are interlocked maritally and parentally, we're partners in business, she manages my playing career, and if I'm lucky, I even get to see her now and then.

How do you see the guitar in the context of general music? Does it have a permanent place, or are we heading for a decline of the sort it had in the mid-19th century?
With the vast and diverse repertoire composed during the 20th century, combined with the best works of the 19th century, 21st-century guitarists should be able to perform concerts of guitar music (as opposed to borrowed repertoire) that should be able to move audiences from tears to ecstasy and back. What more could we possibly ask for? Segovia's dream of guitar tuition in all of our institutions has virtually been realized. As a disseminating vehicle, recordings have taken the place of the 3000-seat hall, which so often defeated our intimate instrument. Just look at how many excellent guitarists are presently vying for professional fame and fortune!

If one believes (and I do!) that the growing quantity and quality of repertoire will demand broader, thus deeper performers, then guitar players of the future will certainly have enough to sustain themselves and their audiences through any lean times.

In your last Wigmore Hall recital, you included a piece for solo guitar and prepared tape. We see a roughly similar phenomenon in London's Underground, where a busker may play accompanied by an amplified tape. What are your feelings about this compositional trend ?
I believe that the advent of electro-acoustical music will some day yield great music, if it has not already done so. The ability to dissect sounds on an almost microscopic level, to subtly develop them, and then reconstruct them with infinite control of nuance — these are all tools, or instruments, if you will, that our composers are just being introduced to.

Much of today's research is being geared toward the intelligent response of computers to performer input. Thus, a virtuoso's every reaction — his attack, timbre, vibrato, dynamics etcetera — can be monitored and measured by the computer. The composer can then provide the computer with information that will allow the computer to react musically to what is being shaped by the player. This procedure, now in its

infancy, is preferable to playing against an unyielding tape. This ongoing instrument building and invention, which many of our best musical minds have devoted themselves to, has very little to do with the 'boom-box' tracks that you're hearing on the Piccadilly Line.

Will this lead to music that has a permanent place in our affections, as the music of the 18th- and 19th-century classicists and romantics has?
I don't think instruments have anything to do with this. The most popular music of the latter half of this century has been produced on electronic instruments, and is listened to through loudspeakers. The best of this 'popular' music seems to have achieved the status of 'classic'. I'm referring, of course, to rock music, which seems to have a permanent place in many people's affections.

In the field of 'classical' music, we have certainly not achieved anything like the accomplishments of the 18th- and 19th-centuries. However, I believe that this is true for acoustic as well as electronic instruments, though this has more to do with the unsettling effect that linguistic uncertainty has visited upon our composers, than on the mere changing of instrumental palette.

I personally love the 20th-century repertoire for its variety and surprises. The absence of 'common practice' has opened the way for very personal expression by those masters who have been successful in forging a language. The guitar is indeed fortunate to have compositions by a broad range of today's composers, and if it is not too early to predict, I feel sure that a good number will be played, loved and cherished by guitarists, long after we are all gone.

David Starobin returned to London a few years later to perform Giulio Regondi's recently rediscovered 10 Etudes, and a new concerto by Poul Ruders. The concert formed part of Classical Guitar's Celebrity Concerts series, and naturally I took the opportunity to talk to David about it before the event. By that time he was playing a copy of a 19th-century guitar by Staufer, also made by Gary Southwell but, in David's opinion, of a superior design to the Panormo copy he had played on his previous visit. The Ruders work, incidentally, was performed on a modern amplified guitar. Two very different works, and two very different instruments. Was there anything that united the two halves of this concert?

David Starobin: Regondi's *10 Etudes* is a work

Courtesy Classical Guitar Magazine

lasting approximately 40 minutes. They were most probably meant to be heard as a set, as Regondi has carefully chosen a contrasting tempo and character continuity, and has also employed parallel and relative key juxtapositions between pieces. Poul Ruders's *Psalmodies* is a concert suite/chamber concerto in eleven interconnected movements, designed as a very grand 30-minute arch. Both of these multi-movement works create an impact that is a cumulative result of their respective large scale forms.

More importantly, both composers have succeeded, in their own very different ways, in achieving a communicative balance between technical means and expressive results. Within his ten passionately romantic outbursts, Regondi has exhibited more compositional 'technique' than in other 19th-century guitar music that I am aware of. A favored device, almost a signature in these etudes, is his use of 'encapsulating codas'. Here, Regondi routinely takes materials from two different sections and combines them, developing and transforming his argument into an all-encompassing recapitulation. He accomplishes this so artfully and smoothly that one is almost unaware of the miracles that have taken place.

Poul Ruders also achieves an intense blend of intellect and heart, employing means far more extreme than Regondi's. In many of Ruders's scores 'remembered musics' bump up against exhilaratingly modernistic

inventions. His masterful technical control always seems to preside over the violent and uplifting path that his scores often follow.

Regondi's 10 Etudes *was recently discovered in the Soviet Union by Matanya Ophee. Other than historical interest, what special qualities does this work have?* These pieces are special in just about every way that it is possible to be special. The set is a 40-minute cycle of Romantic music. How many of those do we have in our repertory? The high musical quality, the range and variety of expression, and Regondi's incomparable guitarism guarantee them the highest place in our instrument's active repertoire.

Thrust before the French and British public as a child prodigy, Regondi was clearly a major talent. Fernando Sor would not be dedicating his 'Souvenir d'Amitié' to just any eight-year old, nor would Leigh Hunt be writing about a nine-year old guitarist in the same breath as Mozart and Paganini, were it not for the appearance of such a phenomenon.

Giulio Regondi was that rare and quintessential mid-19th-century artist — a virtuoso performer gifted with creative vision, and the requisite discipline to realize that vision. As only a portion of Regondi's output for the guitar is extant, the discovery of the *10 Etudes* considerably expands our view of his compositional range. The location of missing Regondi guitar works should become a priority for anyone who truly loves the guitar and its music.

With the republication of Op.19-23 in Simon Wynberg's Chanterelle Edition in 1981, 20th-century guitarists could clearly see that Regondi was a master guitarist. He was a performer whose left hand knew no fear, and whose right hand ranged from the dreamy and lyrical utterances of Op.19's tremolo to Op.23's flamboyant octave displays. With the discovery of the *10 Etudes*, an even broader harmonic vocabulary has been revealed, and an even greater talent exposed. In *10 Etudes*, Regondi's chief concern shifts from the writing of display vehicles to a more subtle virtuosity linked to deeper interior compositional logic. This is not to say that Opp.19-23 lack logic, or that the études are easy works to play. Clearly, the same formidable musician is at work, but writing with very different purpose and result.

You will be performing 10 Etudes *on a copy of a Staufer guitar. What is your reasoning for this choice, and does this make the music easier to perform?*

Well, it certainly does not make the music easy to perform! I play on a copy of a Staufer/Legnani model, which I consider to be one of the best-designed guitars ever built. In addition to its unique sonic characteristics, this instrument features the famous 'flying fingerboard'. With my ratchet key in hand, I am able to adjust the action of this instrument in ten seconds' time. In music of very high velocity the ability to quickly 'fine tune' the guitar's action is very advantageous. With this device, the player can easily compensate for factors such as changing humidity and its effect upon the guitar's top, the particular musical requirements of an individual composition, or even the player's subtlest physical changes, from hour to hour. I hope that some of today's forward-looking guitar builders will allow themselves a backward glance, and experiment with the inclusion of this remarkable invention.

What of the issue of so-called 'authenticity'? Should these pieces be played on a Staufer, an instrument that Regondi himself is said to have played on, or are they better served on a fine modern instrument?
That is a very complex question to answer. One could argue the merits of one side or the other, with any argument being immediately dashed to pieces by the genius of a given player on a given instrument. Clearly, individual taste and choice are governing factors here. However, the study of historical practice is, hopefully at the least, a starting point in our search for reaching solutions.

I personally admire performances that meet the composer's level of creativity with equally vivid levels of performer re-creativity. Experimenting with old and new instruments is one part of this re-creative process. The thinking performer's view of a particular composer or composition would hopefully lead to that individual's choice of instrument.

What other 19th-century composers have you been performing recently, and on which instruments have you been playing their music?
I've just made a CD of Giuliani solos played on a Staufer, and will soon be making a Regondi disc on this same instrument. I've been playing a lot of Sor on Panormo and Lacôte, and I'm doing some Coste on a 6-stringer. I'd like to find a Scherzer 10-string to fill that gap.

The Danish composer Poul Ruders has composed Psalmodies for you. Will you say something about the composer and the circumstances which led to this composition?
I came to know Ruders's music when I conducted his *Four Compositions* in New York. I also remember the impact of a great performance of his *Manhattan Abstraction* that Oliver Knussen conducted at Tanglewood. These two experiences made deep impressions, and I approached Ruders, asking for a little chamber concerto. Rose Augustine commissioned Poul, and two years later the score was completed.

One of the greatest joys of being a musician in our time is our ability to 'access the record' so easily — to have at our ears and eyes a veritable tornado of human creativity, constantly destroying our assumptions and forcing us to reinvent our view of the past. The music of Ruders is one such force for me. His music is as gratifying to listen to as it is to perform. At its best it is truly transporting.

In trying to describe *Psalmodies*, I think it best to print a portion of the composer's own program note: '*Psalmodies*. The word has its origin in ancient Greek: Psalmoidia, i.e. "singing to the harp", and we find the word again in Psalter, derived from "Psallein": playing the strings with the fingers. *Psalmodies* has no specific religious contents or aim; the collection of eleven pieces forms a concert suite displaying a wide range of emotions; from the jubilant to the dismal, the guitar playing the natural leading part "inside" a chorus of woodwinds and strings.'

Have you performed music by other Danish composers?
Yes. I've played quite a bit of music by Per Nørgård, and this season I'll be conducting a performance of Bent Sorensen's *Les Tuchins*, an excellent work which has two fine electric guitar parts. There is a wonderfully active 'new guitar' scene in Denmark, fostered largely by players such as Erling Møldrup and Karl Petersen.

What are your own aspirations for the guitar?
In the area of repertoire expansion, I hope that the current direction continues apace. We have finally begun to attract the best of present-day composers to our instrument, while simultaneously uncovering hidden jewels from our past. In the area of performance, the guitar has found new life amidst the gradually emerging expertise of today's players. My own goal is to be a positive part of this reawakening.

* George Crumb's Canis Mundi was performed several times in 1999, with the composer himself playing the percussion parts.

CC

DAVID TANENBAUM

The son of two musicians, David Tanenbaum was born in New York City in 1956. His route to the classical guitar led through the piano and the cello and, at the age of ten, the electric guitar. Study with Aaron Shearer at the Peabody Conservatory, along with a couple of good prizes at international level, launched him on a successful career on the global platform.

David Tanenbaum was in London to give the first British performance of Hans Werner Henze's new concerto, 'An eine Aölsharfe' (To an Aeolian Harp). It was an unusual way for a young guitarist to make his UK debut, but he had met Henze in the USA, and the German composer had been impressed by his playing. The concerto followed.

The performance was more than usually interesting, with the guitar placed far forward of the orchestra. What it lost in intimate cooperation with the orchestra, it gained in clarity and focus. It was a concert that brought much critical acclaim to both composer and soloist, and by extension to the guitar itself.

A short time previously, the American magazine 'Guitar Player' had put forward the suggestion that the classical guitar was, not to put too fine a point on it, dead. It was not something that I had noticed, and David Tanenbaum's performance of a new concerto by a leading composer certainly suggested that there was life yet in the 'corpse'. My first question asked if he had noticed any significant lack of animation during his travels.

David Tanenbaum: Not at all. I think it's changing a lot. It seems to have reached a certain peak in popularity which perhaps has gone down some, but there are so many people involved that I think there will be peaks and valleys a little bit. People are learning a lot; ideas are being tossed around internationally, and certain directions are being forged.

What always strikes me about the guitar is the incredible dimension of the instrument; how it expresses so much of the music of today — and not just classical — and how interesting some of the crossover is. I think we need to utilize that and express the different colors that the guitar has. I think they are perfect for expressing the music of today.

I started as a pianist. My parents are both classical musicians, and one of the reasons that I feel I'm not intimidated by modern music is that my father is a composer. From three years old I was listening to the most contemporary music. When you do that a lot, you begin to discriminate and perhaps to trust your own judgments. I think a lot of people are put off by new music. They might have an authentic reaction, but perhaps not trust it.

My mother's a pianist, and she taught me when I was four or five. And I also played the cello. Interestingly enough, I was sort of forced to do those things. It was a requirement. I had to take lessons, so I had to practice. I started to rebel. And when I was about ten or eleven I didn't practice so much. I remember doing very badly in some performances in the local conservatory. A teacher suggested to my parents that I be allowed to quit. He thought that I was talented enough that I would drift back into music.

So I did quit everything at that point and sort of rebelliously played electric guitar. I found the classical guitar after that. It was for me a very private musical experience. The instrument was quiet, it couldn't be heard by anyone else if I shut the door. The repertoire was unknown — and that was one of the reasons why I took to it so much. I became fascinated by the different colors that it had. It was full of possibilities.

93

Kingmond Young Photography

Can you tell me something about the Henze concerto, the Aölsharfe? It's very much in my mind after the experience of the concert. You've played it before, in Austria and Germany, haven't you?
Yes. The world premiere was August the 27th 1986, in Lucerne, Switzerland. I played it two days after that in Frankfurt. I played it in Vienna in October with the ORF Orchestra. The performances in Switzerland and Germany were with the Ensemble Modern, which is part of the Junge Deutsche Philharmonia, the Young German Philharmonic, the part that specializes in modern music.

The Vienna performance on January the 9th was a lecture recital on the piece. Henze talked in German about it at length, and we did examples, and then we performed it. The difficulty for me was that I did a solo recital in Austria on January 8th, and played that on the 9th; on the 10th I had to take a polar flight to California and play a concert which I had to do on the 11th. Then on the 12th I came back to London.

This is, I guess, the fifth performance of it. Henze has now cancelled all his conducting engagements so that he can write his new opera, which is based on Mishima's book 'The Sailor who fell from grace with the sea'. The next performance will be the US premiere on March 9th in Los Angeles.

Aölsharfe is a very interesting piece. Bayan Northcott said that he felt that the textures were too difficult; there was too much going on, and it became sort of a harmonic muddle. Henze, interestingly enough, began the last rehearsal of the piece this time saying that he felt that in his last few orchestral pieces he may have indulged himself in too much counterpoint, that there was too much going on in the orchestra and that it was hard to hear. I think that's a danger with this piece. I believe it can be made very clear, but I think it requires an enormous amount of clarifying and keeping the textures very transparent.

It's an interesting challenge for an orchestra. They have to learn to play very quietly with the guitar — even if it's amplified — so that the guitar is absolutely above. So I think it's a challenging piece, and one that can be very successful. But I think it's going to be a difficult one, one that has to be rehearsed very carefully. Henze's procedure was to rehearse with sectionals, and to have me play through almost every movement with each member of the orchestra. So everybody got to hear my part, and I got to hear their parts.

So much of his music is programmatic. This piece is based on the poems of Eduard Morike, an early 19th-century lyric poet. Henze actually sets this music as if it was a vocal setting. In other words, the guitar is playing a line that's supposedly speaking the poetry. These important lines go from one instrument to another, and it's very important to be able to trace them and find out where they are. Sometimes one has to be told that by Henze, sometimes it's a little diffuse and you can't tell right away where the important line is, but it's always important to search for it and to bring it out.

It's very interesting how he chose to set it. As Bream said once, Henze makes very large gestures for the guitar, and he has done so again with *Aölsharfe*. It's very lyrical, very legato in style. The writing for the guitar feels very grounded to the fingerboard. I found the first and fourth movements extremely difficult but very rewarding to work on, because it was almost like a new style, a new kind of guitar playing, one that I had not physically experienced before.

A different style of writing from, for instance, the Royal Winter Music?
Yes. There's always the emotional climate of the poetry or the program aspect that he is trying to create, and I find there is an emotional climate of Shakespeare in *Royal Winter Music*. For instance, when I play one of the Sonatas in a program, for me the music that works best after it is John Dowland, which is music from that time. But the emotional climate of *Aölsharfe* is really more from that early romantic, early Schubert period.
Sometimes it's hard to put your finger on exactly what tools are used that make it so different. Henze is very hard to pin down. He will dip into any kind of method; he'll use a 12-tone row, and then come back to it with a few fragments here and there. He doesn't often stick to one thing throughout a large work.

He uses the Landler, doesn't he? The three-in-a-bar Austrian dance.
He uses that in the third movement, which is a kind of joking movement, a scherzo. When we rehearsed in Germany and in Vienna, the conductors and the orchestra and everybody got that one right away!

But in England it had to be explained.
That's right. But it was very interesting to see this piece from its genesis. We met in 1983. A pianist friend in the Peabody Conservatory introduced me to a lot of Henze's works, and one in particular was *El*

Cimarrón. I always wanted to play that piece, and I think it was in 1979, when I was teaching at my home in California, that the phone rang and it was a singer who was putting together the first West Coast production of *El Cimarrón*. He wanted me to be part of it.

I did that piece on tour. Andrew Porter, the critic of The New Yorker, was doing a six-months sabbatical on the West Coast about the music scene there, and he happened to be at the first performance. There was a reception after the first performance, and he came up to me and was really excited. I waited and waited for the review to come out in The New Yorker, because it would be very important for me, but it never came out. So I wrote to him. He immediately wrote a letter with a very nice quote, explaining to me that the performance was too complex to fit into the space that he had. There were certain things he liked, and he said that my playing was among them, but there were other things he didn't like. But he said, 'I've just seen Henze in New York and I told him about your playing'. So that was how Henze first found out about my playing.

After that I began to play *Royal Winter Music*. I sent Henze many reviews of the piece, and when he came to California for a festival in 1983 I asked if I could perhaps play the *Royal Winter Music* for him. I was very interested in first of all getting what I thought were some mistakes in the score corrected. He's an enormously busy person, and I didn't think there would be a chance. But finally on a Sunday morning, the last day of the festival, he did have some time. We went out on the balcony of his hotel and played. I played the second movement, 'Romeo and Juliet', and he said: 'I'm going to write you a concerto' — just like that!

Certainly I didn't expect it. I wasn't there for anything like that. I was just interested in his thoughts — and I got the music. It was very hard to play on after that. It was an astonishing thing.

Two years later he was asked to write a piece for the Lucerne Festival, because it was his 60th birthday. He wanted to write something for the Ensemble Modern, so he suggested this piece. And that's how it came about. I got a telegram in November of 1985, in which Henze explained that he was going to write the piece. At that point he outlined what his entire schedule would be like for the year. He said I'd get the first movement here, the third movement would come next, then the second movement will come, then please keep July as free as possible, because the last movement will come in middle to late July.

Of course, July wasn't free at that point. The movement did come in late July, five weeks before the premiere. That was the most hysterical time, trying to learn the whole thing.

When I first looked at the score, I must say that it looked completely unplayable to me. I worked with Henze in New York. I'd just done the first movement, and it turned out that the kind of relationship he was interested in was a very creative one where he was working not so much with the details of the instrument or how it could be played, but rather with the romantic sound concept that he had for this poetry, and the sound concept of the balance of the ensemble. He wanted the guitarist to take a very active role in the creating of the piece — you know, rewrite things if you had to.

In the fourth movement there are 11-note and 12-note chords. Unbelievable! I cut them all to six notes, sometimes five notes. The guitar and harp are playing together, and it's just a very big plucked string sound. The guitar is being made as big as possible.

Why do you think he did that? He knows about the guitar. He knows that 12-note chords are impossible. He just wanted to show the harmonic structure that he wanted. He wanted to let me create the chords and find the best place to put them. As you know there are many different ways you can play a B flat seventh chord, for instance.

So it was a lot of fun. I tried to keep the general range of the top line going, but I also tried to experiment and make chords as big as possible. On the last chord, which I think is a very haunting effect, he wrote 'Sons étouffés'— muffled sounds — and asked me to find some way to realize it. I tried tambura and I tried flesh thumb strokes, and I finally came up with a pizzicato stroke with the thumb with the hand then released — a sort of muffled sound that opens up.

There is a lot needing to be rewritten, especially in the first and fourth movements. The second and third, by the way, had very few changes made in them. The structure of the piece is such that the second movement is mostly single-line. The guitar is reduced to a simple single line, the idea being that the guitar from that point starts to feel like it's growing bigger again. It's almost like a deception in the sound, where it starts coming out of the ensemble as the piece progresses. The third movement has a lot of thirds and sixths, and the fourth movement unleashes.

The fourth movement also is the one where the strings finally take the mutes off. I find that to be true of a lot of Henze's music. Sometimes in the last movements, things really reach their peaks, and the most amount of sound is made.

From the audience's point of view, that makes good psychological sense, doesn't it? In the theatre, if the last act of a play is good, the audience tends to forget, or at least to forgive, what has gone before.
Yes, I think so. The other analogy is the solo guitar program, where perhaps you'd start with a thinner-textured renaissance piece, and go towards modern music, where there's a feeling that the sound is getting bigger.

I saw the microphone in front of the guitar at the performance. How much amplification was there in fact? The sound seemed to come from you, not from the speakers.
There was a little bit of amplification of the guitar. They did a very good thing, which was to put the speakers behind the orchestra, so that the orchestra could hear the guitar. Even in the concertos where you can play without having amplification, I worry that the orchestra's playing an accompaniment to a concerto and can't hear the soloist. I've always liked the idea of at least letting them hear you.

This piece was conceived to be done without amplification. That's why the instrumentation is so low. There are no violins, no regular flutes. The instrumentation is alto flute, bass flute, oboe d'amore, cor anglais, bass clarinet, bassoon, harp, one percussion player — although there were actually two people doing this part — viola d'amore, which has a very prominent role, two violas, viola da gamba, two cellos and a bass. It's written to be like an old consort. The oboe d'amore and the cor anglais are two of the highest instruments, the only ones that can really conflict with the guitar. The guitar, of course, is used very high most of the time, so that it can work above the instrumentation. I think it can be heard well without amplification in all but the last movement, in which it joins the ensemble and really does get lost sometimes.

I think that is what a lot of guitarists in the audience felt — that it could too easily become lost. They want to hear it all the time, even when it's in a concertante role.
It's funny, you know, all the guitarists complained to me about the amplification — and no-one else did! I think it's a borderline piece. We did it once without

amplification in Vienna, in the Schubertzaal, which probably has four or five hundred seats. I think it can be heard well there, but there are times — for instance, there's a harmonic section where you're going to lose those very high harmonics sometimes.

It's a real problem. When we did the premiere in Lucerne, the speakers were on the side of the stage. Henze really did not like the fact there was so much of a visual focus on the guitar, yet the sound was coming from a different place. He wanted the sound and the visual focus in the same place. Before the premiere he said, 'You know, you move around when you play', and he asked me to really indulge myself, to act the movements and choreograph them. So he wants a lot of gesture from the guitarist.

I'll have to do it a few more times to decide on the application. I think there are certain halls where it's not going to work without amplification. I really do.

Another aspect was the sideways posture, a bit like a pianist, who of course can see the conductor. It's not so easy for a guitarist.
That's true. He's over there to the left of you, and you're sort of looking over the fingerboard to the left.

But because you were slightly turned, some people in the hall felt that they were being deprived of the guitar.
It's a problem also. And it's tricky enough that I'm still reading it, so that's a problem. I always want to have the music stand not in front of me but to the left.

Would there be a case for having the guitar back among the other instrumentalists and facing the conductor?
Yes, that's possible. Interestingly, in this piece, Henze asks the ensemble to move as far back and away from me as possible. But of course when you're doing that, I think it's important that the orchestra hear you. If they're way back and you're way up and pointing outwards, I think you're going to have to get speakers behind them.

You know, I don't think amplification in itself is necessarily such an evil. I think it can be done really successfully. I felt John Williams did a very good job when he toured the US. Very tasteful. It enhanced the experience rather than take anything away from it.

Is Aölsharfe going to be published soon?
Henze wants it to get out in the world. Schott will

publish it soon. The piece is dedicated to my wife and me, by the way, which is a very sweet thing for Henze to do. Her name is Julie; Henze calls her 'Juliet' — one more Shakespearian angle!

What is he like as a conductor?
Well, I will tell you that technically he's certainly not the greatest conductor I've ever worked with, but he is absolutely musical at all times. His ears are just phenomenal. He tends to be a little bit unpredictable as a conductor, in the sense that he, I think, hears things, or has an inspiration on the spot and just goes for it, and it may not be something that you've rehearsed. One has to be very much on one's toes.

It's such an interesting experience, because there's always a sound idea. The listening is fantastic. I've learned more about the piece in the past week, doing it with him twice, than in studying it for eight months.

He really senses the deepest aspect of one's musicianship. He wants you to bring that out. Every time I've done less than that, or maybe been a little timid, he just says: 'Do more of it'. He never gets in the way of the essence of your musicianship; he just wants it to come out as much as possible. He's like a great teacher.

I think it's that way with orchestras too. He really wants them to listen. He just wants to participate in the listening. It's a very good experience to work with him.

I know that you will be playing this concerto many more times, but will other guitarists also be playing it?
I have exclusive recording rights to it, and the US

premiere, but the general thing is in my experience that you get rights more when you commission the piece yourself. I certainly didn't have the funds to do that, so it wasn't right for me to ask for the rights. Anything that Henze has given me has been given out of generosity — and there's been a lot.

Have you played all the other concertos — the standards?
I have not performed the Ponce concerto, but I've done all the others. I did an interesting concerto job once with the San Francisco Ballet, which did a ballet choreographed to the Rodrigo *Aranjuez* and the *Fantasia para un gentilhombre* — played back to back without a break. They changed the order of the Fantasia a little bit, and in the Aranjuez the order was 3, 1, 2 — ending with the second movement. I did that ten times in one week. Ever since then, I've not been scared of the *Aranjuez*.

Do you play any other contemporary concertos?
I've played the Bennett, which I think is a very nice piece. I think it would work on the other side of the Henze recording, because it's for 13 instruments.

I've had a number of concertos written for me. I haven't premiered all of them. There's a deluge of new concertos now. People have recognized that there's a great need for a bigger variety of concertos, and I hope it continues. It is very important for us to get as much into the mainstream as possible.

How do you persuade orchestras to play something other than the Aranjuez concerto?

Courtesy Classical Guitar Magazine

Well, that's hard work. Sometimes you can ease them into it. When you have a conductor you've worked with regularly, you can sometimes get him to do the Castelnuovo-Tedesco, which is a popular sounding concerto, or the Villa-Lobos. Another way you can do it is to do two concertos, which guitarists are doing more and more. The *Aranjuez*, then the Bennett or something else more modern. The *Aranjuez* is not that long compared to some of the piano concertos. It's a short 20 minutes, so there is time to do more.

The other way is to work with venturesome conductors, which will not often be with the most highlighted big orchestra series but which is a great experience for a guitarist, to work with an ensemble and to give these pieces an airing.

The Henze piece is a very unusual ensemble, and it's sort of caught in between the size of a major orchestra and a small chamber group. I admire the fact that he wrote for these instruments even though it's probably going to limit the number of performances. With a major orchestra, it's going to be featuring nine or ten of their players and four or five specialists. And a chamber group will often have trouble in getting good players on viola d'amore or oboe d'amore who can play modern music. But composers must first write what they hear, and worry about the prospects later.

Sir Peter Maxwell-Davies said to me after the performance that the thing with this piece is to get a recording. I think he's absolutely right. It's a hard enough score to hear; we need to have a recording that's well prepared, to be a document, a reference point. (*Editor's note: David Tanenbaum later recorded this work for Harmonia Mundi, with Hans Werner Henze conducting the Ensemble Modern.*)

You gave a masterclass in the Purcell Room the day before the concert. What did you think of the students?
I was quite impressed with the level of the students. Three of them were, I guess, 17 or 18, finishing their high school studies, and one was just beginning at college level. I thought the playing was quite impressive. With the exception of the student who played the Brouwer piece, I thought there was a need for a little more flexibility and a little more range of dynamics.

In the States, do you notice any significant difference in quality between private teaching and institutional teaching?
That's a very hard one. I think with some more time under our belt, it will level off and there will be more uniformity. Right now there's a great diversity. You can have some very high level teaching privately, and in the universities you can find some pretty bad teaching. I like to think that with enough people and enough ideas going around, that we shall naturally weed out some of the lesser work.

The level continues to rise; young guitarists start at earlier ages, and the educational system is getting better and better — partly, I think, through the transference of ideas. I don't think there's any sort of system that is universal — yet! Perhaps there will be more educational systems as we go along, which people will either adhere to or react against, but that will be helpful, I think.

CC

Benjamin Verdery

Benjamin Verdery was in London to play in the South Bank Summer Music Festival. The director that year was John Williams, who had met Ben in Córdoba and invited him to play in London. Ben's presence in Spain was the outcome of a meeting with Paco Peña in New York. Thus Ben Verdery's first appearance in England was in the Queen Elizabeth Hall before an audience of about 1500 enthusiastic fans of John Williams. Not every guitarist makes his London debut in such heady circumstances, but Ben, something of an extrovert and given to intense enthusiasms, took it all in his stride.

He was invited some years later to the Classical Guitar Festival of Great Britain at West Dean, a large and sprawling millionaire's mansion in the heart of the West Sussex countryside, and it was there that we had our second interview. His work with the ensemble in that week's course was astonishing; some fairly humble amateur players found themselves playing quite extraordinary music — Ben's own Some Towns and Cities, for instance — with an enthusiasm and a precision they would scarcely have believed had you told them about it beforehand. Ben's particular brand of energy is very infectious. Leo Brouwer called him 'A fantastic creative mind in a young country', and you can see why.

To go back to that first appearance in London, Ben played Bach's 6th Cello Suite to a QEH audience that was still shuffling in noisily. Once seated, they applauded vigorously every time Ben paused between Bach's dances. It was enough to break the concentration of many a seasoned guitarist, but Ben did not seem to be aware of it.

Benjamin Verdery: In an odd way you don't really notice it. I was so excited to be playing — my adrenaline was up, of course — that I didn't take note. Towards the end of the Suite was the only time I was a little bit disturbed by the clapping. Because it breaks the flow. But basically it doesn't bother me. I've played in a number of different circumstances where a lot of things have happened, so really it wasn't anything absolutely extraordinary.

I will say that it was tremendously exciting to play Bach to a full house. And of course to be billed with John and Paco in the same concert was a tremendous honor. Overwhelming.

Have you opened a concert with the Bach before?
No. It occurred to me two days before the concert. Usually it's about third in the program, finishing the first half. But I love the music so much, and I thought, well, in a way it's fine for me. Perhaps for the audience it might have been a little much to start with a major piece, so grand. But given the situation, I think it was the best way to do it.

You know how these things happen. To have started with a shorter piece might have implied more of a solo concert, and I was really there only to do one piece. There was an idea that I might split it; play a little Bach and then something else. But we decided it was best to put one whole work on. A substantial work.

What sort of problems did you have to overcome when you transcribed the 6th Cello Suite?
My feeling about Bach and the guitar is that almost everything works. So I really don't give myself any great credit for having transcribed it. Bach is so easily transcribable on any instrument. Anthony Newman once said that Bach sounds great on tuned bathtubs! His music is so universal. I've heard a steel band playing the 3rd Brandenburg. It sounded unbelievably good.

The same applies to the guitar. Especially. Granted, the Cello Suite is a little thinner in texture, so that one would want to add more bass notes. The 6th Suite didn't have much added at all; It's quite sparse. I think I might have done a little more than I did, especially in movements like the Allemande. But I still like the idea of 'implied harmony', not always spelling out the harmony but leaving it implied, as Bach did. And I think that perhaps in order to make it work for the guitar — that is, with so much single-line playing — one should pick the tempi up just a little bit. Of course I listen to cellos playing it, but it's a different instrument. One should consider that it's a guitar, and that's one of the things I did consider in terms of tempi.

To go back to my original feeling, that almost any piece by Bach lends itself to the guitar. It doesn't take any great musical mind to do it. That's why I don't think I'll publish it. A player who's good enough to play that music will want to do his own arrangement anyway.

Some arrangements try to retain the feeling of a cello. A critic in The Times *said it was best to forget the original instrument. Would you agree?*
Yes, though not totally. I do think cellistically in certain spots, but I'm playing a guitar. Not a cello. Not a harpsichord. I probably approach the Suite more from the harpsichord point of view than that of a cello — you know, in the ornaments and things. We can learn, certainly, from listening to the cello. But I have six strings, not four.

After all, Bach must have been the first person to discover that his music worked on other instruments.
Absolutely! It's no secret, now, that you can play Bach on anything. And certainly on a guitar. Bach sounds particularly great on the guitar.

The best definition of a good transcription is that it doesn't sound like a transcription. It sounds like a guitar piece, a flute piece or whatever.

I've heard thousands of transcriptions where the playing is remarkable. It's great that it was done, but to me it sounds ultimately too difficult. It just doesn't sound natural enough. I've done that myself, especially with flute and guitar, because my wife (Rie Schmidt) is a flutist. I've been excited about a piece and had all the best intentions, but after playing it a few times I can see that it just doesn't make it. It's the same with arrangements. You don't really know until you've done it and played it through at tempo.

It's so exciting when you do a transcription that really works. A friend of mine, Arthur Levering, a very good arranger, did a transcription of Poulenc's *Mouvement Perpetuelle* for flute and guitar, and it's a gem. I think it'll stay in the flute and guitar repertoire for ever.

Gerald Garcia is another. I've just heard his arrangements of Chinese folk songs for guitar and violin — unbelievable! It's not an easy thing to do. I'm a beginner in that area. But it's a big thrill when it works out well.

Transcriptions have been done throughout musical history. Not just the Baroque era but right up to Ravel. We're stuck in a pure era just now: don't do this, and don't do that!

I imagine that one of the things you find attractive about John Williams is his readiness to have a go at almost anything that comes along — whether it works or not.
Absolutely! I really cannot applaud that enough. It's the true pioneering spirit. It's wonderful to see.

Would you say it represented a spreading outwards rather than a growing upwards?
No, I wouldn't agree with that. When he gets it right it's fantastic.

We're all spreading out in order to go up. The idea is to go up — or to go wherever. To broaden our own horizons in some way and to make music playable. Again, it's what you choose to do. It's what he chooses to do, and if you don't like it you don't come to the concert.

In an earlier interview you talked about 'stretching' the instrument. How many ways are there in which that can be done? Transcription is obviously one...
Doing what John Williams and Peter Hurford did with the organ is another. Playing with a variety of different instruments, and in different contexts. Stretching the instrument in terms of new music; having composers write for you whom you respect, good composers who have written for other instruments, not just the guitar, and who have a real knowledge of how all instruments work. That's what I mean.

It's really up to the individual. What I love about the world is that there are so many diverse people in it. Everybody does something different. And that's what I love about the guitar. It's an instrument where there are so many different experts in so many different fields. There's no other instrument like that. Flamenco guitar, classical guitar, blues guitar, rock guitar, country, flat-picking, bluegrass — it's incredible! And you'll find real virtuosi in all of those fields.

In addition to your many and varied activities as performer and teacher, you are the Artistic Director of the D'Addario Foundation for the Performing Arts. Will you, briefly, say something about the Foundation's work?

Right now it's just a concert series, in San Francisco and New York. Hopefully we'll perhaps get another city in there. Thus far it's been guitar concerts with different types of artists. We hope to broaden that by bringing in even more. This year I was really enthused with Paco Peña's festival in Córdoba. I've played there twice — and that's another great honor. Paco has an incredibly broad mind, in his musical tastes and in the guitar. This year (1984) he had a number of different types of guitar playing there, like Eduardo Falú, the great Argentinian folk singer, and the group Inti Illimani. I'm not all that familiar with that kind of music, so I would like to see that happening in our series as well.

We try to present a spectrum of different kinds of guitarist. In New York there are so many guitarists of wonderful playing ability, and we do try to put on one or two local artists a year. It's terribly exciting to be involved with it. And it gives a lot of guitarists an opportunity to play in New York. Like London, it's difficult to put on a concert there — and very expensive.

This year we have a really exciting series. Paco Peña, of course. The Assad Brothers — an incredible guitar duo. David Leisner is going to play, a great American guitarist. Each year we like to do a debut, and this year we decided to present the winner of the Toronto guitar competition.

Touching on attitudes and postures for the moment, your style is a very relaxed one...

I did study Alexander Technique. Not long enough! It was absolutely wonderful, the whole business of neck-free. I studied because my playing was tense, so tense that I could barely play. This is what usually happens when we need a change in our life; we get to the bottom before we can pick ourselves up again.

This teacher introduced me to the guitar cushion, which I really love. Aesthetically it doesn't look like much, but it sure feels great to have both feet on the ground. It instantly puts your back straight. Though of course I do look to my left.

For guitarists, tension is the number one problem. I'm continually aware of that. Some people are really so relaxed, it's incredible. John Williams, for instance; I've never seen anyone so relaxed. I don't know if it's natural or what, but it certainly seems natural.

There was a time when I had to make a conscious effort to keep my back straight and to breathe well. I think we forget how to breathe when we're holding a guitar. The guitar cushion has helped. And Alexander Technique. A terrific amount of tension is created from the neck and shoulders area. Even when we sit at a table. I'll be sitting and talking to someone. And all of a sudden I'll let down my shoulders, which have been up and tense. I can't believe that all day long I've been carrying around this tension.

And that applies to the instrument. You've got to realize that it's a very physical activity when you pick up an instrument. If you don't approach it in a delicate way you can strain yourself. That's why we have people with tendinitis and backaches. So it can't but help to improve your playing and make you realize how little effort is needed to play the guitar. I'm continuously aware that I barely have to press down — if it's a good instrument, not one with the strings ten feet off the fingerboard. You don't have to press down so hard. And you realize that you're not going to get a lot of extra volume by digging down into the strings. All that has to do with an attitude of posture. I feel very strongly about it. I don't think teachers talk about it enough.

You rest the instrument on the seat — as Sor is said to have rested it on the table.

I like to do it; it seems sort of natural. And when you have a wooden chair, it's stupendous — because it picks up the vibrations. But it's comfortable that way. And I'm particularly keen on having both feet on the ground.

Obviously the footstool has worked for thousands of great players. For me, it didn't seem so great. And I can use the knee cushion in trains and planes — the footstool doesn't make a very good pillow!

All we have to realize, especially in teaching, is that everybody has a different set of hands. My theory has always been 'a right ball park', as we say in America, meaning that if you're in the ball park you're basically in the right direction. The best way to approach the instrument is, what is natural for that person? What feels correct, if you can use such a word — since it's not very natural to play an instrument to begin with. You can work from there. And then everybody's going to come up with their own ideas. There are a million different ways of looking at it. But you start off with basic principles and work from those, being very sensitive to the fact that every person is different.

Do you enjoy teaching?
I love teaching. I'm teaching ensemble at Manhattan guitar and ensemble, chamber music. It's a lot of fun. Guitar duos, guitar and flute, whatever. Also the State University of New York at Purchase, which is where I went to school. And Queen's. So it sounds impressive, but I actually just have two from here, four from there — you know. I don't actually go to each college. In fact one of my students saw me at a concert and said 'I didn't know you wore shoes' — because I always teach in bare feet. But I really do love to teach.

Will you say something about your guitar and flute duo with your wife, Rie Schmidt?
We've just finished a recording, which should be out soon. French music, mostly transcriptions. We're really excited about that. I hope to finish a recording of a C. P. E. Bach concerto I arranged. He wrote the same concerto for flute, cello and harpsichord. So I stole a bit from this, a little from that, and I think it makes a really neat guitar concerto. It sounds to me as a guitar concerto should sound.

I haven't decided what other concerto I'm going to put on the recording. Some baroque concerto. With the Bach recording already issued, I originally had the idea of a concerto on one side and solo guitar on the other, but the company wasn't so pleased about that; they wanted just the solos.

I feel very lucky that I've had the opportunity to do so much performing. Each time you play you learn something new. Each concert for me has been a learning experience — after which you go home and think about what really went on. If you're aware, you should be able to remember.

I still feel young in concert experience. I feel it's something you can only improve at by doing it a million times and getting more relaxed — so that you can do in public what you can do so well in your own living room.

It's quite serious to get up and play with other musi-

Photo by Gary Wheeler

cians. Of course you respect them musically, but it really is great when you get along. If you don't have a wonderful rapport, it shows in the music. So it's great to play music with my wife — and rehearsal times are ideal. We've really grown as a duo. She's taught me a tremendous amount — she's a better musician than I am. She has an active life in New York. She does a lot of freelance work. She also has a flute quartet, which is a wild sound. Wild! A lot of the pieces sound like the Wizard of Oz. She also plays solo recitals, and is active in a couple of chamber music groups. We're both involved in a contemporary music group, which gives me a chance to play chamber music.

So we can't always travel together. It's difficult, that aspect of being a musician. It's wonderful to play everywhere, but you can get lonely. I think everybody does. It's a funny thing to be the centre of attention for one evening among very nice people — yet you're so lonely. You're having a great time, but.... The funny thing is, when you leave them, you're always sad because you've made really nice friends. You know you're not going to see them again for some time, maybe never again. So both parties become very attentive to each other and don't take each other for granted for a minute. You learn a tremendous amount about that person. It's fascinating. Especially when you get to see how different countries work.

I would love to go to Japan. Especially because my wife is half-Japanese. I have a tremendous interest in Eastern religion and art. And I'd love to go to China. And Africa — but I don't know most of Europe yet.

I'm crazy about England, believe it or not. I guess I'm something of an Anglophile, though I've only been to London. Today I bought the History of England, which I plan to read so that when I come back in March I can go to Westminster Abbey and I'll know something. But there's something about this country I'm crazy about. But I'm also crazy about every place I've ever been. I just recently fell in love with Spain. Last year, in Spain with Paco. I got to see Córdoba and Sevilla and Cadiz — all those places that Albéniz wrote about. And I didn't particularly like Spanish music on the guitar. It was Bach and contemporary music for me, but when I went to Spain and heard Paco and all these people playing.... Guitars — they grow on trees! Every street you go down....

I'm crazy about America too. This year I got the opportunity to travel to little towns there. You think, oh, I'm going to Syllacauga, Alabama — who knows where that is? Well, it was the greatest thing in my life. I played outside on someone's porch, which was like a ranch — like in one of those American films like *Bonanza*, with horses and cattle. And they invited all the local townspeople. We're talking about people who'd probably never heard a classical guitar, not to mention classical music. They brought a 'cover supper' — everybody brings a plate. So you had these huge tables, with all this home-made food, with about 150 people. It was just incredible to be there.

In these little pockets of America, these little states with different mentalities and ideas, every audience is important. Of course, London has that — what New York means to a Londoner, London means to me. But I realized that you have to play your best everywhere, whether it's for schoolchildren at 8 o'clock in the morning or the Queen Elizabeth Hall at 7.45 in the evening. You really have to, as a communicator. People know it if you don't prepare well. You're not doing your job.

Concert musicians sometimes forget. You travel so much, you walk onto the stage, you play your concert, and everybody says how great you are, how well you played — hopefully, that's what happens. And then you leave. Maybe you spend the night at somebody's house. But you forget that people put that concert on; you forget the work it took. Going to a relatively small town like Syllacauga, I saw how people put themselves out. It's only because people love music that they bring you there. You know what I mean? We take

it for granted that there's a hall, that there are people who run the place, put out the publicity and generally put a lot of time into it. I think it's important for the artist to realize that. It gives you more of a sense of responsibility.

Would this sense of responsibility lead you to tailor a program to suit a particular audience?
That can be a very tricky point. In a case like Syllacauga, I think it was important to play tuneful pieces that were close to what they were familiar with. You've got to draw your audience in. The way we were talking earlier, about perhaps opening with a shorter piece before playing the Bach — it's the same thing. You have to get people accustomed to the sound.

In that way you do have to tailor, but when it's a concert series and I'm asked to play, I can say pretty safely that I've never played anything I didn't really love, whether it was contemporary or not. And I usually play two contemporary pieces in every program. Now I realize there are a lot of mediocre contemporary pieces. The main point is to love the music — that's the bottom line.

I get a kick out of playing music by my friends. I'd much rather play a Grade B piece by a friend than a Grade A piece from the 19th century. Again, when it comes to a concert series I think it's important to play what you really feel. The number of times I've been told 'Don't play any contemporary music'! And sometimes I've been told 'Don't play any Bach'.

People sometimes forget about Bach. For me, listening to Bach is not easy. It's my favorite music, but I can't say I've got it the first time I hear a fugue. I'm still hearing voices left and right from the fugue from the *Prelude, Fugue and Allegro*. Each time I hear it I hear something I didn't hear before. We assume that because it's Bach or old that it's immediately accessible. It's just as hard to listen to as a lot of contemporary music.

How would you categorize yourself? What do you call yourself?
I don't know. What *do* I call myself? A musician who plays the guitar. A musician who has chosen the guitar as his mode of expression.

I feel tremendously lucky to be able to play even remotely well. I'm always unbelievably amazed when I watch anyone play an instrument. I don't know how they do it. So I feel really lucky to be able to do it and actually make a living from it. I wake up every morning and say, 'Don't take this away from me'.

CC

JOHN WILLIAMS

My most vivid memory of John Williams is a rehearsal in the BBC studios, Maida Vale. Leo Brouwer was there to conduct a recording of his Concierto de Toronto, with John Williams as the soloist. It was a memorable occasion, with John at his best and the Langham Orchestra responding magnificently to Leo's dynamic direction. An account of it appears in Classical Guitar Vol.7 No.4, but for the purposes of this book I prefer to go back to an earlier occasion, when CG's then reviews editor Chris Kilvington and I interviewed John Williams in his house in North London. The year was 1987, around the time when a heavier emphasis was beginning to be placed on ensemble guitar music in Britain's music schools, with two of which John Williams has close connections: The Royal College of Music, London, and The Royal Northern College of Music, Manchester. He had been to the RCM to see guitar professor Charles Ramirez and vice-director Ian Horsburgh, and happened to remark in passing that he would be happy to come back 'as an old student and past teacher'. And that is exactly what he did, initiating a series of regular visits in order to encourage participation in chamber music.

Invited to comment on this initiative, John immediately launched into an attack — a fully justified one, as every thoughtful observer knows — on the general sightreading ability of guitarists.

CC

John Williams: Sooner or later, guitarists have to face the fact that, note for note, the guitar is no more difficult than a wind instrument or a stringed instrument. Compared to other instrumentalists, 99 per cent of guitarists on that basis are appalling sightreaders, appalling ensemble players, and have bad ears in terms of phrasing. That for me is an uncomfortable truth. We have a lovely instrument and some of us play it very beautifully, etcetera, but those are the facts. An advanced, graduated guitar student phrasing a simple classical theme is a joke compared to a fiddler or a flautist. And there's no reasonable excuse for it.

It's an embarrassing truth, and unless something's done in terms of education it's going to go on getting worse. Ironically, we're entrenching the problem by getting the guitar more and more established in colleges; we're making the gulf even more painfully obvious. We're asking more and more favors of the musical establishment, people who love the guitar. I'm not being patronizing about this, they genuinely love it, and that's why it's there. And the more allowances they feel they have to make for bad musicianship amongst the guitarists, the worse it's going to get.

Chris Kilvington: *Would you agree that people have become very preoccupied with their solo careers? There are far too many excellent and gifted young players around anyway, not all of whom can make it. So perhaps it's either an alternative way of looking at things for them, or the possibility of a career in ensemble.*

JW: Ultimately the thing's going to be changed when the same ethic that applies to primary school and recorder classes is adapted to the guitar, so that as young guitarists go up the educational scale, they don't

lose touch in secondary school with the ensemble. Whereas the wind players and the strings go in to Saturday morning orchestra, the guitar players start losing out. So at all levels it's got to see some change.

It's no good crying over spilt milk, but we can improve. We can improve it even if we're 50-year-old amateurs. Instead of sweating your guts out trying to play a Villa-Lobos prelude that's too difficult, just get a couple of friends and sit down with some ensemble music.

The other big area is repertoire. Guitarists are imprisoned by thinking about whose edition they are going to buy, where's the fingering going to be, and where can they get it. I approached Tony Rooley about four years ago, before going to Spain, and asked him if there was any old lute music that would be suitable for ensemble playing — because I wanted to introduce it into Spain. And he said, 'Well, any of it — all of that old consort music, whether it's broken consorts, viols, recorders, wind, mixed wind or whether it's unspecified.' All that stuff was pretty makeshift, anyway — the Praetorius collection, for instance. Well, he recommended Anthony Holborne, various galliards and things like that. Which is fantastic.

I went into Peters' to get the parts of Haydn's 'Bird' Quartet (Op. 33 No. 3), which I wanted to give to students, and in just two minutes I found two little volumes of old things in five and six parts. I told the college students to try to get into the habit, when they're in a music shop, instead of going to the guitar shelf and looking there, of casting a glance along the old music shelf — which is what I did yesterday, picking up this and that. You can see straight away: it has nice simple lines. What fun! Suppose you're going to a party at the weekend — you don't want to have to practice duets for an hour every day beforehand in order to make it presentable. Go and buy something and sightread it — which is what quartet players do. At the College, we have the Haydn quartets, everything up to Op. 33. We have trios, quartets and quintets etc. It's wonderful. You get so much back from the students. It's new to them.

CK: *Do you find that their musicianship in ensemble is weak until you give them some guidance — no matter how good they may be as soloists?*
Absolutely. The musicianship doesn't exist. There are different cross-sections in different collections of students, but certainly at both the London and the Northern Colleges, I'd say there would have been one or two players at most in a whole guitar department. One or two were aware of it at the summer course in Spain, but couldn't do it very well. Hardly one of them knows how to nod his head or count in. It is appalling, but it is true. We know the guitar is difficult, but these things are simple; they can be taught.

CK: *Will you eventually try to incorporate other instruments into this scheme?*
I think they will do that themselves. It follows on.

Photo by Julian Nieman

There's no reason why you shouldn't have two guitars, two flutes and one fiddle, for example. You get into the problem of volume and difficult blending with wind instruments and, say, viola and cello, and you really can't hear the guitar very well. The guitar's going to have to bash out the notes, and then you get a percussive sound.

The first thing is to get them to do the kind of thing that makes clear the gap between the dynamics in ensemble and the blending of sound that we expect in the guitar, i.e. take three parts that you could easily play on one guitar but which great quartet players would spend five or ten minutes on, blending their sound and dynamics. To play most of the music, unless you get to very late Mozart or Haydn, where you get rather difficult fiddling parts, is technically, nothing for a quartet player. Blending a sound like a C and an open E is something that we accept as a part of guitar technique, but a quartet will take time off for 30 seconds just to make sure their bowing's right. But we never give it a moment's thought. Then you've got the bass line....

The guitar's got to get out of the frame of mind of thinking, 'Why should I do that when I can do it on one guitar?'

CK: *How have the guitarists you've met responded to this kind of work?*
They respond absolutely immediately. It's a bit like a self-evident truth: you point out something that we're all aware of, and everybody says 'Of course. We've been trying to forget it!'.

I've had the odd argument on the basis that it is just a little bit more difficult on the guitar to coordinate the two hands. You've got so many different positions in which to finger the notes, therefore there's more excuse for guitarists finding it more difficult. Within the guitar repertoire, that's true, because the guitar repertoire has been written by various guitarists who have exploited the technique. But we're now talking about note for note, single notes.

With kids, again, I don't know exactly what the different courses are, or the different ways it's being done. But, given the traditional way — as when I started — of going through open strings, scales, and on to easy Aguado and Sor, my feeling now would be that actually that is getting on to so-called easy pieces too soon.

CK: *That kind of thing is done at the cost of develop-ing phrasing and upper fingerboard knowledge. You tend to learn the notes down at the other end, doing basic chords and simple studies. The upper finger-board isn't used in a cantabile fashion.*
That's what I would have thought. It seems to me there must be scope for altering the emphasis of that early teaching, even for kids, so that it takes account of that more.

What about specifically grouping kids together, under direction, at an earlier age than they might have done? So that after, say, four, five or six lessons, where they might start to play a little easy solo piece, they instead play a little ensemble piece? Because that's what happens on recorders in primary schools. They do solos later on, but basically it's an ensemble instrument.

The music is there. You can actually play the recorder repertoire. The big block in changing the curriculum syllabus has always been based on needing guitar editions of it. But it's not necessary, because it's all there: you just use recorder parts, any early music, Haydn quartets, etcetera.

CK: *Some of the people I come across are physically incapable of playing the instrument. Do you feel there's a cut-off point somewhere? How far does egalitarianism go?*
On the one hand, it's a difficult question to answer. On the other hand, related to ensemble playing in general, in its widest application and at all levels, it's an easy question to answer — if you dismiss the false expecta-tions of playing solo pieces which are too difficult. We're all struggling with music which most of the time is relatively more difficult for all of us, compared to what the equivalent stuff would be on another instrument.

It doesn't operate on other instruments. 50 per cent of the time, when you're playing a Beethoven or Mozart sonata, or even large chunks of Schubert and Chopin on the piano, they're actually not that difficult to play. The whole piece may be, but you're talking about half of it, whereas on the guitar you're struggling 95 per cent of the time.

Of course that goes all the way down the scale to amateurs — and, coming back to your point, to people who are not physically cut out owing to their hand shape or fingernails or whatever. It's tragically wrong, the pressure that is put on them, the expectations that they will be able to achieve something of their own.

But in its own way that also applies to a lot of amateur string and woodwind players if they had to play solo. It doesn't apply when they join their mates at the weekend and say 'Let's have a quartet evening'. People who perhaps were music students and then later in life have become, say, doctors or accountants but still love music — they don't play very well, but they can still read through a little quartet the first Wednesday in every month. That is the thing. It dispels immediately and finally that pressure and that expectation. People would love it — if they knew.

With minimal guidance, people can go and get a little ensemble and read through music with a few friends. And that's really what it's all about. What else is music about? It's not about breeding out-of-work solo musicians.

Colin Cooper: *Would you say that ensemble experi-ence improves solo performance?*
That's why I like it in the curriculum at college level. In time it will affect attitudes to other things, but it in no way means a sudden change or alteration in existing curricula or even in existing playing. Hopefully the addition of the thing will act as an unconscious, good influence on the solo playing. It certainly can't hurt it.

CC: *Can you discount the arguments that, playing in ensemble, we tend to lose the color range of the guitar? And that playing transcribed music is some-how not quite the thing — isn't all this irrelevant?*
The color range of the guitar that is supposed to be retained or protected by the status quo is a very artifi-cial one. It's not flexible, as with a string or a wind player. It's a thing of guitar 'sweetness' or harpsichord ponticello; it's not based on a constantly changing melodic color, though obviously one or two players do it instinctively. In terms of the way most students play, it's not. Whereas string players, as soon as they start to get a proficient technique, start to feel it in their bow pressure. We don't have anything like that.

Depending on the psychology of the individual, I think that most people — not all — would find that they look back on those occasions when they've played ensemble music. I know, speaking for myself — and I know that Julian feels the same when we're playing duets or when he's playing with other people — that there is an added dimension which is nothing to do with the achievement of performing on the stage. You do actually get enjoyment from hearing other people play at the same time. You're almost like a listener, because you're participating in something that someone else is doing. I think there's no end to the possibilities.

I don't want to interfere with other people's curriculum, but I think it would be good if Manchester (The Royal Northern College) and London (The Royal College) have got it going by next September. If there is ensemble curriculum every week in both colleges, it would be a valuable precedent. Everyone would have to do it.

CK: *Quite apart from what the students are going to get out of it, which is very considerable, what are you going to get out of it?*
It's very difficult to work out what you enjoy in a job, because your own enjoyment is what propagates the thing in the first place.

It's very exciting. Simple though it is, you get a quartet of students — OK, we've heard a guitar quartet before, playing special music, but suddenly you think of a particular Haydn quartet. I don't know what suddenly made me first think of it. I'd heard it, and I had a score, I think, of the 'Bird', Opus 33 No. 3, and I just happened to look at it, and I thought, well, not only can they do all the consort music and all that, but if they want something more challenging they can do this quartet. Now the excitement when the quartet in Córdoba did this — ! Stefano Cardi was the best player that year, so he played the first fiddle part, which is a bit more difficult than the others. But the excitement of hearing these four players! Within ten days they'd prepared, for argument's sake, all the quartet. In fact they did half the first movement, including the exposition and half the development; they did all of the scherzo, all of the slow movement except the recap in a slightly different key, and they did all the last movement — in ten days! Hearing that was really quite something.

'The Bird' is not the only one; most of the quartets up to Op. 33 go. But 'The Bird' is a lovely quartet musically. We're so used to Sor and Giuliani, who are lovely at their best, and every now and then you get a nice sort of neo-Beethoven diminished progression or Neapolitan sixth or something, and you think, 'That's really nice'. But it's not like Haydn. .

CK: *A Grade three player ought to be able to cope with the viola part. It would be boring for a good player, perhaps, but amateur players have always been glad of those quartets — for the sheer pleasure of being able to do them.*
Exactly. For a lot of the time, the viola player and second fiddle of, say, the Amadeus or the Gabrieli Quartets are playing very boring parts. So it's a bit much for guitarist to start complaining that those parts are boring

CC: *The whole is a good piece of music. Guitarists have to learn how to cope with seemingly boring parts of the whole, and to make them interesting — to themselves as well as to everybody else. It's a change of mental attitude as much as anything else. To a true artist, two bars' rest can be creative.*
Take the modulation I mentioned earlier in the Haydn quartet; as I was saying, you get to that point, and you might have been playing viola, a C and an A in each bar, but you're part of the whole development of the piece, and when you get to this point, it's only one little modulation. But it's such a good one.

CK: *Is there any possibility of your working with a formal quartet for a while?*
Not really, no. First of all, I don't think it's relevant at this stage. And without very close examination of the different pieces, I'm not sure that any of the Haydn and the Mozart quartets would actually justify an actual professional performance. In other words, it's needed as an exercise — a perfect exercise.

That having been said, my instinct is that actually there must be, at a quick glance, three or four of the complete Haydn quartets that would fully justify a guitar quartet performance at a concert. That's only a quick judgment, but I certainly think it's valuable material. And of course a lot of the early consort music.

There are some practical difficulties when you come to the Haydn quartets. First of all, the range of the fiddle where it goes too high: you often have to juggle with the parts for them to fit together successfully. And there's the viola clef, which I don't think people can be expected to have to sightread. And there's the cello part, not because of the bass clef — which everybody ought to be able to read anyway — but where it goes down to C. On these rare occasions you have to put the odd note or two, or even short passage, up an octave. The viola part is easy to write out. It's not like writing out guitar music, where you've got hundreds of notes in each bar. You can write out a whole movement of the viola clef in half an hour, so there's no impediment. So the practical problems are small: the viola clef, the low C in the cello and the odd fiddle parts.

But it is communication and enjoyment We can't continually have the object of all music education being to produce the magic number of solo people who are going to earn a living. That's a crazy approach.

CK: *Every parent with a musical child is faced with a dilemma: whether to apply pressure and so risk losing the child's willingness to work, or whether to let things take their course, with the possibility of equally dire results. How was persuasion applied in your own case?*
I was persuaded quite heavily into practice, being told that I was good, and that it was natural that I should do it. It was sort of assumed that was what I would do, and therefore I should practise. And I used to say, when I was about 20, I would have liked to have *decided* to do it. But looking back, all I can say is, 'Thank God I was pushed into it!' I can't imagine anything better.

But it's a difficult area. There are very, very general guidelines, but there's no rule. You can take a famous violinist who might have been forced into playing scales by his father with a whip over him from the age of two — and there have been a couple of examples of that — and they've turned out to be fantastic fiddlers, but their lives might be an absolute misery in terms of their internal existence. So who's going to make the judgment as to whether it was right or not? I could say, with patronizing hindsight, 'Well, you know, my father never gave me any choice — that's what I was going to be'. And then, immodestly and honestly, I'd have to look back and say 'Actually, yes, he was right, and I'm very glad he did push me into it.' But I couldn't go from that to saying that every child whose parents thinks that he or she is talented should be pushed into it.

CK: *You can only say, in retrospect, that in your case it worked out?*
That's it.

CC: *On the other hand, within the limits of the guitar, you've never been without another option, and your career has gone off in quite different directions from time to time. You aren't confined in the conventional mould of the classical performer, are you?*
No. But that's luck again. It's predisposition; something in my personality. Musically, I've grown up in London, having done the preliminary musical training at college. And I've done a hell of a lot with other musicians, limited though the guitar repertoire is. In

the 60s I did concerts with the singer Wilfred Brown for ten years, which included for a couple of years a religious overseas radio program, where I was doing about five arrangements of songs a week. And playing the very small chamber music repertoire for guitar over and over again with a group called Musica da Camera, and then with the Melos Ensemble, doing new music. I rather took to all that, and I sort of carried on. I still do the odd concerts with the Sinfonietta, even though Tim Walker does most of them. So the different directions for me have come through these situations, and it applies in exactly the same way to anything so-called 'commercial'.

It seems strange to say so, but it's never, ever, been self-conscious or even conscious. Then again, looking back, I think it might have been obvious what I was doing.

CC: *But it was the sort of channelling that could have resulted in a solo career in which you spent your whole existence jetting around and playing the Aranjuez in every city in the world.*
It's also connected very deeply with one's ordinary, social private life. I've been married twice and I've split up twice. I have a daughter who's grown up and a son who's growing up, so I don't want to be away for six or nine months of the year, playing the *Aranjuez* or whatever. I won't go away for more than one three-week trip in a year. I mean, a few days, ten days, a week here, a week there, is OK, but I don't want to do too much. So if you like, it's an added excuse to keep me disciplined!

I don't know what I would have done if I'd been on another instrument. If instead of just *Aranjuez*, I'd had a repertoire of 20 concertos for another instrument — would it have been different? Would I have been more tempted? Would I have been a different person? If—if—if —

CC: *Did the guitar as an instrument give you a little more freedom in that respect?*
Absolutely! That's the luck. But certainly, I am and have always, to my recollection, been able to take responsibility for myself, so if I complain that I've been away too long in the year, well, that's my fault because I've not foreseen it enough. There's been no financial need. There's not many of us on the guitar in that position. And the things I've done happen to be around London, because I've been here for a combination of musical and personal, private and social reasons.

You can't explain yourself all the time either. I had a letter asking me to go Esztergom, but it's August. August is school holidays for kids, and I sort of want to be around. For years and years I never played a single date between July the 20th and September the 15th, when my daughter had her school holidays. We always used to rent a place in France and have lots of friends to stay — you know, trying to live the sort of routine that most people with families do, having school holidays and weekends.

And I wouldn't play at weekends. You're either free or you're not, and that's my way of looking at things.

CK: *Are you interested in any of the East European music that's coming out? Koshkin and Rak, for example?*
I heard *The Prince's Toys* on Radio 3 (*by Nikita Koshkin. John Williams later took the same composer's Usher Waltz into his repertory — Ed.*). It's quite nice, but I've heard lots of things that I like a lot. I quite see myself getting music for the odd occasion, but I can't see myself sweating and practising every day to learn something by memory. It's this gulf between performance and listening; I'm quite happy to listen to someone else playing it without feeling it's incumbent on me to necessarily play it myself.

It's purely personal. I get on to music that interests me particularly. I'm not saying it's better or worse, only that it interests me, involves me. Paul Hart's piece with NYJO (National Youth Jazz Orchestra) is, I think, a wonderful piece; it gives me so much musical and playing satisfaction. NYJO is 40 strong, and I use an amplified Takamine live, but my Smallman on the recording. It was so lovely; it's got everything in it that music is supposed to have.

Paul Hart has written three other little pieces, which are wonderful. One of them's a peach, with just a piano and synth and guitar. Another is piano and guitar, and the other one is just synths with a tiny bit of guitar.

It's very difficult to explain in terms of guitar repertoire what appeals to me musically. I find it very difficult to differentiate between what I like playing and what I like listening to, and one doesn't necessarily involve the other. I might like listening to other guitarists playing. Out of curiosity and out of enjoyment, I'll like hearing them play a new piece — without the slightest urge to learn it or play it myself.

Photo by Julian Niemahl / Courtesy Sony Classics

I've commissioned Steve Gray to write a concerto for me. Steve is the keyboard player in Sky; he's a wonderful musician and, unlike all the guitar concerto composers, he's a real, with a capital R, orchestrator.

CC: *To go back to teaching for a moment — is it all ensemble now, or do you find time to teach solo?*
For the last two or three years I haven't taught solo at all. I'm sick of sitting down in front of people and playing, say, *Asturias*. There are so many ways of playing Asturias . . .

CK: *Do people come along with preconceived ideas of what you might expect and how they ought to do it?*
No, I think they come along expecting directions as to how to play it like I play it! Sometimes you get misunderstandings, because I'm loath to direct people in that way. It is important, but it's ceased to have the importance that the ensemble thing has for me.

It's no good mixing it. In one of these Córdoba courses I was doing both. People were putting up with the ensemble thing so that they could get a chance to play. I thought, no, there's only one answer to this — no solo tuition.

Again, it's that business about regular solo teaching. Instead of a reason, or investigating their own ability to teach themselves and develop their own personality, it becomes a crutch: 'Give me the formula, and I'll play it like you' — that's what it amounts to.

The last couple of times I've done solo teaching, I took to saying: 'Well, look, if you want to know my attitude to this course, whether it's ten days or two weeks, the best thing I'd be able to hear from anyone would be that at the end of the course they never want to, or need to, come anywhere near me again.'

I've found with a few people with whom I've maintained connections at most courses that they know exactly what it is they've wanted or been able to take from me. Stefano Cardi, for example, was fantastic at understanding this. In the end the penny drops; the brightest ones know how to teach themselves.

CK: *We mentioned earlier the comparative shortage of English students at overseas guitar courses, and your course at Córdoba is apparently no exception. Is this something to do with the fact that we're an island race?*
It's to do with all the arts. We're still elitist here. It seems extraordinary that there seems to be such a big gap in attitudes and abilities at these courses. Belgians, Dutch and French also turn up. Whether there's a historical reason for this I don't know, but they turn up and understand. There was an Italian trio in the first year, and they had such flair. Is it that the English students don't travel so well?

CK: *Do you think we're a complacent race?*
I think, generally, yes; and as a result the English guitar scene is behind now, overall. In my observations — and unexpectedly so — behind America as well. America used to be the great lagger. In my younger time, in the 50s and 60s, America really was behind everyone. We always used to wonder, in amazement, how a country with so many facilities and a population of a couple of hundred million could have such an appallingly bad standard. I think the reason was that the only ones pushed into classical guitar were from well-off middle-class families who thought that by buying their kids a Ramírez and sending them to a Segovia 'workshop' in Spain, it would 'buy' them culture and a musical career.

It's just not the case at all now. I think that at last the true wealth of America's cultural and racial diversity is teaching us all a lesson. On all levels, there's a lot of guitar activity all over the place, and of a very good standard. I did pick that up when I was there. The teaching organization in, for example, Dallas is a model. The guitar society there has a full-time paid director who organizes teaching, senior citizens, entertainment, playing at schools, all done by the society. In England, I just wonder.

England overall, musically and educationally as far as audiences, numbers of orchestras and numbers of other practicing musicians — all that outcome of post-second world war egalitarian secondary education and all that — is still musically ahead of everybody else in the western world. With that basis, why is it that the guitar standard, as I see it, is so much lower in musical and technical attitude than in most continental countries?

We have 14 or 15 orchestras in London. Paris doesn't have 14 or 15 orchestras. New York doesn't have 14 or 15 orchestras and the audiences that we have in London — quite apart from the orchestras in the other cities, of a terrific standard: Birmingham, and so on. I don't understand how this terrific musicality is not reflected in the guitar standard.

CC/CK

110

ZAGREB GUITAR TRIO

Put three virtuoso guitarists together. Not any three virtuosos, but three who happen to be friends. Two of them studied with the third, who can also turn his hand to the double-bass, which he plays with equal proficiency. Thus the Zagreb Guitar Trio began with two considerable advantages: they had a flexibility rare in guitar ensembles; and they knew one another's playing intimately.

The Trio (Darko Petrinjak, Istvan Römer, Goran Listes) built shrewdly on those advantages, soon acquiring a solid and wide-ranging repertoire and the ability to work on it without having to spend valuable time on turning three soloists into a precision ensemble — they were that from the beginning.

We met in London. The Trio had just given an outstanding concert at the Artworkers Guild's handsome premises in Queen's Square. The event had been arranged by Robert Spencer, who had taught Darko Petrinjak the lute at the Royal Academy of Music. Robert was himself a remarkable musician: a guitarist, a lutenist, a founder member of the Julian Bream Ensemble, a collector, a lecturer who could discourse brilliantly about Dowland while playing the illustrations himself, above all an enthusiast whose very presence made you glad to be working in and for music.

I felt the same about the Zagreb Guitar Trio. Their technical brilliance, their perfect timing, their total togetherness combine to give them complete freedom to make music, which they do with a unique combination of zest and musical penetration.

Photo by Jens Peter Bark

The Zagreb Guitar Trio met at the Zagreb Music Academy, where Istvan Römer and Goran Listes were students in Darko Petrinjak's class.

'We enjoy each other's company very much,' said Darko Petrinjak, 'so the guitar trio came as a consequence of that, instead of the other way around. There would be no point in changing members.'

There is no leader. When a new work comes up, they draw lots to settle the division of labor — quite literally, out of a hat. It is an Italian carabiniere's hat, with three corners. It ensures that no one member of the ensemble regularly gets an unfairly rewarding part to play, or, conversely, is landed with excessively boring parts. Not that accompanying parts are necessarily boring; but the Trio believe that typecasting is something to be avoided.

It helps that requintos and basses are not used in the Zagreb Guitar Trio. Three standard guitars are more than good enough — although Darko Petrinjak, a double-bass player of virtuosity, has found a number of works for that instrument and two guitars that provide additional interest and variety.

Each of the three members of the Trio is a soloist in his own right. They teamed up in 1984. It would have been earlier, but Istvan Römer had health problems; first a tumor on a finger, and later a problem with eyesight, both necessitating surgery. The tumor was a worry, with possible amputation looming up. 'Is music so important for you, my boy?' the surgeon asked. Istvan began to think in terms of the trumpet, needing only three fingers on one hand, but fortunately things turned out well and he was soon fully restored to his maximum ability — and a pretty good ability that is, as various competition successes prove. Three months after the operation, he won first prize at Mettmann. Later, both eyes had to be operated on in order to save his sight. It was a depressing time, but it had the advantage, he says cheerfully, of keeping him out of the army.

Solo playing takes up most of their time. Darko Petrinjak, born in 1954, is a lutenist as well as a guitarist and double-bass player. He took his post-graduate studies in guitar under Hector Quine at the Royal Academy of Music, and lute under Robert Spencer. At the RAM he was awarded the Julian Bream Prize and recital diplomas (the highest award for a performer) for both guitar and lute. For three years he taught guitar at the Birmingham School of Music, and since 1981 he has been Professor of Guitar at the Zagreb Music Academy. He played in the London/Zagreb Consort with Robert Spencer, and also plays chamber music with double-bass. He has shared concerts with the violinist Yfrah Neaman. His third solo record was issued around the time of our meeting, with music by Biberian, Blake Watkins, Koshkin and Barrios. He composes, too, and has written or ar-ranged about a hundred compositions for guitar trio, two guitars and double-bass, guitar and voice, guitar and violin, guitar and cello, and solo guitar. His recordings include solos, duets with a mezzo-soprano, a duo with cello, and of course those with the Zagreb Guitar Trio.

Goran Listes, born 1961, is married to an Italian and lives in Rome. As well as studying at Zagreb with Petrinjak, he studied at the Academy of Music in Graz, Austria, where his teacher was Marga Bäuml. His competition successes include first prize at the 19th Yugoslav Competition of Music Artists and at the 15th International Jeunesses Musicales Competition, in Zagreb and Belgrade respectively. His solo activi-ties have taken him to Cuba, Spain, Greece, Bulgaria, Austria, Belgium, Poland, West Germany and the USA. In 1989 he won the Fernando Sor International Competition in Rome. He devotes a lot of his time to composing, and his compositions include a Passa-caglia and Fugue, which has been performed by the Hand/Dupré Duo. He has issued a solo recital record on the Jugoton label, of music by Scarlatti, Bach, Josipovic, Koshkin and Barrios. He is an active solo-ist, like the other members of the Trio, and also duets with soprano Mirjana Bohanec and with cellist Ksenija Jankovic.

The third and youngest member of the Trio is Istvan Römer — like Goran Listes, a Hungarian name. He was born in 1962. Also like Listes, he studied both at Zagreb with Petrinjak and at the Academy of Music in Graz with Marga Bäuml. After graduating from both institutions with high honors, he obtained a number of competition successes, among which were Mettmann (first prize), Palma (first prize), Vina del Mar, Chile (first prize), Maria Callas, Greece (second prize), and Gargnano (third prize). He plays in a duo with the cellist Walter Despalj, and they have issued a record-ing of duets. He has also made a solo recording of music by Bach, Papandopulo, Granados and Bogdanovic.

It is clear that the activities of the Zagreb Trio take up only a part of the professional careers of its members, although a very important one. But when they are working as a trio, it is the most enjoyable time for them. 'Company makes another spirit', was the way Goran Listes put it. 'We exchange things' — and more things than music. It was a sharing that went beyond professional commitment.

Darko said their playing came naturally. 'So we don't talk about it very much. Maybe with very modern pieces, then we have to do a little bit of talking, just to find the right way to approach the piece. But the standard repertoire just comes off very naturally, with very little to be talked about.'

It was different when they started; then they had to spend quite a lot of time, as all ensembles do. Now they know one another's playing well enough to be able to anticipate.

For repertoire, they necessarily use a lot of transcrip-tions. 'But every now and then an original work pops up,' said Darko. 'For example, Chanterelle Editions have issued the works of Zani de Ferranti, which contain a Polonaise for three guitars.' Then they had a piece by Gragnani — 'very standard, but we still enjoy playing it very much. We have a Diabelli piece, which we've slightly rearranged so that the interesting part is shared between us. It is a great experience to have new

Courtesy Classical Guitar Magazine

pieces — either discovering them or asking people to write them. In that sense we've been very lucky. We've got three pieces from Nikita Koshkin, written for us, which are really very good. One piece by John Duarte (*Little Suite op.95*, recorded by the Trio on Jugoton LSY 68105), a number of pieces by Yugoslav composers.'

The Duarte piece was much liked. 'A very successful piece,' said Goran Listes. 'Whenever we play it, everybody enjoys it.' Including, he added, other composers.

Darko Petrinjak plays the double-bass as proficiently as he plays the guitar. That means that he plays it very well indeed. He praised his teacher in Yugoslavia, Josip Novosel, who taught him so much. 'It's a very interesting combination. We've asked people like Brouwer, Sérgio Assad and Ernesto Cordero to write pieces for this combination.'

Goran pointed out that another aspect of the double-bass was that in conjunction with the two guitars the Trio could tackle a number of baroque works by Bach, Handel and others: virtually anything for two violins and continuo could be arranged for bass and two guitars.

Here is a tip for guitarists seeking to improve their technique, courtesy of the Zagreb Guitar Trio: go to some piano masterclasses. The movements of a pianist's hand have some similarities to a guitarist's. And of course the piano shares with the guitar the problem of and how to get it. Then, too, as Darko Petrinjak pointed out, there were problems common to the violin and the guitar — accents, for instance. 'Sometimes they have to play a lot of notes on one bow, but only one on the next bow — one that mustn't be any louder. This is what guitarists very often do, put accents on wrong notes because of some technical reason such as a change of position.'

So many things to learn, we all agreed. But would a sensible guitarist learn them from a pianist or a violinist, in the light of what had just been said? It would depend on who it was, said Istvan Römer, adding — with a certain humor — that perhaps you could even learn something from a guitarist.

At the time this interview took place, Yugoslavia was still united, at least nominally. Comparatively little was known about its contemporary guitar composers, and the Zagreb Guitar Trio were able to suggest a few names that would be worth further investigation. Darko Petrinjak was particularly helpful here, with an impressive list. For instance, there is the Sarajevo composer Vojislav Ivanovic, a profile of whom appeared in CG in August 1988. His enchanting *Café No.6* was published in the same issue, one of a set of six subsequently published by Chanterelle of Heidelberg.

Then there is Boris Papandopulo, Yugoslavian despite his Greek name, who was born in 1906; he composed a concerto with string orchestra, a trio-sonata for two guitars and double-bass, and three Yugoslavian dances for solo guitar, published by Gerig Verlag of Cologne and recorded by Istvan Römer.

The works of Dusan Bogdanovic are gradually becoming known. His works include *Blues and Variations*, two *Sonatas*, *Lento and Toccata*, and *Introduction, Passacaglia and Fugue of the Golden Flower*. *(Since this article was published in 1990, Bogdanovic's name has come to the fore. His numerous works, often with a element of jazz, are performed widely and receive high acclaim.)*.

Miroslav Miletic has written a sonata for violin and guitar, a consort trio for three guitars, a concerto with orchestra, and a suite for solo guitar. Other names to look out for are Marko Ruzdjak, Silvio Foretic and Andelko Klobucar.

The recordings of the Zagreb Guitar Trio are, it need scarcely be said, very good. There is however an electric quality about their live performances, an atmosphere that induces alertness and receptivity in their audiences. It is very difficult to recapture this quality in a recording, and that single fact is probably the strongest argument there is in favor of live performance.

Musicians sometimes strive after a kind of uniform perfection that will pass muster not only in the recording studio but also on the concert platform. I formed the impression that these three men from Yugoslavia would never succumb to that particular temptation. Their concerts are characterized by a blend of excitement and enjoyment, and the result is a life-enhancing exhilaration for the audience.

CC

ABOUT THE EDITOR

COLIN COOPER was born in Birkenhead, England, in 1926. His training as an aeronautical engineer was interrupted by active service in the second world war, after which he turned his hand to writing, becoming active in rural community drama and, later, national radio. A television play won a prize in 1969, by which time he was writing sci-fi and crime fiction for various London book publishers.

Music was a powerful attraction from an early age. At various times he studied violin, viola, piano and mandolin, but it was not until, at the age of 36, he discovered the enormous potential of the guitar that he felt able to concentrate in one specific direction. He studied the instrument with Gilbert Biberian and became a teacher in the Inner London Education Authority's adult education scheme. In 1972 he joined a partnership (soon dissolved) formed for the purposes of creating Guitar magazine (later Guitar International), the first four issues of which were published from his house in north London. He has contributed to many other international publications including the Tokyo magazine Gendai Guitar, for which he wrote a monthly column for 15 consecutive years.

In 1982 Colin Cooper accepted an invitation from Maurice Summerfield to be the first News Editor of a new monthly magazine, Classical Guitar. He later became Features Editor and, over the ensuing 19 years, played a significant part in the general shaping of the magazine's policy.

His continuing interest in the developing guitar scene takes him to many international guitar festivals. He has lectured in countries as diverse as France, Italy, Croatia and Turkey, and frequently serves on the juries of international guitar competitions.